Saving Nelson Mandela

PIVOTAL MOMENTS IN WORLD HISTORY

This series examines choices made at historical turning points—and
the figures who made them—and reveals the effect these choices had,
and continue to have, on the course of world events.

Americanos
Latin America's Struggle for Independence
John Charles Chasteen

A Most Holy War
The Albigensian Crusade and the Battle for Christendom
Mark Gregory Pegg

Saving Nelson Mandela
The Rivonia Trial and the Fate of South Africa
Kenneth S. Broun

Saving Nelson Mandela

The Rivonia Trial and the Fate of South Africa

KENNETH S. BROUN

OXFORD
UNIVERSITY PRESS

OXFORD
UNIVERSITY PRESS

Oxford University Press, Inc., publishes works that further
Oxford University's objective of excellence
in research, scholarship, and education.

Oxford   New York
Auckland   Cape Town   Dar es Salaam   Hong Kong   Karachi
Kuala Lumpur   Madrid   Melbourne   Mexico City   Nairobi
New Delhi   Shanghai   Taipei   Toronto

With offices in
Argentina   Austria   Brazil   Chile   Czech Republic   France   Greece
Guatemala   Hungary   Italy   Japan   Poland   Portugal   Singapore
South Korea   Switzerland   Thailand   Turkey   Ukraine   Vietnam

Published by Oxford University Press, Inc.
198 Madison Avenue, New York, NY 10016

www.oup.com

Oxford is a registered trademark of Oxford University Press

Library of Congress Cataloging-in-Publication Data
Broun, Kenneth S.
Saving Nelson Mandela : [the Rivonia trial and the fate of South Africa / Kenneth S. Broun].
p. cm. — (Pivotal moments in world history)
Includes bibliographical references and index.
ISBN 978-0-19-974022-2
1. Rivonia Trial, Pretoria, South Africa, 1964.
2. Mandela, Nelson, 1918– Trials, litigation, etc.
3. Trials (Political crimes and offenses)—South Africa.
4. South Africa—History—1961–1994.
I. Title. II. Series: Pivotal moments in world history.
KTL42.R58B76   2012
345.680231—dc23   2011026021

9 8 7 6 5 4 3 2 1

Printed in the United States of America
on acid-free paper

To Margie and to the Rivonia Trial defendants and their lawyers

Contents

People Involved in the Rivonia Trial

Defendants

THE defendants in the Rivonia Trial were listed in the indictment as Accused 1 through 10 and usually referred to at the trial by their numbers rather than their names.

1. Nelson Mandela
2. Walter Sisulu
3. Denis Goldberg
4. Govan Mbeki
5. Ahmed Mohamed Kathrada
6. Lionel "Rusty" Bernstein
7. Raymond Mhlaba
8. James Kantor
9. Elias Motsoaledi
10. Andrew Mlangeni

Defense lawyers

Bram Fischer, *advocate (lead counsel)*
Vernon Berrange, *advocate*
George Bizos, *advocate*
Arthur Chaskalson, *advocate*
Joel Joffe, *attorney*
Harold Hanson, *advocate*
George Lowen, *advocate*
H. C. Nicholas, *advocate*

Prosecutors

Percy Yutar, *deputy attorney general, Transvaal*
A. B. Krog

Judge

Justice Quartus de Wet, *judge president of the Transvaal Provincial Division*

The Police

Hendrik van den Bergh, *commander, Special Branch*
Captain T. J. Swanepoel
Lieutenant Willem Petrus van Wyk
Sergeant Carl Johannes Dirker
Sergeant Donald John Card
Sergeant Jonathan du Preez

Key State Witnesses

Bruno Mtolo (Mr. X)
Patrick "Abel" Mthembu (Mr. Y)
Joseph Mashifane
English Tolo Mashiloane
Cyril Davids
Caswell Mboxela

Defendants' Wives and Family Members

Winnie Mandela, *Nelson Mandela's wife*
Albertina Sisulu, *Walter Sisulu's wife*
Hilda Bernstein, *Lionel Bernstein's wife*
Esme Goldberg, *Denis Goldberg's wife*
Annie Goldberg, *Denis Goldberg's mother*
Juni Mlangeni, *Andrew Mlangeni's wife*

Other African National Congress (ANC) or Communist Party of South Africa (CPSA) Leaders or Activists

Robert Hepple, *CPSA, originally named in Rivonia indictment*
Harold Wolpe, *CPSA leader, arrested after Rivonia raid but escaped*
Arthur Goldreich, *CPSA leader, arrested after Rivonia raid but escaped*
Chief Albert Luthuli, *ANC president general*

Oliver Tambo, *ANC leader (in exile)*
Ruth First, *CPSA leader*
Joseph Slovo, *CPSA leader (in exile)*
Michael Harmel, *CPSA leader*

South African Government Officials

Henrik Verwoerd, *prime minister*
John Vorster, *minister of justice*
Eric Louw, *minister of foreign affairs until December 31, 1963*
Hilgard Muller, *minister of foreign affairs after December 31, 1963*
G. P. Jooste, *foreign secretary*
Rudolf Werner Rein, *attorney general, Transvaal Province*

American Officials

Lyndon B. Johnson, *president*
Dean Rusk, *secretary of state*
McGeorge Bundy, *assistant to the president*
Maxwell Taylor, *chairman of the Joint Chiefs of Staff*
Adlai Stevenson, *ambassador to the United Nations*
Joseph C. Satterthwaite, *American ambassador to South Africa*

British Officials

R. A. Butler, *secretary of state for foreign affairs*
Hugh Stephenson, *ambassador to South Africa*
Leslie Minford, *consul general in Johannesburg*
Lord Dunrossil, *Foreign Office observer at trial*

Others

Arnoldus Johannus Greeff, *prison guard*
AnnMarie Wolpe, *Harold Wolpe's wife and James Kantor's sister*
Molly Fischer, *Bram Fischer's wife*
Canon L. John Collins, *dean of St. Paul's Cathedral, London, head of Defence and Aid Fund*

John Arnold, *British barrister, observer at trial*
Thomas Kellock, *British barrister, observer at trial*
Judge Charles Fahy, *American observer at trial*
Nadine Gordimer, *author working with defense*
Jaja Wachuku, *Nigerian foreign minister*
Alan Paton, *author testifying at sentencing hearing*

Introduction

ON FEBRUARY 11, 1990, Nelson Mandela walked out of a South African prison, a free man for the first time in twenty-seven years. He immediately assumed the leadership role that would move South Africa from a system of apartheid to a struggling but viable democracy. No one person, not even Nelson Mandela, was solely responsible for this miracle. But no one can doubt the crucial role that he played in the process that brought a new era to South Africa, or that his intellect, sturdy leadership, and political savvy made this process far more peaceful than anyone had predicted would be the case. In 1994 Mandela finally got the opportunity to serve as president of the Republic of South Africa under its new constitution.

That Nelson Mandela would ever be freed was almost out of the question in 1964, when he was sent to prison. Mandela and his codefendants faced charges brought under the recently enacted Sabotage Act, the violation of which carried the death penalty. The South African government had proudly announced that it had brought to justice men who had planned and begun to carry out a campaign for its violent overthrow. The country's press celebrated the success of the police in catching the criminals, who represented a very real threat to the way of life of white South Africa. Foreign representatives were told by informed sources that the maximum sentence for the top leadership was possible, indeed likely. Most observers—white and black, government supporters and opponents—thought that Mandela and the others would all be hanged.

South Africa in 1963 was the product of more than three hundred years of racial and ethnic conflict. European settlers began coming to South Africa in the late 1600s. The native population was almost immediately segregated and subjugated. Wars were fought between the settlers and the black people inhabiting the land—wars that were inevitably won by the better-armed Europeans. The white settlers were eventually successful in establishing themselves as a ruling minority throughout the area now encompassing all of southern Africa.

The Anglo-Boer War of 1899–1902 was fought for control of the country between two European groups—each of which oppressed the black population within the areas of their control.[1] On one side were the English, who were interested in making sure that the British Empire extended to the tip of Africa and included its vast mineral resources—especially gold and diamonds. On the other were the Afrikaners—a mixed European people who spoke a language, Afrikaans, reflective of the Dutch ancestry of many of them—who were mostly interested in settling the land and farming it, often on the back of black labor. The Afrikaners were referred to as Boers—Afrikaans for "farmers." By the late 1800s, the Boers had set up independent republics in the heart of South Africa. The English won the war in a long, hard, and bloody fight. The Boer republics were merged into what would become the Union of South Africa and later the modern day Republic of South Africa. A large number of children and wives of Boer guerrillas were sent to concentration camps where more than 20,000 died of undernourishment or poor hygiene. Three-quarters of the dead were children.[2] English speakers were to dominate South African government for nearly a half century. Many Afrikaners came to view themselves as second-class citizens.

Black natives were part of the South African scene of continuing hostility between the English and the Afrikaners—tolerated only to the extent that they would serve the white people of both groups. The blacks were a majority of at least 80 percent, but their role was to provide cheap labor for the white mines, farms, and businesses, as well as domestic servants for their homes. Other ethnic groups also inhabited the country, including the so-called Coloured, a mixed ethnic group speaking Afrikaans and largely concentrated in the area near Cape Town; and Indians—South Asians who began coming to South Africa in large numbers in the latter part of the nineteenth century first as indentured laborers and later as traders. Although somewhat better treated than the native black population, Coloureds and Indians usually lived separately from both white and black South Africans and were treated as inferior to the whites.

Europeans owned almost all of South Africa's fertile agricultural land. Schools and public facilities were segregated by law and custom. There was de facto segregation of living areas, although some mixed areas existed. The major cities such as Johannesburg and Cape Town were exclusively in white control. Blacks came to the cities to work—especially in the gold and other mineral mines surrounding the city of Johannesburg. Blacks mingled with whites, but only as domestic servants and other laborers.

In 1963, less than 20 percent (3,250,000) of the total South African population of more than 17 million was white—roughly two-thirds Afrikaner and one-third English speaking. The black population was estimated at 11,640,000 (68.3 percent), with 1,650,000 Coloured and 520,000 Asians.[3]

By the middle of the twentieth century, Afrikaners were still hurting from what they perceived as oppression at British hands during and after the Anglo-Boer Wars. The political situation changed dramatically in 1948 with the political ascendancy of the Afrikaner-dominated National Party. Afrikaners were now in control of the government. They seized the opportunity both to preserve their culture and to quash what they saw as increasing English softness on issues involving the black population.

The National Party leadership escalated and institutionalized the prevailing segregation and subjugation of non-Europeans in what became known as apartheid. Apartheid had many aspects. The overall goal of the policy was total separation of the races—a separation that exceeded even the pernicious Jim Crow laws of the American South in scope and force. Of course words such as "oppression" or "subjugation" or their synonyms were never used by the regime. But the intent of the policy was clearly to maintain the status of non-Europeans as inferior. Apartheid legislation referred to the nation's blacks as "Bantus." Bantu is a language grouping that includes the languages spoken by many of South African blacks, including the very large Zulu and Xhosa groups. The term was one used consistently by the government and resented just as consistently by the people to which it referred, who preferred to be called simply black. Bantustans (homelands for native blacks) were created, a move that was intended eventually to deprive most black South Africans of any citizenship rights within the Republic of South Africa. The principle was that blacks were to be citizens of the Bantustans and, in essence, guest workers within South Africa proper. The Coloured population was totally denied the right to vote—a right it had had in parts of the country. The Group Areas Act dictated where various racial groups could live. The Bantu Education Act and similar legislation sought to insure that blacks would receive no education not befitting a domestic servant. Rigid racial laws governing all aspects of life were enacted. Estimates were made in the early 1980s that 60 percent of the laws of South Africa governed relations among the races.

Until 1994, South Africa had no effective constitutional limitations on the ability of Parliament to enact whatever racist legislation it believed would advance its agenda. Legislation denying basic civil rights could be adopted without fear that some court would strike it down. And as the apartheid policy began to take hold of the country, civil rights were increasingly curtailed.

The apartheid South African government touted its judicial system as independent—and to some extent it was. In 1956, Nelson Mandela and some 160 other people were charged with treason. The "Treason Trial" went on for five years in various stages. The defendants were free on bail for much of that time. The charges were weak by any criteria. The state could not prove that the defendants sought the violent overthrow of the government. None of the major antiapartheid movements had yet engaged in violence or even in planning for violence. The defenders and their supporters were simply seeking basic human and civil rights within their country. The judiciary was independent enough to ensure that the state was put to its proof. Many of the defendants were discharged long before the end of the proceedings. The Treason Trial ended in March 1961 with the acquittal of the thirty remaining defendants including Mandela.

Yet, as we will see, the independence of the judiciary did not mean that the judges had sympathy for those charged with opposition to the ruling regime. Judges appointed by the apartheid government were, with some notable exceptions, individuals who were, by upbringing and education, totally supportive of its views. Even to the extent that they might personally differ from the policies, they were sworn to obey the law. To many white South Africans, that meant a literal interpretation of the law unencumbered by notions of natural law or human rights.

Formed in 1912, the African National Congress (ANC) was traditionally a moderate voice that avoided mass demonstrations or confrontation of any kind. In the 1950s, it came under the influence of its Youth League, led by Mandela and others. Under their leadership, the ANC became increasingly more militant and confrontational. At the same time, leaders like Mandela shifted from a Black Nationalist stance that avoided working with white, Indian, or Coloured activists to one that sought allies wherever they could be found. Among those allies were members of the multiracial, but white dominated, Communist Party of South Africa. The party itself was made illegal in 1950, but its membership stayed involved in the struggle through other forms. Some of its members were devoted to a worldwide Communist movement led by the Soviet Union; many others were drawn to the party because they saw it as the only reasonable outlet for their opposition to the South African government's oppression of its own people.

In 1955, the Congress of the People rally in Kliptown, Soweto—part of the vast black settlement or "township" near Johannesburg—adopted the Freedom Charter, a set of principles for a democratic South Africa. The principles of the Freedom Charter were adopted by a diverse set of anti-apartheid groups including, in 1956, the ANC.

Despite the Treason Trial of leaders actively involved in opposition to the apartheid laws, protests continued and built in size and success in the late 1950s and 1960s. A group calling itself the Pan African Congress (PAC) split from the ANC in 1959. The PAC espoused a more militant Black Nationalist creed than the more traditional ANC. In 1960, the PAC organized a mass protest against the hated passes that all blacks were required to carry. The protest culminated in the watershed Sharpeville incident in March 1960. During a protest in the Sharpeville township near the industrial city of Vereeniging south of Johannesburg, police fired into the crowd, killing sixty-nine people and wounding many others.

In reaction to the shootings, black militancy rose, as did white fear of the black population's response. White flight from the country increased greatly. New laws were enacted to curtail resistance to the government. The ANC and PAC, together with other organizations seeking rights for black populations, were declared illegal. Draconian security legislation was enacted.

One law prohibiting dissent was already on the books—the Suppression of Communism Act, adopted in 1950. The law, which took advantage of the post–World War II fear of Communism in South Africa and throughout the West, banned the Communist Party. It broadly defined Communism to meet the special needs of the South African regime. The act not only prohibited activities aimed "at the establishment of a despotic system of government based on the dictatorship of the proletariat," it also prohibited activity "which aims at the encouragement of feelings of hostility between the European and Non-European races of the Republic."

In 1962, Parliament enacted the Sabotage Act, prohibiting acts of sabotage. Persons charged under the act were denied rights guaranteed to defendants in other trials. Mandela and his codefendants were to be charged and tried under this act.

In addition, the General Law Amendment Act was adopted in May 1963. Clause 17 of that act permitted the minister of justice to detain any person suspected of a political crime for ninety days in an isolation cell until he or she answered questions to the satisfaction of the minister. Once the ninety days were up, the suspect could be detained again under the same act. The successive number of detentions was unlimited— detention without trial could last, as then–Justice Minister John Vorster exclaimed, until "this side of eternity." All of Mandela's codefendants were initially detained under this act. Mandela was already in prison at the time of their detentions.

The 1963–64 trial of Mandela and his codefendants represented in many ways the culmination of South African history to that point. The nation was heading headfirst into a conflict brought on by three hundred years of racial conflict, an Afrikaner population frustrated by the loss of their independence and fearful of the destruction of their culture, and a black population that had seen its plight worsen day by day and year by year. Fifteen years after the National Party took control of South Africa's government and began to institute apartheid, the time was ripe not only for a definitive judicial sanction for government opponents but for a verdict that would ensure that these enemies of the state would be out of the way forever.

The trial—the Rivonia Trial, as it was called, named for the Johannesburg suburb in which many of the illegal meetings took place and the arrests were made—was no model for procedural justice, but neither was it a kangaroo court. Some forms of trial familiar to lawyers in the Anglo-American world were present—including, most importantly, the right to cross-examine witnesses.

It was a pivotal moment in South Africa's history, and one of high drama. A team composed of lawyers of great intellect, legal ability, and integrity defended the accused. They applied their considerable skill to a cause in which they deeply believed. The accused, through both their statements to the court and their testimony, demonstrated strength of character and devotion to a cause that even a hostile judge could not, in the end, ignore. The character and conduct of the judge before whom the case was tried illustrate both the strength and weaknesses of the South African judicial system. The judge may well have been independent of the government and its prosecutor, but his own prejudices guided him through much of the proceedings. International opinion and the actions of foreign governments figured in as well. White South African opinion was clearly in favor of the prosecution and harsh sentences for the accused. International opinion was almost unanimous in its support for them, particularly in the newly independent African states and the Communist bloc. There was also considerable attention to the trial on the part of the major Western powers—or at least concern that death sentences would sour relations with African and other Third World people. The question was how the West—and in particular the United States and United Kingdom—might attempt to influence the trial's outcome.

My own interest in the Rivonia Trial was generated by several circumstances. I have been a trial lawyer and I have taught classes on evidence and trial advocacy in the United States for forty-three years, serving as both a member of the board of trustees and as director of the National Institute for Trial Advocacy (NITA). Almost every year of the past twenty-five, I have traveled to South Africa to participate in programs sponsored by the Black Lawyers of South Africa. The programs are designed to improve the advocacy skills of its trial lawyers, who were deprived of adequate educational opportunities during the apartheid years. We have trained more than a thousand young lawyers in the skills they would need to represent their clients in court.

My quarter century of involvement with South Africa, both before and after the end of apartheid, has given me an appreciation for that country and its struggles, in and out of the courtroom. I have of course observed the remarkable role Nelson Mandela played in South Africa's history and in its destiny. I was deeply honored that he agreed to write an introduction to my first book about South Africa, *Black Lawyers, White Courts*, which told the story of some lawyers who helped shape that destiny.

I was drawn to the Rivonia Trial because I was aware of its significance in South Africa's history. But I also became interested in the trial because of the respect I have for great advocacy. I met two of the lawyers who represented the defendants at the Rivonia Trial, George Bizos and Arthur Chaskalson, on my first trip to their country in 1986, and have known about and admired their abilities in a courtroom. The lead defense counsel at the Rivonia Trial, Bram Fischer, remains a legend in South Africa to this day.

Something happened in the course of the trial that began in October 1963 and ended in June 1964—the Rivonia Trial—something that ultimately saved the lives of Mandela and his codefendants and, ultimately, the very soul of their country. This book is an attempt to uncover what that something was.

Saving Nelson Mandela

1

Arrests and Escapes

TODAY, THE JOHANNESBURG suburb of Rivonia—about ten miles north of the city's center—has been absorbed by the upper-class commercial center of Sandton. With its sleek corporate headquarters and lavish homes, the area resembles an upscale suburb of Houston. But in 1963, Rivonia was a sparsely developed exurban community. The area was still largely *veld*—grassland with occasional scrub trees. Within it was Liliesleaf Farm, a twenty-eight-acre property with a spacious main house set back from a dirt road. Behind the house were a large thatched-roof cottage and an assortment of outbuildings.[1]

As far as the neighbors knew, Liliesleaf was owned and occupied by an affluent white family, the Goldreichs. Arthur Goldreich was an artist, architect, and industrial designer who created commercial space for Greatermans, a large department store chain. He and his family frequented the local polo club and hosted dinner parties. They had the usual assortment of black servants to tend both the house and grounds, including, at one point, a gardener called David Motsamayi.

But neither the farm nor the Goldreichs were what they appeared to be. Arthur was a longtime active member of the illegal Communist Party. In 1961 and 1962, he had traveled extensively through the Communist bloc nations, including the Soviet Union and China, gathering information on running an insurgency and on the manufacture of armaments.[2] Goldreich had redesigned the main room of the thatched cottage as a meeting place for the leadership of the Communist Party and the ANC, now working together on the possibility of military action against the government through its combined organization, Umkhonto we Sizwe, commonly referred to as MK.

Elaborate deceptions had been used in the purchase of the property. Michael Harmel, a Communist Party leader, handled the transaction in July 1961. A lawyer named Harold Wolpe set up a dummy company for the purchase. The nominal owner of Liliesleaf was not Goldreich but rather

Vivian Ezra, another Communist who had somehow escaped the attention of the security police.

The only clues to a casual observer of what went on at the farm were the number of visitors, many of them black. Blacks generally didn't socialize with whites in 1960s South Africa—or, for that matter, in subsequent years. A neighbor later told the police that Mr. Goldreich seemed a nice enough man, but she was surprised that he seemed to have a great many African friends who came and went at all hours. "His Bantu visitors are very well dressed. My young son goes over there sometimes to play with the Goldreich children, and he says they often have mixed parties in the lounge—Europeans and Bantu hobnobbing and drinking together."[3]

And indeed there was hobnobbing. Since 1961, most of the leadership of the Communist Party and of the ANC and many other activists working with MK passed through the cottage's gates. Among them was Bruno Mtolo, a saboteur from Durban and leader of MK's Natal branch, who was to become the key state witness at the Rivonia Trial. Some stayed, posing as workers. The purported foreman at the farm was a longtime Communist Party activist named Thomas Mashefane. The gardener, "David Motsamayi," was in fact Nelson Mandela, who lived on the property until early 1962 when he was smuggled out of the country.[4] These were the days when Mandela was known in the South African press as the "Black Pimpernel," for his being sought everywhere and managing to escape capture.[5] Mandela/Motsamayi spent his days tending the garden and reading about world revolutions, as well as about the struggle of the Boers against the English. He often spent his nights in meetings outside of Rivonia, coming back before dawn to assume his humble role as a gardener.

Other activists used disguises when they ducked in and out of Lilieslief. Ahmed Kathrada, a young leader in the South African Indian Congress, posed as a Portuguese citizen named Pedro Perreira, and sported a handle-bar mustache, dyed red hair, and theatrical makeup that reddened his complexion. A government apologist later noted that he "could have passed for a White man."[6] Similarly, Walter Sisulu, code name "Allah," sported a Hitler-like mustache, had his hair straightened, and, in the words of the same government author, could have been a "Cape Coloured person."[7] ("Coloured" was a separate racial classification of mixed-race people used in the complex lexicon of apartheid. "Cape Coloured" is a cultural group of mixed race people who speak Afrikaans and live in the Western Cape Province.) Sisulu's father had in fact been white, although Sisulu always viewed himself as a black African, as did the South African government. Along with Mandela, Sisulu was one of the two most important ANC leaders not in exile. The Communist activist Denis Goldberg grew a beard; the ANC leader Govan Mbeki, code name "Dhlamini"[8] and father of future South African president Thabo Mbeki, dressed as a common farm laborer.

But despite the disguises and elaborate deceptions, security at Lilieslief had become surprisingly lax. The location and use of the house was supposed to be on a need-to-know basis. By July 1963, "need-to-know" had degenerated, and this information filtered fairly openly through the ranks of those involved in antigovernment activities. Documents were kept long beyond their usefulness to anyone, other than to the police as evidence in potential prosecutions. The Communist Party leader Joe Slovo had assured Mandela that his diary and other incriminating documents would be destroyed.[9]

In fact, they were never destroyed or even removed from Liliesleaf Farm. Among the documents seized in the raid were a sixty-two-page notebook entitled "Part One: How to Be a Good Communist," a diary of Mandela's trip abroad in 1962, and a note describing plans for a jail escape.

Bram Fischer, who was to lead the defense team at the Rivonia Trial and was himself a leader in the Communist Party, became increasingly alarmed by the sloppiness of his fellow activists, who, after all, were involved in a capital crime conspiracy to overthrow a government that was willing to use all its power to crush opposition. Nonetheless, they often acted in an amateurish way. Fischer's complaints were noted but not acted upon. Lax security had existed even in 1961, when Mandela was living at the farm. Mandela returned one night to find the Communist Party leader Michael Harmel, who was staying at the house, asleep with the front door open, the lights on, and the radio blasting. When Mandela woke him, Harmel complained, "Nel, must you disturb my sleep? Can't this wait until tomorrow?"[10] British barristers observing the trial would later comment to British Embassy representatives that they were astonished at the "amateurish ineptitude of all of the conspirators." In their view, the defendants had gratuitously provided the state with voluminous and invaluable documentary evidence against themselves.[11]

Because of concerns about security at Liliesleaf itself, the MK leadership obtained two other properties. One was a place called Travallyn, located near the old mining town of Krugersdorp, some twenty miles west of Johannesburg. The property was to be used as an arsenal in the battle against the regime. Denis Goldberg moved there ten days before the raid.

His job was to obtain the needed weaponry. The other was located in Mountain View, another suburb not far from central Johannesburg. It was to be a safe house, used to shelter activists on the run from the police. It would serve that purpose even after the Rivonia raid.

Nelson Mandela was not among the activists meeting at Liliesleaf Farm in 1963. He was already imprisoned in the penitentiary on Robben Island, located just outside the Cape Town harbor. After the ANC was declared illegal in 1960, Mandela went into hiding—spending some of that time at the Rivonia farm. He left the country for several months early in 1962 but returned a few months later to resume his underground activities—including meetings with ANC and MK leaders. He was apprehended in August 1962 and charged with illegally leaving the country and with inciting laborers to strike. He was sentenced to five years imprisonment. A year later he was to be brought back to Pretoria to stand trial yet again.

Lieutenant Willem Petrus van Wyk joined the Special Branch, the South African security police, in 1960. Van Wyk had previously been on regular police duty, and he had come to know Nelson Mandela and Joe Slovo in their capacity as criminal defense lawyers. He had a friendly relationship with them, of the kind that, surprisingly, frequently exists between the police and defense counsel. But his new duties cast him as their pursuer, a role he undertook with more courtesy than was normal for the security police, but also with diligence. He developed an extensive network of informers—a network that eventually paid him enormous dividends.[12]

The newly named head of the Special Branch was Hendrik van den Bergh, called "Long Hendrik" by his men. Van den Bergh had been imprisoned during World War II for Nazi sympathies and had been a cellmate of Justice Minister John Vorster. The lone opposition member of the South Africa Parliament, Helen Suzman of the Progressive Party, who died in 2009 at the age of ninety-one, called van den Bergh "South Africa's own Heinrich Himmler." Long Hendrik ruthlessly sought to close down any possible threats to the governing regime. He brought a degree of sophistication to the Special Branch by hiring some college graduates. He also purportedly visited France to learn the torture methods of the notorious intelligence section of the French General Staff, the Deuxième Bureau.[13]

Despite his extensive network of informers and the arrest and imprisonment of Mandela, Lieutenant van Wyk and his commander were frustrated by their failure to destroy the antigovernment movement entirely.

Major Communist leaders were under house arrest, including Lionel "Rusty" Bernstein. Others, including Joe Slovo, had at least temporarily fled the country. But, other than Mandela himself, the ANC and MK leadership had largely avoided apprehension. Sisulu, Mbeki, and Goldberg were all fugitives from the law. Even detentions of family members, such as Sisulu's wife, Albertina, had not resulted in the arrest of the more politically significant leaders.

Van Wyk's luck changed with the capture of an informant picked up near the border with Bechuanaland (now Botswana).[14] This border crossing was a frequent escape point and, almost as frequently, a place at which fleeing dissidents were seized. The informant said he knew where to find Sisulu and others and was willing to sell that information for six thousand rand, the equivalent of about $12,000. Van Wyk got clearance to make the payment if the information proved correct. The man told them that the hideout was in the northern suburbs, that there was a church nearby, and, more cryptically, that it was marked by a sign with the word "IVON." Van Wyk spent several nights cruising the area with the informant, hoping that he could pinpoint the precise location. After several nights, the informer recognized the neighborhood, and a sign reading "IVON"—"RIVONIA,"—with the "R" and "IA" faded out. The "church" turned out to be a gabled house.

Plans began immediately for a raid that van Wyk hoped would yield at least some of the targets of his search. On July 11, 1963, he gathered a squad of fifteen police officers and an Alsatian police dog named Cheetah. They approached the property in a van marked with the logo of a dry cleaning service. Two officers named Kleingel and van den Berg, wearing white lab coats, sat in front. On the road to Liliesleaf the party stopped at the Rivonia police station to borrow a blanket, which they hung behind the front seat to hide the others inside the van.

Van Wyk had originally planned not to obtain a search warrant for the premises, fearing a breach in security that would alert his targets. However, his immediate superior officer, Colonel "Tiny" Ventner, worried that a liberal judge might throw out the fruits of the raid. Ventner ordered van Wyk to obtain a warrant. An officer was dispatched to the court in central Johannesburg to get the appropriate paperwork completed. As a result of this, the raid was postponed from just after lunch until 3 p.m. The delay turned out to be fortunate for van Wyk. Had the raid taken place as planned, the only dissident leader present would have been Ahmed Kathrada. The others did not arrive until shortly before 3 p.m.

As the van approached the property, a black servant blocked the entrance, telling them that no one has home. Kleingel asked directions to the Sleepy Hollow Hotel. Officer van der Berg, who was driving, slipped the gearshift into reverse and had started to turn around when van Wyk ordered him to stop: "Ons slaan toe!" (Let's close in!)

Concern about security had convinced the MK leadership that continuing to hold meetings at Liliesleaf Farm was not a good idea. The July 11th meeting was to have been the last. Ahmed Kathrada stayed at the farm the night before.[15] Denis Goldberg came over midafternoon from the relative safety of Travallyn, bringing Walter Sisulu, Govan Mbeki, and ANC activist Raymond Mhlaba in a Volkswagen microbus. Bob Hepple, a lawyer and Communist Party member, arrived in his station wagon. Rusty Bernstein, who was under limited house arrest, drove directly to Rivonia in his old Chevy after his mandatory check-in with the police at the Marshall Square station in Central Johannesburg. He left the station at about 2 p.m. and must have arrived at the farm sometime after 2:30 p.m.

The meeting was to take place in one of Liliesleaf's outbuildings, a thatched cottage. At 3 p.m., all but Goldberg were gathered in the cottage, some seated around a coffee table covered with incriminating documents. Goldberg, the engineer, was in the main house, reading Robert Jungk's *Brighter Than a Thousand Suns*, the story of the atomic scientists and the Manhattan project.[16] Various servants, some of whom were connected to the ANC and some who were unaware of the nature of the activities at the farm, were scattered around.

The van entered the yard, and the front and back doors flew open. Policemen filled the yard; their dog ran toward the houses. Someone shouted a warning. Sisulu, Mbeki, and Kathrada jumped out of a ground-floor window. Bernstein pulled papers from his pocket and dropped them on the table in front of him. Hepple stuffed documents into a small and unlit coal-burning stove. His attempts to light the stove failed. The defendants would later tell their lawyers that among the documents stuffed into the stove was the plan for Operation Mayibuye ("comeback" or "return" in Zulu), which was to provide the most damning evidence against the accused at the trial. One of the raiders, Detective Sergeant Carel Dirker, would testify at the trial that the document was found in the middle of the table around which the men had gathered. Sisulu, Mbeki, and Kathrada ran toward the woods, but halted when they were ordered to do so. Hepple, Bernstein, and Mhlaba were arrested in the cottage. Goldberg was apprehended in the main house.

Van Wyk recognized most of those arrested, including Sisulu, despite his mustache and straightened hair, and Mbeki, in a workman's cap and grimy overalls. Van Wyk's second in command, Dirker, patted down Sisulu and said, "I've got you now."[17] He had been harassing Sisulu's family for months in an attempt to find him. But van Wyk failed to recognize everyone immediately. He asked one of his fellow officers who the red-haired man was. Kathrada gave his characteristic grin, jogging the lieutenant's memory: "Good heavens!" he exclaimed. "Kathrada!"[18]

More arrests took place later in the afternoon. Just before sunset, Arthur Goldreich returned home. Seeing the police cars, he tried to back out of the driveway but was blocked by police and arrested. His wife, Hazel, arrived a short time later with the children and a friend. She was also arrested, as was Hilliard Festenstein, a physician who came to the house, ostensibly to return a book, later that evening.[19] Eight servants and farmhands were also placed in custody. The white prisoners were taken off in the dry cleaning van, the blacks in a separate vehicle.

The haul of men and documents surprised even the Special Branch police. Not only were those arrested the leading dissidents still in South Africa, the stash of documents exceeded their wildest expectations. More than two hundred documents were seized, ranging from Mandela's diary, notebook, and false passport to an MK disciplinary code and a notebook in Goldreich's handwriting labeled "Theory of Demolition." The real catch was the Operation Mayibuye document, which outlined a detailed plan for guerilla warfare and intervention by sympathetic foreign powers. The documents firmly tied Mandela to the Rivonia activities, permitting new charges to be brought against him. There were lists of names and addresses, presumably networks of MK associates. Documents also led the police to Travallyn and the small arsenal there.

The police also uncovered other items supporting claims of sabotage, if not outright revolution. There was a manual entitled "British Coal Mine Explosives," as well as nitric acid, ammonium nitrate crystals, benzene, aluminum pipes, time fuses, and rubber gloves. More benign if equally incriminating discoveries included a duplicating machine, six typewriters, and reams of blank paper, as well as a radio transmitter and poles that could serve as masts for broadcast. There were, in addition, 106 maps, pinpointing police stations, army bases, railway lines, and other potential sabotage targets. The only weapon found at Liliesleaf Farm was an air gun.[20] It was, nonetheless, an incriminating haul.

* * *

All of those arrested at Rivonia were held under the ninety-day-detention law in solitary confinement. The extent of their solitude and other aspects of their treatment during confinement varied widely over the next three months. White prisoners were treated more leniently than the blacks.

In addition to those arrested at Rivonia, the Special Branch began to gather other ANC and Communist Party leadership into their net. Harold Wolpe, who had been involved in the purchase of Liliesleaf Farm, was arrested trying to flee into Bechuanaland. Mandela was brought to Pretoria Local Prison from his Robben Island prison cell and treated as a ninety-day detainee. Early in August, Ruth First, a Communist leader and the wife of Joe Slovo, was detained and confined to the white women's section of the same prison.

The Pretoria Local Prison, where most of the detainees were kept, was a short-term holding facility in the nation's administrative capital. Of course, whites were kept separately from blacks. Attempts by the wives of white detainees to get extra clothing to Govan Mbeki and Raymond Mhlaba were initially rebuffed. A black person later delivered the clothing.

After two chilly nights at the notorious Old Fort Prison in Johannesburg, Ahmed Kathrada was transferred for some unknown reasons to the Pretoria prison—the black section, of course, given that he was no longer red-headed or Portuguese. After an icy shower, he was placed in solitary confinement in a cell approximately eight square feet in area. His solitude was virtually complete at first. He was allowed one hour of exercise a day. His only conversations were with Special Branch police, who tried to turn him into a witness for the state. Their tactics were of the classic good-cop/bad-cop variety. Inspector van Zyl, whom Kathrada had met under friendly circumstances in his hometown of Schweizer-Reneke, passed along messages from his family and suggested that he shouldn't protect "kaffirs" and "Jews." The bad cop was Captain "Rooi Rus" Swanepoel, who threatened him with violence and used racist epithets. Kathrada could see the other black prisoners from Liliesleaf Farm but could not communicate with them. No books other than the Bible were allowed for this Muslim man, who was not permitted to have written contact with the outside world.[21]

Toward the end of the ninety days, the restrictions eased somewhat. Food was delivered to him, and he could send his clothes out to the laundry. More lenient warders permitted some communication among prisoners. Notes were smuggled in and out with packages. Kathrada would learn both of the escape of some of his comrades and the fate of another, Looksmart Ngudle, who died while in detention. Ngudle's death made

Kathrada fully aware of the likelihood that he would either be killed in prison or, after a perfunctory trial, hanged.[22]

Rusty Bernstein was also kept in Pretoria Local Prison. Solitary confinement frightened and depressed him. The persistence of his wife, Hilda, eventually resulted in a few visits from her, ostensibly to discuss family and "business" matters such as the sale of a car,[23] but his human contact was limited to these brief visits and the inevitable interrogations. In the absence of books or regular communications, he was unable to concentrate on anything other than his plight, which was what his captors intended. Hilda and Bram Fischer, who together with others had formed an escape committee, agreed with Rusty that escape from the Pretoria prison was impossible.[24]

Denis Goldberg was initially confined to Pretoria Local Prison under conditions similar to those of his black comrades. However, at some point in the detention period, he was transferred to the jail at Vereeniging, the industrial town thirty miles or so south of Johannesburg near the site of the Sharpeville massacre. Although Goldberg was still kept in solitary confinement, the security at Vereeniging was somewhat more lax than in Pretoria, lax enough for him to venture an escape attempt. Goldberg pried open the bars of his cell using the padlock on the door as a lever. He got over a fourteen-foot wall—Goldberg would later remember it as at least twenty feet high—topped with glass and barbed wire and ran toward the woods near the prison. But another prisoner alerted the guards, and he was brought down by police dogs only a few hundred feet from freedom.[25] After he was transferred back to Pretoria, Esme, his wife, noticed the torn and bloody clothing in his laundry. The police told her of the abortive escape and warned of the consequences of any further attempts.[26]

Harold Wolpe and the Goldreichs were kept at Marshall Square, the Johannesburg holding jail, and also put under solitary confinement. But the circumstances in Johannesburg differed markedly from those in Pretoria or even Vereeniging. After first being confined to a small cell without a cot or chair, Wolpe complained, and he was transferred to a cell with a bed and toilet facilities. The warders permitted food and clean clothes to be brought in from the outside almost from the beginning of his detention. His wife, AnnMarie, visited frequently. The Marshall Square warders, who had no love for the arrogant Special Police, regarded the prisoners as misguided intellectuals of a better class than the hardened small-time criminals who ordinarily populated their facility.[27] They eventually permitted regular contact among not only the white prisoners but their Indian comrades as well—Laloo Chiba, Abdullah Jassat, and Mosie Moola, who had been arrested on matters unrelated to the Rivonia conspiracy. The five of them had regular meetings, which were openly permitted by their guards. They conferred about the possibility of escape and actively planned for it.[28]

Their ideas might have come from the script of a bad prison movie. They fantasized about shooting their way out with a gas gun, or cutting their way through the bars with a pair of steel cutters hidden inside the cavity of a roasted chicken or with razor blades stuffed into a loaf of French bread—all to be smuggled in by AnnMarie Wolpe. The razor-blade idea actually came from a Peter Sellers film, *Two-Way Stretch*. They rejected the gun plan as idiotic; the cutting tools actually made their way to the prisoners—inside a chicken—but barely made a dent in the bars.[29]

Astoundingly, one of the craziest plots actually worked. Wolpe and Goldreich, together with Jassat and Moola—Chiba had already been released—bribed their sole nighttime guard, eighteen-year-old Arnoldus Johannus Greeff, into helping them. Greeff would enter Goldreich's cell, lead them out of the building, and then pretend as if he had been knocked out. Hazel Goldreich was invited to join in the plan; she sensibly declined, believing that it wouldn't work and that even a successful escape would forever separate her from her children. The escape committee, led by Bram Fischer and Hilda Bernstein, was told of the plan and was appropriately dubious of its chances for success. Although it did not go exactly as planned, the escape took place. Goldreich and Wolpe eventually made their way to the MK safe house in Mountain View and then across the border into Swaziland. Jassat and Moola blended into Johannesburg's Indian community and also remained free. Despite a 10,000-rand price on their heads, Goldreich and Wolpe were ultimately flown to Bechuanaland. They eventually made it to Dar es Salaam, Tanganyika, and then to freedom in England.

In the meantime, young Greeff bowed to questioning and gave a complete account of the plan. He was charged with accepting a bribe and aiding escape. The prosecutor in his case was Percy Yutar, who was to lead the prosecution of the Rivonia defendants. Greeff was convicted and sentenced to the maximum six years. Lord Dunrossil, an official observer to the British Foreign Office, believed that there was no great political significance to Greeff's trial, "though it has no doubt come as a shock to some Afrikaners that such a seemingly loyal son of the *volk* could be bribed in this way to let important political prisoners escape. What does emerge is that Goldreich is clearly a quick-witted man of considerable patience and resource."[30] Greeff was released a few years later without completing his sentence. He did not get the promised four thousand rand until Nelson Mandela became president of the Republic. The money was paid by the ANC, which by then ruled South Africa.[31]

AnnMarie Wolpe was arrested in front of her children and taken to Marshall Square for questioning about her complicity in her husband's escape. She admitted sending razor blades to her husband but denied any other role in the plot. Oddly, despite her obvious involvement, she was released the next day, never again to be arrested.

But another person was to pay dearly for the embarrassment the escape caused the South African police establishment. Shortly after Wolpe and Goldreich reached the comparative safety of Bechuanaland, the offices of James Kantor, Wolpe's brother-in-law and law partner, were raided. Hundreds of files dealing with Kantor's criminal and civil representations, as well as financial records, were seized. Kantor had had nothing to do with the escape. He had permitted his brother-in-law to use his weekend retreat at Hartebeesport resort area near Johannesburg while on the run from the police after the Liliesleaf Farm raid, but not after Wolpe and the others fled Marshall Square. Other than sharing a law practice with his Communist brother-in-law, Kantor had had no involvement in antigovernment activities. He was what he seemed to the community—a successful, socially well-connected, apolitical lawyer. Nevertheless, after his office was raided, Kantor was himself detained under the ninety-day law. He was later charged, along with the other Rivonia defendants, with sabotage and violation of the Suppression of Communism Act. It was the price someone in the Wolpe family had to pay for compromising the system.

Shortly after Kantor's arrest, Justice Minister John Vorster said that despite the escapes the state would pursue its case: "There can be no doubt that two of the big fishes have got away, but some very important ones still remain in our net. It will be more or less like producing Hamlet without the Prince, but the show will go on just the same."[32]

2

The Lawyers and the Judge

The Defense

LIKE THE UNITED Kingdom, South Africa has a divided bar; at the time of the Rivonia Trial, "attorneys" and "advocates" played very different roles in the judicial process. Attorneys—like solicitors, their British counterparts—were the office lawyers. They worked directly with clients. They were responsible for legal work not directly involving the courts—drafting contracts, wills, and trusts, and other non-litigation-related paperwork. When courtroom work was required, especially in the higher courts, the attorney would employ an advocate, the equivalent of a British barrister, and would work with that advocate in the preparation of the case. In 1963, only an advocate could appear for a client in those trial courts trying serious civil and criminal matters, or before the appellate courts. The attorney was responsible for making sure that the advocate was paid for courtroom work. Attorneys could team up with one another in law firms. Advocates were all solo practitioners. They had offices in specially designated buildings located near the central courts—the South African equivalent of the British Inns of Court.

By October 1963, thirty-year-old Joel Joffe had worked as both an advocate and as an attorney, most recently as the latter, which is what he was at the time of the Rivonia Trial. At one point he had been James Kantor's law partner. He was unsympathetic to the apartheid government but had no involvement in politics and had handled few cases with any political implications. Like many of his well-educated, English-speaking contemporaries, Joffe's reaction to the South African situation was to plan to emigrate to Australia. His visa for entry to Australia was pending and plans for the move were under way—Joffe and his wife, Vanetta, had gone so far as to sell their house. When Kantor was arrested and detained under the ninety-day law, his family asked Joffe to step in as the caretaker of his practice. Joffe wound up sharing the office with the security police, who combed through the office records—papers, ledgers, account books and receipts, and financial statements. The records pertained both to Kantor and to Kantor's brother-in-law Harold Wolpe, who was by now well away from South Africa. Joffe describes his work in Kantor's office as the "sinister and cheerless task" of burying the ashes of what had been a thriving and lucrative practice.[1]

Several weeks after Joffe began work at Kantor's office, Hilda Bernstein, the wife of defendant Rusty Bernstein, visited him. Both Hilda and Rusty had been active in the Communist Party of South Africa, both before its banning in 1950 and then, surreptitiously, in its various later incarnations. Hilda's election to the Johannesburg City Council in 1944 as a Communist was a unique event—no Communist had ever been elected by the all-white electorates of the nation and, at least as long as the electorates remained all white, none would be again.

Several other lawyers had already turned down Hilda's request for representation because they were either too busy or afraid to become involved in this monumental and controversial case. Even Joffe was hesitant, fearing that representation would be a waste of time. As everyone knew, the trial would be a mere formality. "Everything pointed clearly to a certain conviction for everybody involved. It was not just that there was a mountain of evidence, if the press leaks were to be believed, but the documents from Rivonia alone were sufficiently damning for everyone concerned to be sentenced with the utmost severity of the law."[2]

But, as Joffe listened to Hilda's story of attempts to get information about her husband's status, he was "less surprised than sickened by her account."[3] The head of the Security Police had refused to tell her even whether her husband would be charged. She had received permission to visit Rusty on two occasions, but the conversations were closely monitored and limited to business and financial matters.

Joffe was outraged and agreed to undertake the representation. Within a few weeks, others connected with the prisoners contacted him: Albertina Sisulu, Walter's wife; Annie Goldberg, Denis's mother; and Winnie Mandela, Nelson's wife. He agreed to represent them all, except for Kantor—who would need separate counsel—and Bob Hepple. Whether Hepple would be a defendant or state witness was unclear.

Rusty Bernstein thought Joffe an "inspired choice." He was a mild and unobtrusive man who combined "a fierce sense of right and justice with great empathy." Joffe became more than the attorney organizing the trial. He became the guardian of the financial and personal affairs of the families of the defendants. The need for assistance to the families was to become more and more important as the trial went on.[4]

As the attorney, Joffe's primary task was to put together a team of advocates to represent the prisoners in court[5]—assuming that there would be charges, rather than an endless series of ninety-day detentions. At this point, endless detention was clearly a possibility.

Joffe first choice was Bram Fischer, perhaps the most admired advocate in the Johannesburg bar. Fischer, forty-five, had "taken silk," meaning he was QC, or Queen's Counsel, a designation given to a small number of lawyers ranked by their peers as among the best in the profession. Fischer was also a dedicated and active opponent of the apartheid regime. The families that had hired Joffe all suggested that the Rivonia team be headed by Fischer, who had been a lead advocate in the Treason Trial, the marathon proceedings that had occurred in fits and starts between 1956 and 1961, ending with the acquittal of all the defendants, including Mandela.

Fischer was therefore in many ways the obvious choice for Rivonia. He was one of the most outstanding lawyers in the country. He was a much sought-after advocate, representing not only those charged with antigovernment activities but also large commercial interests. His clients ranged from accused traitors to the mining magnate Sir Ernest Oppenheimer. Fischer came from the Afrikaner aristocracy. He was the son of a judge president of the South Africa's Orange Free State and a grandson of a president of the Orange River Republic, one of the Boer republics brought into the Union of South Africa.

Paradoxically, Fischer was also an ardent Communist. His conversion to Communism began in the early 1930s while he was a Rhodes Scholar at Oxford. Some South African intellectuals embraced the Party primarily for its support for the rights of black people. They were willing to overlook concerns about abuses committed in the Soviet Union and elsewhere in order to be part of an organization fighting the racism that saturated South Africa. Bram Fischer's devotion to the Communist cause went beyond identification with its support for a nonracial society. He was a true believer. He unhesitatingly followed the Soviet line, dismissing reports about Stalin's excesses as "propaganda put about by the Western press."[6] When others sought to soften his South African Communist Party affiliation, casting it as based only upon the Party's support for political rights and equality for black people, he would ask them not to "apologize to anyone for [his] political beliefs."[7]

Praise for Fischer flowed from the mouths of those with whom he came in contact. Hilda Bernstein described him as having "a complete and undeviating honesty that compelled him to do what he believed to be right, regardless of any personal difficulties."[8] Rusty Bernstein recalled his "enormous compassion."[9] Mandela remembers that "he showed a level of courage and sacrifice that was in class by itself."[10] Sisulu observed, "His manner made it difficult for people to say no."[11] Fischer remained polite and dignified, even in his dealings with the police. Joffe recalls, "Bram was the most popular man at the Johannesburg bar. Nobody had hard words to say about him though some, particularly amongst the Security Police, had harsh words for his politics."[12] In addition to his charm, gentleness, and sincerity, Fischer had other traits even more important for an advocate about to represent people charged with a capital offense. Joffe comments that he had "a painstaking, conscientious mind, a clear insight, tremendous drive and ability, singleness of purpose and immense courage and integrity."[13]

In 1954, after the Party was outlawed, Fischer's political beliefs caused him to be banned from public meetings. His wife and political soul mate, Molly, was under a similar order. But Fischer continued his law practice unabated and with great success in both commercial and human rights cases. In 1961, he was elected chairman of the Johannesburg Bar Council.

Beneath his public façade, however, Fischer was a leader of a revolutionary movement that had begun to deal in violent acts. He had been an active participant in the planning of the very antigovernment activities with which the prisoners in the Rivonia Trial were to be charged. It was pure coincidence that Fischer had not been at Liliesleaf Farm on the day of the raid. Under principles of legal ethics—as applicable in South Africa as elsewhere in the Anglo-American legal world—a lawyer subject to being charged as part of the same conspiracy as his client has a conflict of interest that would, at least without the client's consent, bar him from the representation. Although Joffe was unaware of Fischer's own participation in the illegal acts, the accused and their families knew how deeply Fischer was involved in MK. They so valued his representation that they were willing to gamble on his ability to avoid both jail and the pitfalls of self-protection that might have tempted a lesser man. They knew that Fischer's heart and mind were in their cause, not in saving his own skin.

Fischer's involvement in the activities at Liliesleaf Farm nonetheless made him a highly vulnerable lead counsel. His arrest and detention were distinct possibilities, and he knew it. This made him initially reluctant to take on the case—more out of concern for how an attack on him would harm the accused than for his own safety. He was ultimately persuaded to lead the defense team by Joffe and two brilliant young advocates, George

Bizos and Arthur Chaskalson, whose services Joffe had secured to assist in the defense. In a meeting in Chaskalson's office, Chaskalson made the point to Fischer that as an Afrikaner Fischer was in the best position to defend clients who, it could be argued, had acted no differently from Afrikaner patriots in their opposition to British rule.[14]

Despite their relative youth, Bizos and Chaskalson had been involved in a number of political cases and were already considered among the best lawyers at the Johannesburg bar. As a child, Bizos had escaped the Nazi occupation of his native Greece, fleeing with his father in a small rowboat that drifted in the Mediterranean for several days before being picked up by a British destroyer; the Bizoses had helped hide some New Zealand soldiers trapped in their village by the Nazis. Since becoming an advocate 1954, Bizos had handled more political cases than any other lawyer in Johannesburg. An outgoing man with an easy manner, he would serve not only as a valuable member of the legal team but as public relations person for the defense.

Chaskalson had been at the bar for ten years. He was tall, good-looking, and athletic. Those traits, in combination with an incisive legal mind, had made his success as an advocate a sure bet. In his earlier years, he had represented corporate and insurance-law clients—cases that conferred wealth and status. He began to take on political cases not as a form of protest against the state but from a sense of duty. His skill in examination was to be invaluable.

Later the defense team recruited another prominent and venerable (he was sixty-five) Johannesburg advocate, Vernon Berrange. Berrange was known as a devastating cross-examiner. Joffe noted that he could "strike terror even into the most belligerent of policemen."[15] He too had been an important part of the Treason Trial defense team, as well as an advocate in countless other political trials. Berrange had been in London during the early stages of the representation but joined the defense in time to use his abilities as a cross-examiner, abilities that would be crucial in a case such as this, in which the defense could anticipate that many of the state's witnesses would either be persons who had themselves been subject to ninety-day detentions or police officers with a strong motive to distort or embellish the truth.

Like Fischer, Berrange faced risks by becoming involved in the Rivonia Trial. He had been named as a member of the Communist Party, membership in which was outlawed by the government under the Suppression of Communism Act. The government was then drafting legislation that would disbar "listed persons" from the practice of law. Representing Mandela and the others greatly increased the chances of his losing his profession.

George Bizos has noted that during a United Nations debate on the Rivonia Trial, "a delegate from a small tyrannical regime had asked what sort of justice could the Rivonia accused expect if they had lackeys of the Verwoerd government appointed as their lawyers."[16] The statement not only appalled the defense team, it was also clearly untrue.[17] Indeed, no group could be further from being lackeys of the South African government than the lawyers who agreed to represent the defendants in the Rivonia Trial. Their diligence, expertise, and sympathy for the accused were models for lawyers in political trials, and remain so. In 1966, Canon L. John Collins of St. Paul's Cathedral in London—whose group provided whatever meager funding was available for the defense counsel—praised the work of the Rivonia lawyers as "one of the bright spots over these last ten dark years."[18]

The Prosecutor

The prosecution team was lead by Dr. Percy Yutar, deputy attorney general of the province. Yutar had prosecuted on behalf of the state since 1939. With a doctorate in law—he insisted on being addressed as Dr. Yutar—he was said to be the most qualified prosecution lawyer in South Africa.[19] A sympathetic judge called him "one of the most respected and colorful figures in South Africa's Administration of Justice,"and, further, a lawyer who had been "the undoing of many a reluctant or truculent witness."[20] A newspaper article, entitled "The Yutar Legend," described him as "far and away the most qualified legal brain this country has ever possessed." The subhead of the article read: "Ruthless avenger is also gentle."[21]

That sympathetic judge had described Yutar as "square-shouldered, ramrod-erect, baldish and deceptively calm of voice and mien."[22] Less benevolent observers depicted him as "small, dapper, balding man with a deformed left hand and a supercilious smile."[23] His left hand had been mangled in an electric mincing machine when he was working in his father's butcher shop. His style was to be strong, fast, and derisive. His opponents in the courtroom described his voice not as calm but as a sad falsetto—especially when things were not going well for him—occasionally rising to a high-pitched squeak. He thirsted for publicity and enthusiastically courted the press. His ambition was to become the first Jewish attorney general in South Africa.

Yutar was one of eight children in a family of Orthodox Lithuanian immigrants. There were close to 120,000 Jews in South Africa at the time of the Rivonia Trial. Roughly 80 percent were Jews who immigrated to South Africa from Lithuania and nearby areas in the early 1900s and their descendants. Most were part of the English-speaking community, although Jews had fought on both sides of the Anglo-Boer War.[24] Yutar was one of the few Jews to hold a high government position in an Afrikaner-dominated civil service in which anti-Semitism was never far below the surface. The president of South Africa's largest synagogue for more than a decade, he proudly wore a signet ring in the shape of the Star of David.[25] He was always anxious to prove that Jews—and Percy Yutar in particular—were good and loyal citizens of white South Africa. He was openly contemptuous of Jewish Communists, of which there were many, including Rivonia defendants Rusty Bernstein and Denis Goldberg, as well as the escapees Wolpe and Goldreich.

Yutar's ambition, his craving for publicity, his politics, and his hostility toward the defendants would manifest itself throughout the trial. Interestingly, and a little curiously not all of this played well with the trial judge.

Justice Quartus de Wet

His official title was judge president of the Transvaal Provincial Division of the Supreme Court of South Africa. Quartus De Wet (his name is Latin for "fourth son"; his older brother was Tertius) sat in sole judgment of the law and facts. His was the only vote that counted. Although jury trials were still possible in South African at the time of Rivonia, the law under which the defendants were charged did not permit a jury.

Defense counsel viewed de Wet as a mixed bag—not the best they could have hoped for their clients but certainly not the worst. An Afrikaner whose family had been prominent figures on the political scene, Quartus's father had been a high-ranking government official. Justice de Wet was not a member of the ruling National Party, the party responsible for instituting apartheid in 1948; he had been appointed to the bench in 1947 as a member of the United Party.

The United Party was the party of the well-regarded statesman Jan Smuts (1870–1950). Smuts was a hero of the Boer War; he led British forces against the Germans in World War I; and he was named a field marshal in World War II. He is the only person to sign the treaties ending both world wars. He was also one of the leading forces behind the formation of the United Nations. Smuts and his party were racists in every modern sense of the word. They believed in the superiority of white culture. But, unlike the Nationalists, they did not seek to codify their racism in a rigid set of laws intended to permanently subjugate the black people of the country.

The British Consul General, Leslie Minford—who was to be a keen observer at the trial—believed that, despite de Wet's United Party background, his political leanings were Nationalist. But Minford noted that de Wet was not a member of the far-right Afrikaner Broederbond.[26] The difference in attitude was enough to give the defendants and their lawyers some hope of fair treatment.

An earlier incident involving Nelson Mandela as a lawyer also gave the defendants some hope. In 1955, Mandela appeared before an Afrikaner magistrate named Willem Dormehl. Dormehl refused to allow Mandela to represent a client in his courtroom without producing the certificate indicating his right to practice as an attorney. After Mandela brought the certificate and the trial began, Dormehl frequently interrupted his examinations with shouts of "Hey you!" and finally "Hey you! Sit down!" On Bizo's advice, Mandela petitioned the Supreme Court, which oversaw cases heard by magistrates, to have Dormehl removed from the case. The petition came before de Wet, who was outraged by Dormehl's behavior. "Everyone knows that Mandela is an attorney," de Wet noted. He ordered the magistrate to remove himself, adding, "This is the sort of thing that brings the administration of justice into disrepute in our country."[27] In addition, in 1961, de Wet granted Ahmed Kathrada bail in an amount he could easily pay and criticized the security police for "their unwarranted persecution" of him.[28]

Yet the reaction of counsel to de Wet's selection as the presiding judge was still ambivalent. Joffe describes the judge's reputation as "strange." He was known to dispense rough justice on the basis of common sense based upon a "mixture of obstinacy and prejudice." In court, he appeared self-willed, disliking interruptions and procedural objections. Minford described him as a judge who made his mind up fairly rapidly about the merits of the case.[29] Furthermore, although not a puppet of the government, he had all of the prejudices common in white South Africa.

Apartheid South Africa had one of the world's highest capital punishment rates; between 1960 and 1990, more than 2,500 persons were hanged.[30] Yet, although de Wet had imposed the death sentence, he was not generally known as a hanging judge. A story had circulated that a death sentence he imposed had been set aside by the then–governor general of South Africa, who had deemed the defendant innocent. According to the story, de Wet ultimately agreed with the decision to overturn the sentence and afterward became more reluctant to impose capital punishment. Another story, also apocryphal and perhaps involving the same case, told of de Wet catching a police witness in a fabrication.[31] The incident, it was said, caused him to be wary of police testimony.

But de Wet's inconsistent behavior and his protectiveness of a society in which he believed made both counsel and the defendants far from confident that his selection guaranteed leniency. His behavior would puzzle defense counsel throughout the trial, making it difficult for them to predict how he was likely to rule on a given issue. The obviousness of his racial preferences began to dominate the view of him held by the accused and their counsel as the trial wore on. The fundamental assessment of de Wet as difficult, arrogant, and independent of government control yet guided by the prejudices of his upbringing would remain fairly constant.

The key personnel of the Rivonia Trial were now in place.

3

Reaction

WHEN JOEL JOFFE was contacted by Hilda Bernstein and he agreed to represent her husband, Rusty, he told her that he was a lawyer, not a politician. "I will do the job as well as I am able. But public opinion is so heavily against your husband and the others that in the end this is likely to count heavily." "Public opinion, against the Rivonia prisoners?" she responded. "Mr. Joffe, I think we speak a different language. You're talking of white public opinion. I am talking of majority public opinion, which is not against, but *for* the Rivonia accused."[1]

And of course she was right. The white-dominated media were strongly in favor of the prosecution. The Rivonia raid was a stunning and welcome development for most white South Africans—a major breakthrough in the nation's fight against terrorism. Fear of a total onslaught—*totale aanslag* in Afrikaans—by the country's blacks had risen dramatically since the Sharpeville uprising in March 1960. Since then, there had been widely publicized incidents of sabotage. No loss of life had been credibly connected to either the ANC or the South Africa Communist Party; nonetheless, many whites believed that widespread killings were imminent and that those arrested at Rivonia—as well as Nelson Mandela, despite his being in a prison cell on Robben Island—were mostly likely to carry out or to instigate such acts of terrorism.

The white South African press—constituting virtually the entirety of the nation's press—gave the raid and the lead-up to the trial extensive coverage. Front-page banner headlines appeared for weeks after the Rivonia raid in both the Afrikaans- and English-language press, heralding the successful operation to rid the nation of dangerous terrorists. Daily accounts of Wolpe and Goldreich's escape and travels through Swaziland and Bechuanaland filled the nation's newspapers—together with the announcement of the substantial reward for their recapture—through the time of their eventual arrival in London.

Government ministers spewed a steady stream of venom against the Rivonia accused on radio and in the newspapers. Officials—from the minister of justice to the head of the Security Branch—proclaimed the defendants' guilt. The white population was led to view the convictions and hanging of the prisoners as certainties—and assured that this would secure their way of life.

Shortly after the raid, the commissioner of police, Lt. Gen. J. M. Keevy, told the *Rand Daily Mail* that the information collected in the Rivonia raid "would lead to a further weakening of the already crumbling organizations of subversive movements who were threatening the peace and security of the Republic."[2] The Afrikaans-language *Die Burger* proclaimed that the police were convinced they had dealt the troublemakers "a terrible blow."[3] Minister of Justice Vorster predicted from his holiday seaside resort that, based upon the Rivonia raid, "there would be no internal uprising in South Africa this year." He added, "This year was set aside by the Communists, the ANC and other subversive organizations as the time to wreck law and order and create chaos in South Africa." Vorster told the *Star* that he was "confident that every subversive organization would be run to the ground and smashed."[4]

Such a media campaign was unprecedented in South Africa. The tradition of not commenting on pending cases was a strong one. But of course there was not yet a pending case, given that the accused were simply being "detained" under the ninety-day laws without formal arrest and without charges being brought against them.

But as Hilda Bernstein had remarked to Joel Joffe, black opinion was very different. The black press was tiny and far less effective than the word of mouth that traveled through the townships surrounding the cities and into rural locations. News that the principal leaders of the fight against white oppression were on trial for their lives spread quickly. Despite the fact that the date and time of the first hearing was kept secret until very near the day it occurred, the large and supportive crowd of blacks was evidence that, as Hilda Bernstein said, the majority of the opinion in the country was *for* the Rivonia accused. It was much the same in the rest of the world.

The Rivonia Trial made headlines in the West. The major English-language newspapers carried stories of the arrests and the first day of trial. The *New York Times*, for example, ran a detailed story on the beginning of the trial, noting that the defendants faced the death penalty.[5] British newspapers, including the *Times* and *Guardian*, covered the arrests and the trial.

They also covered Wolpe's and Goldreich's escape, as well as their subsequent news conferences describing their ordeals. Interest in the proceedings was sufficient for several other newspapers—including the *New York Times*, the *Washington Post*, and the *Observer* (UK)—to follow the proceedings. Defense counsel tried to present the best possible image of the defendants and their cause. At their request, the novelist Nadine Gordimer, who was to win the Nobel Prize in Literature in 1991, edited autobiographical notes written by the accused for distribution to the local and international press. Gordimer's notes were also passed to the British Foreign Office, among others.[6] The coverage served not only to make many in the United States and Great Britain aware of the trial but also as a springboard for antiapartheid protests for the next thirty years.

Nonetheless, the portrait of Rivonia painted by the world's media was complex, contradictory, and very much influenced by Cold War politics. The only two powers with any effective leverage on South Africa were the United States and Great Britain. Whether the governments of those nations would seek, directly or indirectly, to intervene on behalf of the defendants was uncertain at best. And even if they were to do so, whether or not South Africa would accede to such pressure—even from its most important allies—was equally uncertain.

Leaders and diplomats of all nations, including the Western powers, uniformly condemned South Africa's racial policies. The United Nations was the most common forum for proclaiming their vehement opposition to apartheid. In August 1963, just a month after the raid on Liliesleaf Farm, Adlai Stevenson, the United States ambassador to the United Nations, denounced the apartheid policy as "abhorrent."[7] Sir Patrick Dean, the British UN ambassador, declared it an "evil."[8]

Yet rhetoric had not been translated into meaningful steps to limit the South African regime's ability to enforce apartheid. As more African states gained their independence in the late 1950s, those states, in conjunction with Asian nations and supported by the Communist bloc, sought resolutions condemning South Africa and calling for sanctions against it. Such resolutions were either defeated or watered down to meaninglessness by the Western powers, led by the United States and Great Britain. South Africa, abhorrent as it was, was a bulwark against Communism. Philip Crowe, the United States ambassador to Pretoria from 1959 to 1961, was quoted in *U.S. News and World Report* as stating that South Africa's contribution to the "free world" was not only her military strength but her willingness to serve as a base for the West in a limited war in which the Suez Canal would most certainly be closed. He described South Africa as "one of the few strongly anti-Communist nations on that continent," and stated that the "majority of the forty-odd nations between Cairo and Cape Town are either neutral or subject to Communist influence."[9]

After the Sharpeville massacre, the Afro-Asian bloc was somewhat more successful in getting the UN to use tougher language. In April 1960, the Security Council adopted a resolution calling on South Africa to abandon apartheid and to introduce measures to encourage racial harmony. Great Britain as well as France abstained from the vote, but the United States voted in favor.[10] In August 1963—again, shortly after the Rivonia raid—the Western powers permitted passage of a Security Council Resolution 181, calling for the liberation of all persons imprisoned, interned, or subject to other restrictions "for having opposed the policy of apartheid," and "solemnly calling" upon all states to cease shipment of arms.[11]

Of course, the Rivonia Trial defendants were charged with more than simply opposing apartheid. And the Western powers interpreted the arms-shipment language of the resolution to apply to the shipment of arms "suitable for enforcement of apartheid."[12] At the urging of the United States Joint Chiefs of Staff, discussions of possible arms shipments continued within the State Department for several years.[13] On July 19, 1963, Secretary of State Dean Rusk summarized U.S. policy as reaffirming "our dedication to eradication of apartheid by peaceful means while avoiding measures against South Africa to which we could not agree in principle."[14] The United States was clearly opposed to the expulsion of South Africa from the United Nations as well as to mandatory sanctions in any form. The arms embargo wasn't made mandatory until 1977.

But the world publicity on the arrests and the beginning of the Rivonia Trials affected the debate in the United Nations. On October 11, 1963, just as the trial began, the United Nations General Assembly adopted Resolution 1881 by a 106 to 1 vote, with only South Africa dissenting. The resolution called for an end to the repression of persons opposing apartheid. Paragraph 2 of the resolution "requests the Government of South Africa to abandon the arbitrary trial now in progress and forthwith to grant unconditional release to all political prisoners and to all persons imprisoned, interned or subjected to other restrictions for having opposed the policy of apartheid." This time, Britain, the United States, Australia, and France all voted in favor of the resolution as a whole, but, in a separate vote, abstained from the approval of paragraph 2—the part of the resolution applicable to the Rivonia Trial. The British representative stated that his country "should have preferred to speak not of 'arbitrary trial' but of 'trial based on arbitrary laws.'"[15]

The passage of UN Resolution 1881 contributed to the "laager mentality" attitude of many white South Africans, especially Afrikaners—*laager* being Afrikaans for circled wagons. As reported in the *New York Times*, the *Rand Daily Mail* of Johannesburg ran the headline "The West against South Africa" reporting on the resolution.[16] The pro-government Afrikaans paper *Die Vaderland* asked in an editorial, "Is the whole world now finally against us?"[17]

Still, the passage of the resolution, and especially its timing, elated Bram Fischer. Early on the morning that news of the resolution appeared, Fischer drove to his junior counsel George Bizos's house with the South African *Rand Daily Mail*'s account of its passage. He shoved the paper in Bizos's face and said excitedly, "Take this to them and tell them that they will not dare to hang them after this!"[18] Others were less sure.

The reluctance of Britain and the United States to agree to sanctions against South Africa—despite verbal repudiation of its racial policies—was well established. The relationship between Britain and South Africa was especially complex. There was substantial economic interchange—imports and exports, as well as the brokering of gold in London—between the two nations. In 1963, Britain exported almost £200 million and imported more than £115 million in goods to and from South Africa. British companies had invested almost £270 million in South Africa, almost as much as in the rest of Africa combined.[19] British investment in South Africa was greater than in any other country except Australia, Canada, and the United States.[20] Virtually all of South Africa's gold was marketed through London.[21] In addition, despite a history of hostility between the British and the Afrikaners who now led the country, there were close economic, political, and personal relationships.[22] Sports competition between the countries, especially between the English and English-speaking South Africans in cricket, was a deeply entrenched part of the culture of both nations.[23]

British support for the South African government began to wane to a significant degree in the late 1950s and early 1960s. Sentiment in Britain against the Nationalist regime began to rise, probably based more on the anti-British history of the Nationalist leaders than on any fundamental disagreement over the concept of white domination.[24] In addition to this sentiment, Britain, as the nominal leader of the Commonwealth, found itself needing to adopt policies palatable to the African and Asian nations that were also a part of the Commonwealth. Newly independent African states such as Ghana and Nigeria were, not surprisingly, outspoken critics of the South African regime. South Africa voted in 1960 to declare itself a republic, rather than a union under the queen. That decision, and South Africa's unwillingness to moderate its racial policies, led to its withdrawal from the Commonwealth at the same time as its status as a republic became effective on May 31, 1961.[25]

The termination of South Africa's Commonwealth membership did not end British support for the government, with which it maintained political and especially economic relations. By the mid-1960s, British public sentiment, especially among the Tories, began to shift back in favor of a continuing relationship with South Africa.[26]

Although in the 1960s American economic involvement was less significant, investment by U.S. companies in South Africa was growing. In addition to gold, the country produced crucial minerals, including uranium oxide. Perhaps more importantly, the United States was taking the lead in the West in the Cold War. Nations were asked to line up on one side or the other, either for or against the West or the Communist powers, and of course South Africa was viewed as a bulwark against Communist advance in Africa. Some twenty-four years after Mandela's 1962 arrest, a *New York Times* article reported that a retired agent had boasted that the CIA had provided South African intelligence with full details of Mandela's movements. Mandela's biographer, Anthony Sampson, found the report "credible."[27]

The United States and Great Britain retained military relationships with South Africa. The Royal Navy used the naval base at Simon's Town on the Cape Peninsula.[28] U.S. Navy ships regularly used the main ports of Cape Town and Durban. South Africa participated in joint military exercises with Western forces.[29] There was a U.S. missile tracking station and communications facility at Pretoria, providing the terminus of the Atlantic Missile Range arterial long-haul communications system. South Africa also provided NASA with a deep-space-probe and satellite tracking station.[30] In short, the Republic of South Africa was clearly an ally in the West's defense against Communist expansion.

The apartheid regime was accustomed to verbal condemnation and to attempts by the Afro-Asian bloc to add teeth to the rhetoric. Such condemnations brought no noticeable change in its policies, nor did the South African government heed in any meaningful way the antiracist rhetoric coming from the United States or Great Britain. South Africa responded only by attempts to lobby Americans and Britons to see its side of the story.[31] Such attempts were usually laced with arguments emphasizing that the Pretoria government stood firm in the fight to keep the Communists out of southern Africa. The continuing attempt to portray the Rivonia defendants as Communists during the trial was very much a part of this propaganda effort.

Despite the South African government's apparent immovability, it was not completely immune to antiapartheid sentiment in London and Washington. The views of the African and Asian nations affected the conduct of its major Western supporters. After all, the West needed to keep as much good will in the Third World as possible in order to bolster its standing in its ongoing Cold War competition with the Communist bloc. As future events would show, Pretoria knew that it could not endure total isolation. But just how serious a threat the South African leadership believed that isolation to be, in light of American and British economic and military interests, is another matter. The fear of isolation from its Western friends may have had some influence on South Africa's conduct of its internal affairs, but, at least in 1963 and 1964, that influence was likely limited.

Correspondence between the British Embassy and its Foreign Office in October 1963—before the trial began in earnest—set the tone for British and American involvement during its course. Leslie Minford was the British official most involved in the proceedings, and he told the embassy that Rivonia was apt to be the most significant trial to date, "for its own intrinsic revelations and counter-revelations, for its powerful influence on internal and international opinion, for its repercussions on race and political relations inside South Africa and for its possible effect on H.M.G.'s [Her Majesty's Government's] policy vis-à-vis South Africa, bilaterally, intra-Commonwealth and at the United Nations." He thought that it would contribute more to "sharpening the animosities" between South Africa and the rest of world than any other single event.[32]

Lord Dunrossil, the British Foreign Office observer, wrote his office that there was little doubt that the South African government would make a major public show of Rivonia, seeking to show that the acts of violence were planned and executed and that "Communists were heavily involved."[33] He added that the difficult problem for Western observers was that many of the principals accused were Communists, as was Bram Fischer. Dunrossil recommended against official intervention, believing that such action would be "counterproductive."[34]

4

Preparing for Trial

IN THE EARLY days of their representation, defense counsel could only guess at what lay ahead. They did not know who would be charged or what the charges would be. There was even the possibility that there would be no formal charges at all—simply an endless series of ninety-day detentions, lasting until eternity, or at least until the prisoners were dead from natural causes.

What they knew or suspected came from rumors floating around the legal and antigovernment communities and from newspaper reports. They knew the names of at least most detainees. Family members and friends on the outside could confirm their detentions. Government leaks told them that Nelson Mandela had been brought from Robben Island. Mandela's probable inclusion in any prosecution suggested to Joel Joffe and the others that charges would relate to acts that had taken place long before the raid on Liliesleaf Farm in July. Nonetheless, Joffe had the prescience to realize that charges would likely be brought under the Sabotage Act, which had been passed the previous year.[1]

The Sabotage Act contained provisions that would seriously complicate the task of defense counsel.[2] The act permitted a significant departure from the usual requirement in South Africa, as in Great Britain and its former colonies, that the state prove a defendant's guilt beyond a reasonable doubt. Under its provisions, the burden was on an accused to prove his innocence by showing that the commission of the act "objectively regarded" was not calculated or intended to produce certain stated effects, including bringing about any social or economic change in the nation. Furthermore, prosecution under the act would be a summary proceeding, meaning there would be no preparatory examination before a magistrate. Preparatory examinations, normal in South African criminal cases and comparable to a preliminary hearing in an American trial, would determine whether there was enough evidence for the case to go forward. The preparatory hearing would have provided defense counsel some idea of what they were up against. It also would have provided ammunition to cross-examine witnesses, such that it could be established when and if their testimony at trial varied from the testimony given at the preparatory examination.

The Sabotage Act carried a minimum five-year prison sentence and a maximum penalty of death. However, unlike a charge of treason, where every overt act had to be proved by two witnesses, violations of the act could be established by the testimony of a single person. Furthermore, charges of treason required a three-judge panel. In a case under the Sabotage Act, a single judge would try the case, with or without assessors, at his discretion. There was no option of a jury trial—although it is unlikely that the defense would have chosen one in this case, given the likely prejudices of an exclusively white jury pool. If the accused was acquitted under the Sabotage Act, he could be tried on other charges with regard to any of the acts alleged in the sabotage trial. In other words, the act permitted double jeopardy.

Lacking specific information, counsel met, discussed, read the press accounts, and listened to the rumors. Some things could be done—such as seeking funds to finance their defense. A trial was likely to last months, during which time the lawyers would not be able to take on other clients. There were no public funds available—no Legal Aid, no government payments to defense counsel. Furthermore, attorneys were responsible for paying the advocates employed to represent the clients in court. Failure to pay an advocate might result in an attorney, such as Joffe, being blacklisted—and thus unable to employ other advocates—despite the willingness of advocates like Bram Fischer to forego their fees.[3]

The lawyers turned to the only available source—the Defence and Aid Fund. The fund, operating in South Africa and relying on funding from Great Britain and Europe, was an outgrowth of the Christian Action organization, led by Canon L. John Collins, dean of St. Paul's Cathedral in London. The problem was that Defence and Aid had thus far refused to fund representations where the charges involved included violence or threat of violence. Joffe approached Canon Collins with the dilemma. Collins's willingness to consider the request was influenced by the fact that he and Mandela were friends; indeed, they had had a meeting in London in 1962, shortly before Mandela's arrest. Collins realized that the Rivonia Trial was to be a "vital case." He agreed to help. He solicited funds in England—as Joffe remembers it, from "little old ladies involved in the church"—and, eventually, Sweden. Ultimately, £19,500 was raised.

The funds were less than one-fifth of what the lawyers would have ordinarily received for such extended representation.[4] Even with this payment, Joffe was later threatened with blacklisting for failure to adequately compensate counsel—a charge that certainly originated with persons other than the advocates Joffe had engaged.[5]

Joffe sought information about his clients and the possibility of charges against them from whatever sources he could, including the offices of Colonel George Klindt, the head of the Johannesburg Security Police. He learned that Percy Yutar was ensconced in those police offices—which meant that he was almost certainly preparing for the trial against the Rivonia defendants. Joffe's direct inquiries were answered only with silence, however. Everything had become an official secret. They told him they did not know if charges would be brought, who might be charged, or when anything would happen. But they did give him the unsolicited information that no harm would come to him if he undertook the defense of political prisoners. Joffe thought they protested too much—why even mention the possibility of harm to a lawyer who was simply seeking to represent his clients?[6]

During his attempts to get information from Yutar, Joffe had an exchange with him. When they were behind closed doors, Yutar began a "little song of praise," as Joffe described it, for the Security Police, in whose offices he had been working. Yutar noted, "I have been at The Grays [the Security Police office in Johannesburg] for three weeks now, and I have not heard a single word of anti-Semitism from any of these people." Joffe responded that an absence of anti-Semitism was not a cause for special praise. "If you were a policeman, Joffe," replied Yutar, "wouldn't it make you anti-Semitic to have people like Bernstein and Goldberg going around stirring up the Bantu?"[7] Perhaps, thought Joffe, Yutar's prosecution of this case involved more than him simply doing his job as a prosecutor.

The fact that the white defendants and the prosecutor in the Rivonia Trial were Jews was not only reflected in the exchange between Yutar and Joffe. Denis Goldberg relates that, during his interrogation after his Liliesleaf Farm arrest, he was told by his questioner, "Goldberg, you will hang and one of your own will hang you."[8]

By October 7, the rumors suggested that something was about to happen. Joffe placed a call to Yutar. He was told that the trial would begin in Pretoria the next day. Pretoria, thirty miles north of Johannesburg, seemed an odd location for the trial. Based on Yutar's presence in the Johannesburg office and the arrests in nearby Rivonia, Joffe had assumed that all of the documents and investigation had come out of that office.[9] But in other, more important respects, Pretoria was not a surprising choice. Johannesburg was the financial and cultural center of the country, with a strong liberal bent. Pretoria was a civil servant's town, the heart of Afrikaner control of government operations. The five-year-long Treason Trial had been moved from Johannesburg to Pretoria to diminish the protests. Crowds and antigovernment protests would be easier to control than in Johannesburg—or "Jewburg," as some called it.[10]

Joffe and advocates Chaskalson and Bizos drove to Pretoria the next morning. Fischer was in court on another case, and the lawyers agreed that his presence would not be essential to deal with the formalities of an opening hearing. When they arrived at the Palace of Justice, the lawyers were surprised to find nothing to indicate that a major trial was about to begin. Indeed, the courthouse gave the appearance of a normal working day. No one seemed to know anything about those arrested at Rivonia, let alone a scheduled trial. After an hour's wait, the frustrated lawyers asked to see the Transvaal attorney general, Rudolf Werner Rein, Yutar's immediate superior.[11] Rein said that he couldn't help them. He had been told nothing. "I can understand your annoyance, gentlemen, but this is Yutar's case, not mine, and you'll have to take the matter up with him. Frankly, I am sick and tired of being blamed for Yutar's bungling."

In his indignation, Rein did let slip some useful information that perhaps explained the delay in the beginning of the proceedings. Yutar had asked Rein to sign an indictment against the prisoners. Rein had found the indictment to be a poor piece of work, slovenly drafted, and marred by legal defects. He had refused to sign it, returning it to Yutar for redoing, a rebuke that must have galled the man who had been lauded in the press as the most qualified lawyer in the country.

Rein agreed to call Yutar while the defense lawyers sat in his office. They heard him ask, "What is the charge, sabotage or high treason? Who will be the accused?" Hanging up, Rein told them that the prisoners had been released from ninety-day detention and that the case would begin the next day. He related that Yutar would not tell him who would be charged or what the charges would be. The lawyers asked for an explanation of why they had been left standing at the courthouse that day. Rein couldn't answer the question; Yutar had apparently not felt it necessary to apologize. Rein was able to tell them that if they went to the Pretoria Jail, they would be brought any prisoner who was to be charged in the case.

The jail was therefore their next stop, and there they encountered another hurdle, one that would be in place through the entirety of the trial.[12] The authorities told them they could see those prisoners who were to be charged, but that they would have to interview the black prisoners separately from the whites. Prison rules forbade racial mixing for any purposes—including contacts with their lawyers. Apartheid was applied even more rigorously in the prison system than in the outside world. Calls were made to higher-ups in the prison authority, and eventually the decision was made to breach the rules—this once. It was apparently too important to the state to have the trial seem to represent the fairness of the South African legal system for even the racist rules to stand in their way. Nonetheless, counsel's battles to consult freely and privately with their clients would continue throughout the months of the trial.

After what seemed an interminable wait, eleven prisoners, black and white, were brought to meet with the attorneys in a consulting room. The effects of the almost ninety days of confinement were immediately apparent to defense counsel. Bernstein and Kantor seemed particularly distressed and disoriented. Mandela was dressed in the clothes allotted to the black prisoners on the island—a khaki shirt and shorts and flimsy, open-toed sandals. Bizos and Chaskalson, who had known Mandela well before his most recent imprisonment, remarked at his loss of weight and weakened physical condition. But simple human contact—with each other as well as the outside world in the form of their lawyers—turned the meeting, a reunion of old friends, into an almost happy occasion. Joffe remembers that his clients seemed to be rediscovering the joy of speech.

The prisoners told the lawyers that they had been released from their ninety-day detention the previous day. They had been informed that they would be brought into court and formally charged within forty-eight hours of their arrests, deemed to be at the time of their release from detention. The first item of business was for the accused to decide whether they wanted these lawyers to represent them.

All but Jimmy Kantor and Bob Hepple immediately agreed. Everyone realized that Kantor was in a different position from the others. He had never participated in antigovernment activity. He shared none of the political baggage of the other defendants. He was clearly innocent of any charges that might be brought against him. Everyone—the other accused and their lawyers—agreed that he should have separate counsel in order to enable him to conduct a very different kind of defense. Kantor then left the meeting.

Hepple presented a thornier problem. He had been involved in anti-government activities, although more as a messenger than an important player. Hepple appeared uneasy from the beginning of the meeting. He admitted to the group that he had been asked to give evidence against the others and that he was considering doing so. Given the likelihood that those ultimately accused at the trial would face hanging, no one felt it right to try to dissuade him from breaking from their ranks. Joel Joffe would later comment, "He had to decide for himself, in his loneliness, whether to face trial and the disastrous consequences which might flow from it, or to seek indemnification by giving evidence against his colleagues and friends. Nobody at that moment seemed prepared to give him any advice."[13] Any such advice would have been too heavily tainted with self-interest. After delivering his revelation that he might turn on them, Hepple left. There were now the nine defendants, Bizos, Chaskalson, and Joffe.

There wasn't much time for serious legal consultations at this first meeting—and they were all hampered by how little they really knew about the charges that would be brought. Much of the conversation centered on practical matters and the prisoners' concerns for their families. During the course of the trial, in addition to his considerable input into trial strategy, Joffe in particular would spend endless hours assisting the defendants' family members with a variety of issues.

The lawyers did take time to emphasize the seriousness of the situation. Bizos took the lead, telling the clients that they would face charges of either treason or sabotage, or both. Both carried the death penalty.[14] Ahmed Kathrada remembers Bizos saying, "Be prepared for the worst." Mandela recalls that from that moment on they lived in the shadow of the gallows. "The mere possibility of a death sentence changes everything." Yet others had suspected from the time of their arrest that hanging was a real possibility. They had not been misled by the failure of the state's prosecution of the marathon Treason Trial—where Mandela and others had also faced the possibility of a death sentence. That trial was doomed from the start by inadequate evidence, yet the defendants, including Mandela and Kathrada, recalled that the "specter of the gallows had loomed large in our minds."[15] Mandela notes that he and the other defendants believed that death was "the most likely outcome" of the Rivonia Trial. "Far less crimes than ours had recently been punished by life sentences."[16] During the long months of the trial, prison officials never let him forget that he might hang. One night, a warder rapped on his cell door at bedtime. "Mandela, you don't have to worry about sleep," he said. "You are going to sleep for a long, long time." Mandela waited a moment and replied, "All of us, you included, are going to sleep for a long, long time." [17]

George Bizos remembers that there were as many as two thousand death sentences in some years after the National Party took over in 1948, although many were ultimately commuted. He recalls that hundreds of persons faced death at the time of the trial. There had been no executions for purely political crimes, but severe sentences were the rule.[18]

Joffe remembers that his clients appeared unfazed by Bizos's blunt assessment of the likely charges and possible penalties: "With the knowledge they had, both of the law and the evidence which had been found at Rivonia, they must already have reached [these conclusions] for themselves."[19] There was a short pause after Bizos spoke, and then Denis Goldberg chimed in. He said he had learned much from the police during his interrogations. It was clear to him that he had no possible defense. He volunteered to take it all on himself and to plead guilty, if doing so would help anyone else go free. Joffe believes that Goldberg spoke with "absolute sincerity." But no one other than Goldberg himself gave his proposal serious consideration. The offer was quickly brushed aside.[20]

There was little else regarding the trial discussed at the meeting, and the remainder of the time was spent exchanging news of families and their welfare. The prisoners did tell the lawyers that they expected others involved in antigovernment activities to be charged along with them. Ruth First was most prominently mentioned. First and her husband, Joe Slovo, were leaders in the South African Communist Party, and both had been charged in the Treason Trial. First had been detained shortly after the Liliesleaf Farm raid. The press had floated rumors about her being charged with those arrested in Rivonia. After the meeting ended, the next step was to go to Women's Prison to try to talk to her.

But the lawyers failed in their attempt to visit First. The matron told them that First was in solitary confinement and that there were orders from the police directing that no one was to see her. Their insistence that they were her lawyers fell on deaf ears. A suggestion that the matron call the attorney general was rebuffed; she never took orders from the attorney general. The Security Branch had left Ruth First in her custody, and she would follow their orders not to permit First any visitation whatsoever.

Eventually, the matron was persuaded to phone the Security Branch, which simply confirmed her original orders that no contact with the detainee was permitted. In fact, the confrontation was something of a relief to the lawyers. They had been permitted to see the men at the Pretoria main prison with the understanding that they were the people who were to be charged in court in the next day. That Ruth First was not permitted to consult with them likely meant that she would not be included in the charges. They were right. Ruth First was ultimately released from her detention and was not charged with the others.[21] Later that year, she joined her husband in exile, initially in England and then in Mozambique. In 1982, Ruth First was killed by a bomb in a parcel sent to her from South Africa.

Counsel's first appearance in court was scheduled for the next day.

5

The Trial Begins

SHORTLY BEFORE 10 a.m. on October 9, 1963, Nelson Mandela and ten other prisoners emerged from the cells beneath Court Three in the imposing brownstone Palace of Justice in Pretoria. Flanked by two guards for each prisoner, the men walked up the steep flight of stairs that came out in the middle of the high-ceilinged courtroom. They were led into the specially built prisoners' dock facing the judge, their backs to the gallery of spectators. As the lawyers had seen the day before, Mandela, though he retained his athletic, heavily built frame (honed as an amateur boxer), was miserably underweight. He had lost twenty-five pounds in prison. His usually well-rounded face was hollow-cheeked and his skin now hung in bags under his eyes. His ordinarily deep glistening brown color had become a pale yellow.[1]

The other defendants were haggard and tense.[2] Some looked years older than they had just a few months before. The ninety days in isolation had taken their toll, as had the intense interrogation and lack of even the normal amenities of prison existence—adequate sanitary facilities, reading materials, and contact with other prisoners. Until charged, most had no contact with anyone apart from their guards.

As if to counteract his awareness of the prisoners' outward appearances, Mandela turned to the public gallery, where relatives and friends had gathered, and flashed his magnificent smile. His infectious laugh and easy smile would remain with him throughout the ordeal of the trial to come and beyond. He saw the prisoners' black supporters segregated to one side of the courtroom. There was no physical barrier, but there might as well have been. Blacks were herded to one side and whites placed on the other. Mandela remembers them shouting *"Amandla! Ngawethu!"* (Power! It shall be ours!) and *"Mayibuye Afrika"* ("Africa come back"). (Others remember this happening later in the trial.) In any event, according to Mandela, "Seeing our supporters was the best medicine I could have had."[3]

The prisoners arrived at the Palace of Justice about an hour before emerging into the courtroom. They traveled the mile or so from the Pretoria prison in a heavily fortified police van, with a steel divider running along the center to segregate the four white prisoners in the front from the seven blacks in the rear. The van was in the center of a convoy of at least a dozen police trucks led by a limousine carrying police officers. The police in the trucks carried Sten guns; there were dog handlers with Alsatians. Police with machine guns lined the route from the jail to the courthouse. Another unit of police with revolvers and tear gas canisters was nearby.

Given the celebrity and importance to the antiapartheid movement of those about to be tried for their lives, the security surrounding their arrival at the courthouse was not surprising. The show of force was as much a message of strength meant to be perceived by both the government's supporters and challengers as a precaution against any attempt to free the captives or a guard against disruptive demonstrations. But escape was undoubtedly not far from the minds of the police, given what had already happened.

A crowd of the defendants' supporters had gathered in the center of South Africa's administrative capital, in Church Square between the Palace of Justice and the statue of Paul Kruger, the founder of the Transvaal Republic, the Boer republic at the heart of the Anglo-Boer Wars. The inscription beneath the Kruger statue quoted from one of the Afrikaner hero's speeches. It read, in Afrikaans, "In confidence we lay our cause before the whole world. Whether we win or whether we die, freedom will arise in Africa like the sun from the morning clouds."

The crowd was large, yet somewhat smaller than it would be later in the trial. The exact date and time at which the trial was to begin had not been well publicized. Many of the blacks traveled in old buses and crowded taxis from the black townships that surrounded Johannesburg and Pretoria. Some carried signs reading "We Stand by Our Leaders." Among the small group of whites also present, some carried signs proclaiming, "*Laat hulle vrek*"—"Let them die like animals."[4] Those black supporters who could fit into Courtroom Three entered and either took seats on the backless wooden benches in the gallery or stood at the rear of the room. The police took names and addresses of all of the spectators in the galleries and photographed them as they left. In addition to the mostly black supporters, the domestic and international press was well represented, as were various foreign governments.

The convoy carrying the defendants avoided the crowd gathered in front of the building and instead drove around it, through the courthouse gates to the courtyard beyond. The iron gates were shut and locked. The police led their prisoners to the cells below the courts—again segregating them by race. They remained in the courthouse basement for the two hours until the proceedings were to begin.

After the defendants were brought in, everyone in the courtroom rose, and Judge Quartus de Wet, clad in the red robes of a judge about to try a criminal case, came on the bench. He came alone, although he could have asked two "assessors" to sit with him to advise him on factual determinations. There would be no jury trial. George Bizos and Bram Fischer believed the fact that de Wet had elected to come into court without assessors made it less likely that he would impose the death sentence—surmising that he would want someone else to share the onus of such a decision.

Only the court personnel, the judge, the lawyers, and the defendants would hear well what would go on in the sixty-foot-long courtroom. Hilda Bernstein, wife of defendant Lionel Bernstein, described the judge's bench as "an elaborate pulpit of wood, carved and posted like an old-fashioned bed," on which the judge was "enthroned." Beige curtains, draped and pleated from floor to ceiling, were on either side of the bench. "The voices of prosecutor, defending counsel and judge alike disappear and are lost." Most of the audience, including the families of the defendants, would have to guess what was taking place based on pitch of voice, expression, or gesture.[5]

Percy Yutar called the case: *The State v. the National High Command and others.* Yutar produced an indictment, handing a copy to the court. He also passed a copy to defense counsel. This was the first time either the defendants or their lawyers had seen the charges, although the prosecution had already given a copy to the newspapers. As predicted, the principal charges were under the Sabotage Act of 1962.

Bram Fischer had arrived that morning. He looked briefly at the indictment and immediately rose to ask for a postponement to prepare a defense. He noted the complexity of the document he had just received. The charges referred to a large number of acts in almost every part of South Africa. Numerous coconspirators and agents, scattered throughout the country and abroad, were named. The accused had been in solitary confinement for three months and were in no condition to assist in their defense without a period of recuperation. The state, on the other hand, had had three months since the arrest of most of the accused to prepare its case. It also had the police and the Department of Justice to assist it. Fischer added, "There is an old saying that justice must not only be done, but must be seen to be done. The accused in this case are people who carry the deep respect of a very large proportion of the population and for this reason alone justice should be seen to be done. There should be no urgency to bring them to trial. We want justice to be seen to be done."[6] Fischer asked for a postponement of six weeks, noting that at that time he could give the court an idea of when he would hope to be ready.

Yutar jumped to his feet in opposition. In his falsetto voice—with which the defendants and their lawyer would become all too familiar—he spoke of witnesses who had to be called by the end of the month. "I fear for their safety."[7]

Judge de Wet split the baby in half; the case would be adjourned for three weeks.

The day was not over. The court immediately reconvened to hear a bail application on behalf of defendant James Kantor, who had of course not taken part in any antigovernment activities and had been brought in merely because he was the brother-in-law of Harold Wolpe.

Kantor's defense team was led by H. C. Nicholas, QC, another lawyer of distinction with experience in defending persons charged with antigovernment activities. Kantor's defense was totally separate from that of the other accused. Nicholas, with full confidence in his client's innocence, voluntarily handed a copy of Kantor's statement to the police to the court. Everything claimed in the indictment was totally unknown to him. At the end of Nicholas's address, Judge de Wet asked Yutar if there were any indications that Kantor had been involved in the acts of sabotage of which the other defendants were charged. Yutar again leaped to his feet. There was no doubt, he said, that Kantor was fully involved. The prosecutor could unequivocally assure the court of that. Kantor's bail was denied without further hearing.

Afterward, Nicholas angrily approached Yutar and asked the basis for his assurance to the court. Yutar told him that he had an affidavit, one that had been taken from a "responsible policeman." The document was not produced, not then or ever. Yutar said it stated that Kantor had attempted to recruit Africans in the townships to undergo military training as guerrillas.[8] Defense counsel later established the patent falsity of this secret affidavit, secured by ruse by the security police, although not in time to help with Kantor's bail applications.

The eleven defendants, Kantor among them, were led away and taken back to the jail and their segregated cells. The defense had three weeks to prepare to keep them from being sentenced to death.

6

A Pyrrhic Victory

THE INDICTMENT PRESENTED to the defendants and their counsel on October 9, 1963, confirmed Joffe's guess that the accused would be charged under the Sabotage Act, which, in addition to carrying the possibility of a death sentence, gave procedural advantages to the state that it did not have in other criminal prosecutions.

The document leveled sweeping charges.[1] It alleged that the defendants had acted in concert and conspired with some seventy other persons and several organizations, including the African National Congress and the Communist Party of South Africa. With these other individuals and organizations, the defendants had "incited, instigated, commanded, aided, advised, encouraged or procured other persons" to commit acts of sabotage, preparatory to and in facilitation of, armed invasion and guerilla warfare. It alleged more than 235 acts of sabotage. The defendants were also accused of soliciting and receiving money from various persons and bodies, inside and outside the country, in support of a campaign for the repeal or modification of certain laws that would achieve the "objects of Communism" as defined in the Suppression of Communism Act of 1950, a broad definition encompassing almost any social, economic or political change.

Seven of the accused—Mandela, Sisulu, Mbeki, Kathrada, Goldberg, Bernstein, and Mhlaba—were charged with being members of the "National High Command, The National Liberation Movement, [and] the National Executive Committee of the National Liberation Movement Umkhonto we Sizwe." All were accused of being part of the overall conspiracy; Kantor was also charged in his capacity as a partner in the firm of James Kantor and Partners. The "National High Command," though a nonexistent entity, was named as a defendant.

The judge had given the defense team three weeks either to attack the indictment or to be ready to begin the trial. The indictment gave them little notice of the real nature of the case that would be presented by the state. There would be no preparatory examination or preliminary hearing that would enable them to learn more. And the defense also knew that, under the act, it would have the burden of showing that any given act was not committed for the purpose of furthering any political aim.

The response to the indictment was based as much on a political decision as a legal one. Chaskalson, Bizos, and Joffe were focused on the law. By widely accepted standards of South African criminal law, the indictment fell far short of the kind of specificity ordinarily required. But Bram Fischer and all of the accused had far broader goals in mind. To them, the trial was first and foremost an opportunity to get the message of the oppression of apartheid out to the South African public and the world at large. To Mandela and most of the others, that message was far more important than their personal fate.

For all its vagueness, the indictment presented a broad and, in large measure, true picture of most of the accused's activities. Mandela, Sisulu, Mbeki, and Goldberg had surely planned for sabotage and recruitment of military trainees. Except for Kantor, who had separate counsel, the others were at least part of the group that had been planning antigovernment acts. But it was important, especially in the eyes of the defendants themselves, that the point be made that the violence planned and carried out against the government was a last resort; there had been no other way to resist government oppression. South Africa's draconian suppression of dissent had made peaceful dissent impossible.

The issue for the accused and their counsel was whether a legal attack on the insufficiently articulated charges would detract from the power of the message they wanted to send. Ultimately, they decided to challenge the legal sufficiency of the indictment. The charges were too vague to permit an adequate response by the defense. In attacking the document, the defendants were making the statement that persons charged with political crimes would not be railroaded. All the processes of the law still available to them would be brought to bear. Such a defense was necessary to protect not only those defendants who might still be found not guilty—for example, Bernstein and Kathrada, whose involvement in planning for an armed struggle was far more peripheral than the others—but also others who might be charged in the future. Legal attacks at this point might diminish what was defense counsel's greatest fear—although not necessarily the greatest fear of the accused themselves: that their clients might be hanged.[2]

The first step in the challenge was to ask the prosecution for greater particulars, a request permitted under the South African and other legal systems based in English legal tradition. Which of the accused or co-conspirators were alleged to have carried out which of the listed acts of sabotage? The defendants also sought details of the alleged conspiracy among the accused and other persons and between the African National Congress and the Communist Party. The state's answers gave no assistance whatsoever. The typical answer was that "these facts are peculiarly within the knowledge of the accused."[3] As Joffe put it, the responses said, "You are guilty. Therefore you know what you did. Therefore we don't have to tell you."[4]

With little satisfaction of its request for particulars, counsel moved to quash the indictment on the grounds that it did not inform the accused adequately and with reasonable clarity of the precise charges or allegations they had to meet. The hearing on the sufficiency of the charges would be held on October 29.

The weeks before the hearing were filled with legal work by counsel, especially by Fischer, who pored over the contents of the indictment, and by Arthur Chaskalson, who developed the legal case for it to be quashed. The lawyers—often just Bizos and Joffe—continued to meet with their clients. Certain that their warders were closely monitoring their conversations, they learned to use code words and gestures instead of direct statements. Mandela referred to Fischer, with a tilt of his head and lowering of his hand, as "the short one."[5] The lawyers and defendants also wrote key words on paper—to be pointed to rather than articulated—and burned those papers in ashtrays at the end of each conference.

The prison authorities were distressed by the burning of papers, which inspired some of the defendants—including Mandela—to pull a prank fondly remembered by all involved through the years. The notorious and especially brutal interrogator Captain T. J. Swanepoel of the Security Police had come personally to observe the conferences from the door of the consultation room. Noticing his presence, Govan Mbeki, wrote on a piece of paper, "Isn't Lieutenant Swanepoel"—deliberately demoting him—"a fine looking chap." He passed the note to Mandela, who studied it for some time and then whispered to the others. He dropped the note in the empty tin that served as an ashtray. Swanepoel rushed in saying "I think I left my ashtray here. I always have the same ashtray with me in this place." He took the tin and unburned paper and dashed out of the room. He did not personally observe the conferences again for several weeks.[6]

The hearing on the defendants' motion to quash the indictment began in dramatic fashion, duplicating in many ways the accused's first appearance in court earlier that month.[7] They again walked up the stairs leading from the cells below to their dock in the middle of the courtroom. Each prisoner was accompanied by one or two of his own personal guards who were to sit with them throughout the trial. Dozens of plain-clothed guards were to take up places between the prisoners and the public. Security Branch police in civilian dress were placed through the courtroom and massed at all exits and entrances.

No step could prevent the Africans in the courtroom from erupting in excitement and adoration at the sight of their heroes. Mandela was the first to emerge and gave the spectators a thumbs-up and the clenched-right-fist salute of the African National Congress. As some accounts maintain he had done on October 9, he boomed out, "*Amandla!*" (power) in his deep, rich voice, and the African audience replied immediately in chorus, "*Ngawethu!*" (it shall be ours). The call and response was repeated by all of the accused, except Kantor and Hepple, who simply smiled at friends and family in the crowd and remained silent. The crowd was only fully silenced when the orderly shouted, "Order in the Court" and Justice de Wet entered.

Bram Fischer began the proceedings with a careful dissection of the indictment. There was nothing flamboyant about Fischer's delivery. "Unlike the public concept of a lawyer, he is no orator," Joffe said about Fischer. "To listen to him is difficult, as he hesitates over a word, groping for precisely the right one before he uses it, thinking slowly and deliberately between sentences."[8] There were no gestures, no dramatics in his presentation. He was deeply conscious of the importance of his arguments on behalf of men who were both his clients and his close personal friends. As one of Fischer's biographers, Martin Meredith, describes his argument, "He picked his words with care, hesitating to ensure he chose precisely the right word, thinking slowly and deliberately between sentences, pausing for long periods after making one point before framing the next."[9]

Fischer's attack was clinical. He attacked the indictment for its generality and its obscurity. He pointed out that some of the alleged acts of sabotage had been committed before the Sabotage Act had been enacted and that Nelson Mandela had been charged with 156 acts of sabotage somehow committed while he was in prison. He noted that there was no such entity as the "National High Command," though it had been named as a defendant.

Fischer then turned to the state's response to the request for particulars, highlighting its answer that the facts were "peculiarly within the knowledge of the accused." He said, "Unless the State says who carried out each of the acts, how is the defense to meet the charges? Either the State knows who committed the acts, or it does not. If it does not know, then it should not charge them with the acts. If it does know, it should tell us."[10] At this point, he came as close to sounding angry as he ever did, declaring that the response to the bill of particulars demonstrated that the state had decided that the accused were guilty and that there was no point in a legitimate defense.

Joffe remembers that Justice de Wet began to show signs of irritation and impatience as Fischer continued with his argument. At one point he closed his papers and put his pencil on top of them, as though he had already made up his mind. Joffe could not guess at that point whether the judge was with them or against them.[11]

A clearer indication of the judge's thinking emerged during the next argument, this one by Advocate George Lowen on behalf of Jimmy Kantor. Lowen was a far more dynamic orator than Fischer. He had been a lawyer in Germany and had escaped the Nazis in the early 1930s, after appearing for the defense in some trials of opponents to Hitler's regime, and he was willing to inject drama into his arguments. There was a special basis for Lowen's emotion in this case: Kantor was a friend, and he was most certainly innocent of all the charges. Joffe recalls that Lowen literally thundered into the attack: "The adjectives rolled out." The state was "presumptuous, nay ludicrous" in its reply to the request for particulars. With sarcasm, he read one prosecution reply after another: "These facts are not known; these facts are peculiarly within the knowledge of your client."[12]

Finally there was an exchange that tipped Justice de Wet's hand. Lowen pointed to Question 5 submitted by Kantor. "The answer given by the State is dash, dash, dash, exclamation mark!" Justice de Wet looked up and remarked, "In my copy there are four dashes, Mr. Lowen." Lowen read the judge's feelings, and, as would any good lawyer who has realized that he has won a judge over, cut short his argument.[13]

But the drama of the day was not confined to defense counsel's dissection of the indictment. After Lowen's argument, de Wet asked defendant Hepple whether he too wished to attack the indictment. Hepple was unrepresented but was himself a lawyer. Before Hepple could respond, Yutar rose from his seat and announced that the state was withdrawing the charges against Hepple.[14] Hepple, he said, would be the first witness for the state against the accused. Although a ripple of noise went through the public galleries, the other accused—whom Hepple had warned of his intentions the night before the opening of the trial—looked unmoved. Hepple rose, deathly pale. As he left the dock, he muttered to the defendants, "Good luck."[15]

With the arguments for the defense and Hepple's dismissal out of the way, Yutar began his defense of the charges. Instead of taking on the legal arguments so painstakingly articulated by Fischer and Lowen, the prosecutor attacked the application by questioning the genuineness and sincerity of the defendant's position. He argued that the motion and request for particulars had been made simply to harass and embarrass the state. If the defense lawyers were anxious to know the precise details of the allegations against the accused, he would be prepared to hand over a copy of his opening address to the court.[16]

An opening address in a South African court serves the same function as an opening statement in any Anglo-American court. It is a speech in which the party summarizes the evidence that it intends to introduce at the trial. The point of it is to inform the trier of fact—in this case the judge—of what the party plans to prove in the case. An opening address is unlike presenting evidence. It is not intended to inform the other side—in this case persons accused of capital offenses—of the evidence against them. It is most certainly not an official document that formalizes the criminal proceedings.

Fischer began to rise to object to Yutar's suggestion, but didn't have to open his mouth. Justice de Wet was apparently as amazed as Fischer. "I can see no reason why I should allow you to hand that in, Mr. Yutar," he told the prosecutor. "Have you any authority that I can do that? Your opening address is not a document that you are entitled to hand in."[17]

Yutar retreated. He was only concerned about accommodating the wishes of counsel, he replied; the refusal of his offer drew him to conclude that the defense really didn't want further particulars. To that, the judge responded, "That piece of advice is quite irrelevant. This is a legal argument as to what particulars the defense may be entitled to, and the matter is irrelevant."[18]

At this point, Yutar began simply to catalog the evidence he intended to produce—in essence, to make an opening statement. By this time, his voice had risen to its famous falsetto.[19] He was immediately stopped by de Wet. "If the State wishes to make allegations like that they should be made in the proper manner."[20]

The court recessed for lunch, and afterward, despite the judge's pronouncement, Yutar again continued to outline the proof he intended to introduce. This time defense counsel let him go on without objecting, hoping to get as much information as possible about the state's case. Again, however, de Wet stopped Yutar soon after he began. "The whole basis of your argument as I understand it, Mr. Yutar, is that you are satisfied that the accused are guilty. And you are arguing the case on the assumption that they are guilty and that they had known of all these documents. You cannot beg the question and say that you have got the proof and ask the court to decide on the preliminary matter on the basis that the accused are guilty."[21]

Yutar had clearly lost. He tried to bargain with de Wet to save the indictment. He begged the court not to "squash" the indictment, apparently forgetting in his distress that the correct legal term was "quash." His error was especially amusing to defense lawyers in light of Yutar's reputation as the most learned lawyer in South Africa. His voice cracked. He offered to give the defense whatever further particulars the judge wanted. He would drop the "National High Command" as a defendant. De Wet responded that it was not his responsibility to tell the state what particulars were required to make a good indictment. If the indictment was defective, it would be dismissed.

And Justice de Wet did just that. The judge noted that he had never come across a response to a bill of particulars in a criminal case in which the state had been permitted simply to say that the evidence is "peculiarly within the knowledge of the accused." He added, "The accused are assumed to be innocent until they are proved to be guilty. [The state's response to the request for particulars] presupposes that he is guilty and he will not be told anything about the offense."[22] The indictment was quashed, and the defendants, very temporarily, were free men.

The defendants' freedom lasted just long enough for the police to reach them. Denis Goldberg had time to lean down and kiss his wife, Esme, before Detective Sergeant Dirker of the Security Police grabbed hold of him and began to haul him off to the underground cells. Joffe sought to intervene, and Dirker roared at him, "Joffe, if you ever interfere with me again while I am performing my duties, I'll arrest you!" Joffe responded that Dirker better learn what his duty was. His clients had been discharged. At that point, Captain Swanepoel leaped into the dock, thumped one of the accused on the shoulder, and announced, "I am arresting you on a charge of sabotage." One by one, each man was shepherded down the stairs to their cells.[23]

The day ended with a hearing in which applications by Bernstein and Kantor for bail were denied. De Wet, who had come back out of chambers to hear the bail applications, had seemed favorably disposed to grant Kantor bail. As that was about to happen, Major van Niekerk, a senior police officer, came into the room, took a scrap of paper from his pocket, and huddled with Yutar and the rest of the prosecution team. Yutar then rose to his feet, waving Niekerk's document saying, "I cannot, I dare not read the whole of it. It is to this effect, My Lord: that there is a movement afoot to get Kantor and whatever other accused who gets bail out to Lobatsi [in the British protectorate of Bechuanaland]." The note was never given to defense counsel. There was a brief recess, and the purported contents of the note, with no further details, were set out in affidavit form. Kantor was denied bail. Bernstein's request was quickly denied as well. Both men remained prisoners.[24]

A new indictment was certainly coming. It arrived two weeks later. In a brief hearing, another judge, Justice Oscar Galgut, rejected defense efforts for a postponement sufficient to give them adequate time to prepare. It was in the interests of the accused, he said, that the case would go on as soon as possible. After all, the defendants were in jail. The trial was set to commence in two weeks.[25]

The new indictment added some information, including twenty-one pages of annexures detailing 193 (instead of the 235 originally charged) separate acts of sabotage.[26] A new charge—preparing for the commission of acts of violence in the future—had been added. The "National High Command" was no longer a defendant. One hundred twenty-two people were alleged to have acted as agents of the defendants in committing these acts, but yet again the indictment did not state which of the alleged agents committed any particular act. Further requests for particulars resulted only in the information that "the acts particularized in the annexure were committed by the said agents and servants in their respective areas."

Defense counsel moved to quash, and the hearing on November 25 again began with a dissection of the new indictment by Bram Fischer. Justice de Wet, for his part, seemed like a new person. Gone was the sarcasm directed at the prosecution and the willingness to require the state to comply with legal standards. He again put his pencil down and closed his book. This time, however, the gestures did not indicate a favorable attitude toward the defense. Joffe noted that while Fischer had presented a devastating argument against the indictment, they all could tell that "he was talking into thin air."[27] The separate motions to quash on behalf of most of the defendants and by counsel for Kantor were quickly denied. A request for further postponement was summarily denied and the trial was set to begin in earnest the next day.

Joffe has struggled to explain the dramatic turnaround in the judge's attitude. In contrast to his chastisement of Yutar at the first hearing, de Wet was deliberately rude to both Fischer and Harold Hanson, who was arguing for Kantor. Joffe notes that de Wet "tolerated outrageous antics from Yutar with indifference, even with a grin on his face and at times had seemed to encourage those antics by nodding agreement when no agreement was called for."[28]

No one has offered an adequate explanation for the change in de Wet's conduct. Although Joffe is certain that Yutar took instructions from the political authorities of the state, he is not willing to make the same claim about the judge. "I do not believe that Mr. Justice de Wet took or would take instructions from anybody. He was an arrogant man, proud of his position as a judge and of the fact that his father had served as a judge before him."[29] But Joffe would also state, long after the trial was over, that even if he was independent of the government, de Wet nevertheless knew what it wanted.[30]

Justice de Wet's change in attitude may simply have been the result of the recognition that a trial on these charges was inevitable and further delay useless. It was not difficult for anyone in South Africa to discern the strength of the government's commitment to this prosecution.

There was one other significant development that day. During the argument regarding the postponement of the trial, Yutar stated his opposition to delay: "The State cannot guarantee the security of witnesses if the case were postponed." He then made the announcement, timed to make the afternoon edition of the newspapers, that Robert Hepple, who was to have been the first state witness, had been threatened by the accused or their supporters and had fled the country.[31]

News soon surfaced that Hepple had arrived in Dar es Salaam, in what was then Tanganyika, that same day. His version of the reasons for his departure from South Africa was very different from Yutar's. He had not been threatened by the accused or their supporters; he left out of fear of the police. They had made promises that they had broken. He said he had no intention of testifying against the accused, men he admired and supported.[32] Future accounts of the trial would reveal that Hepple's escape had been arranged by Bram Fischer.[33]

There was one more surprise for the defense. When they arrived on the next day, November 26, expecting the trial to begin, Yutar asked for a week's postponement "in order to help Kantor's counsel."[34] Joffe notes that the prosecutor began to fawn on Kantor's counsel while remaining rude to the other defense lawyers. The reasons behind Yutar's motion for postponement and his change in attitude were not difficult to discern. The suggestion had been floated to Kantor that if he told the police everything that Bernstein and Goldberg had discussed during exercise periods in jail, the charges against him would be dropped.

Kantor may not have been a man of deep political beliefs or convictions, but he had personal integrity. Goldberg remembered many years after the trial that Kantor—in a conversation that took place in the dual-facility latrine available to the defendant—had refused to talk to him about Goldberg's role in sabotage planning for fear that he might be forced to reveal that information.[35] The weeklong continuance was granted, but Kantor continued to refuse to testify for the state.

The trial was in fact to begin a week later—without Bob Hepple and without Jimmy Kantor as state witnesses.

The dismissal of the first indictment on October 29 had given the defendants some hope that Judge de Wet would be at least evenhanded in his conduct of the case. Foreign observers were similarly impressed.[36] But subsequent events—the immediate rearrest of the defendants and the perfunctory treatment of the equally vague second indictment—lent themselves to a more cynical analysis. The quashing of the first indictment could serve as an example to be held out to a skeptical world that the procedure under which the trial took place in South Africa was fair, without in any way diminishing either the likelihood of conviction or the severity of the penalty ultimately imposed by the court.

The Case for the Prosecution

THE FIRST DAY of the trial began with pleas by the defendants and an opening address by Percy Yutar. All of them revealed much about the strategy and goals of each side.

The defendants were each asked to make a formal plea to the indictment. Nelson Mandela set the tone: "The government should be in the dock, not me. I plead not guilty." Walter Sisulu followed along similar lines: "It is the government which is guilty, not me." When Justice de Wet rebuked him, asking him to plead either guilty or not guilty and not to make political speeches, Sisulu added: "It is the government which is responsible for what is happening in this country. I plead not guilty."

De Wet was visibly annoyed by the defendants' pleas. Yutar, for his part, appeared horrified. Muttering could be heard from the police sitting in the court. Yet each defendant responded to the request for a plea in similar terms. Jimmy Kantor offered the only exception, simply responding, "I plead not guilty my Lord."[1]

The defense was going to try this case with the goal of avoiding the death sentence for all of the accused and, if possible, gaining acquittal for a few of them. But it was not going to miss the opportunity to put apartheid on trial in the court of world opinion.

Yutar's intention was not dissimilar—to put the spotlight on events and issues outside the courtroom. To the surprise of defense counsel, technicians from the South African Broadcasting Company—SABC, the government-controlled radio system—appeared in the courtroom and began to set up microphones to broadcast Yutar's opening to the people of the republic. Objections were raised by the defense. Yutar, sensing that the judge would not permit radio broadcast over defense objections, quickly disassociated himself from the whole idea. His audience would be limited to courtroom spectators and the readers of newspaper accounts of his words.[2]

The reasons behind Yutar's attempts at public broadcast soon became obvious. His opening address, and indeed his conduct of the entire trial, would seek to do more than establish the guilt of the accused. The trial would tell the nation and the world about the Communist-inspired danger that these people and their followers posed to good people everywhere.

From a lawyer's perspective, Yutar's opening address was his best work of the trial.[3] It dramatically set out the evidence and yet was uncharacteristically concise. It gave the court a graphic picture of the planning and execution of acts of sabotage—acts calculated to bring down the government of the Republic of South Africa.[4] It also gave the defense its first meaningful indication of the nature and extent of the prosecution's case.

The accused, announced Yutar, plotted and engineered acts of violence and destruction throughout the country, directed both against the offices and homes of state and municipal officials as well as against communication facilities. Their purpose was to bring about "chaos, disorder and turmoil." They planned for this turmoil to be followed by the operation of trained guerrilla-warfare units, and—at an appropriate juncture—by an armed invasion of the country by the military units of foreign powers. Proof of his case would come both from witnesses called at the trial and from documents found in the Rivonia raid and in subsequent raids on two other properties—Travallyn and Mountain View.

In his opening, as throughout the trial, Yutar was careful to emphasize that all planning was done by ANC leaders in close cooperation with leaders of the Communist Party of South Africa. The preparations for sabotage and terrorism incorporated the "cell system" and the characteristic secrecy of the Communists. His intended audience was not only the white people of South Africa but Western leaders whose fears of rampaging Communism in Africa trumped their objections to apartheid.

But Yutar's address was much more than simply a plea to anti-Red hysteria. He referred to documents that showed extensive planning for sabotage, including the manufacture of at last seven different types of explosives and 106 maps of the country with proposed targets marked—police stations, post offices, Bantu administration offices, the homes of Bantu policemen and administrators, electric power stations and facilities, telephone lines and cables, and railway lines and signal boxes. Finally, the opening sketched the outlines of testimony from the witnesses who would called and, he said, connect each of the accused to these acts of sabotage and plans for an uprising against the state.

The defense's most significant problem was that much of Yutar's description of the defendants' activities was both true and provable. If any of the accused testified, several would be forced to admit to most of the critical portions of the charges—specifically, that they had planned and directed acts of sabotage against government and communications sites, and had arranged to send young recruits abroad for training in guerrilla warfare. Indeed, the defense lawyers were instructed not to contest testimony from state witnesses that the defendants knew to be true. There would be no attempt on the part of counsel to avoid a conviction, at least for the leaders, Mandela, Sisulu, and Mbeki.[5]

As Yutar's opening statement showed, the prosecution wanted to expose that the antiapartheid movement was dominated by international Communism. And as the pleas entered by the accused demonstrated, counsel and their clients would seek to put the government and its apartheid policies on trial for all of South Africa and the rest of the world to see. The defendants may have broken the apartheid government's laws, but the policies of that government—its racial oppression and total intolerance of even peaceful dissent—left them no other choice.[6]

But there were things that experienced and capable defense lawyers could do for their clients and for the cause in which they and their clients believed. Effective courtroom tactics could reduce the likelihood of the death penalty for some of the accused and perhaps result in the acquittal of some others. Although Kathrada and Bernstein were present at Liliesleaf Farm on the day of the raid, for example, they were not as closely linked to the documents and the activities they reflected as Mandela, Sisulu, Goldberg, Mhlaba, and Mbeki were. And Motosoaledi and Mlangeni would have to be tied to the activities by the testimony of state witnesses.

Even with regard to Mandela, Sisulu, Goldberg, Mhlaba, and Mbeki, all clearly implicated by the documentary evidence, the defense would stress two points throughout both cross-examination and its rebuttal case: first, the plans set out in the Operation Mayibuye document had been prepared for discussion but had not yet been adopted; and, second, all acts of sabotage were planned in a way that would not put human life at risk.[7] The establishment of these points would not be enough to acquit any defendant, but proof of either or both might be enough to persuade the judge not to send the defendants to the gallows.

Although much of what the dozens of state witnesses would say would be truthful, some was embellishment, and some was totally false. The defense would continuously remind most of the state witnesses of the fact that they had been held, or were still being held, in detention. Their release from detention would likely depend on the state's satisfaction with their testimony at the trial. Yutar's claim was that they were being held as a matter of "protective custody." The defense pointed out that there was no such procedure under South African law, but the court let the explanation pass.[8]

Jimmy Kantor presented a different set of problems for his lawyers, who operated separately from counsel for the other accused. Kantor was not involved in the movement, but his brother-in-law and law partner, Harold Wolpe, was up to his ears in all of the activities. Several of the key incriminating documents were either in Wolpe's handwriting or prepared in part by him. But there was very little to link Kantor to Wolpe's part in the conspiracy, other than his law partnership and family ties. The state would have to prove some willful participation on Kantor's part—a task that would prove very difficult.

The heart of the state's case against the accused involved incriminating documents found at Rivonia and the other locations, documents that were brought into evidence throughout the trial.[9] Yutar's introduction of these documents departed significantly from the procedure ordinarily followed in South African courts—and other courts following American or English procedure. That procedure generally required that a witness authenticate each document unless the opposing party agreed to its authenticity.[10] In the ordinary course of a criminal trial, the opposing party is given an opportunity to review the documents prior to their actual introduction into evidence. But the prosecutor in the Rivonia Trial, with the consent of the judge, had a different way of operating. The documents were simply read to the court piecemeal, without authentication by a witness, without review by defense counsel, and without indication as to when in the course of the state's evidence they might be produced.[11] There would probably have been ample evidence that could have been offered to authenticate virtually all of the documents—at least all of the important ones. But the procedure used by Yutar put defense counsel at a serious disadvantage. It was difficult to prepare to attack a document if defense counsel could not anticipate when that document was likely to be introduced, or view it before it was shown to the trier of fact. Procedure aside, even if no witnesses—other than those connecting the accused to the documents found in the raids—testified, the documentary evidence was likely sufficient to convict most of the accused.

There was no more sensational evidence than a six-part document labeled "Operation Mayibuye." Two officers testified that they had found the document—lying open—on the table in the center of the thatched cottage at Liliesleaf Farm on the day of the raid.[12] Operation Mayibuye called for seizing control of the country through acts of sabotage followed by guerrilla warfare—a struggle that would be assisted by the active participation of sympathetic states around the world. A critical paragraph of the document reads:

> The following plan envisages a process which will place in the field, at a date fixed now, simultaneously in pre-selected areas, armed and trained guerrilla bands, who will find ready to join them local guerrilla bands with arms and equipment at their disposal. It will further coincide with a massive propaganda campaign both inside and outside South Africa and a general call for unprecedented mass struggle throughout the land, both violent and non-violent. In the initial period, when for a short while the military advantage will be ours, the plan envisages a massive onslaught on pre-selected targets which will create maximum havoc and confusion in the enemy camp, and which will inject into the masses of the people and other friendly forces a feeling of confidence that here at last is an army of liberation equipped and capable of leading them to victory.[13]

The document continued by outlining programs to train fighters and the organization of an entire guerrilla army. Plans for seeking funding and propaganda support from abroad were set out. The importance of communications and transport were emphasized. At least seven thousand men would be in place ready to join an external force when it arrived. At one point, the plan referred to a "selection of targets to be tackled in an initial phase of guerrilla operations with a view to causing maximum damage to the enemy as well as preventing the quick deployment of reinforcements."

A "Logistics Department" was to manufacture and compile a stock of arms, ammunition, explosives, and other supplies, as well as to organize the training of personnel to use the equipment collected. All this was to have been done by May 30, 1963—a little more than a month before the date of the Rivonia raid.

The Operation Mayibuye document was, logically enough, the focal point of the state's case. The thrust of its message—that the accused had engaged in sabotage, sending abroad young black men for training in guerrilla warfare, securing materials to be used both in sabotage and guerrilla warfare activities, and soliciting funding for all of the above—was corroborated by other documents. All of the documents introduced into evidence were found at one of the raids in locations that would tie them to many of the defendants. Several were in the handwriting of some of the accused and their alleged coconspirators.

Another document, labeled "Outlines for a Brief Course in the Training of Organizers," was found in the car of the escaped detainee, Arthur Goldreich, with additional copies found at Liliesleaf Farm. The paper outlined the struggle of the black people of South Africa, but also discussed the political indoctrination of organizers as well as guerrilla warfare and tactics.[14] Govan Mbeki would admit that he had drafted part of it; Goldreich wrote the remainder.[15] Multiple copies of a related, sixteen-page stenciled document were found at Liliesleaf Farm, in Goldreich's car, and at Travallyn. It stated, among other things, that the organization MK—Umkhonto we Sizwe—was born "to wage a revolutionary armed struggle to overthrow white supremacy." "Sabotage on a national scale should be used principally in disrupting communications, transport, railroad, railroads, railroad installations, etc." The document stressed the importance of sabotaging communications: "We must constantly undermine that strength by knocking out railroads, bridges, electric-lights, telephones and in general everything that is necessary for his normal way of life."[16] Additional documents found in the raids and introduced at the trial corroborated, first, the plans for sabotage, and later, for full-scale guerrilla warfare. Others, some in Arthur Goldreich's handwriting and some prepared by defendant Denis Goldberg, dealt with the acquisition and manufacture of explosives, including landmines and hand grenades. Such evidence was persuasive—indeed devastating—in a case in which the principal charges were sabotage and conspiracy to commit sabotage. Although the principal authors of many of the documents were the escapees Goldreich and Harold Wolpe, other defendants apprehended in the Rivonia raid were tied to them either by their handwriting or their presence at Liliesleaf Farm on the day of the raid.

Though he had been in prison for many months prior to the raid, Nelson Mandela was incriminated by his own handwriting on documents that some of the MK leadership, including Bram Fischer, had so passionately wanted destroyed before they could fall into the hands of the Security Police. But they were not destroyed, and their contents were enough to serve as the basis for Yutar to brand Mandela and the other accused as part of the international Communist conspiracy.

In early 1962, after going underground following the Treason Trial, Mandela had made an extensive tour of African nations, to learn about revolution and to make and cement contacts with sympathetic leaders in

the recently emerged or emerging nations of the continent, including
Julius Nyerere of Tanganyika and Kenneth Kuanda, the future president of
Zambia. A careful man, Mandela made detailed notes about what he had
learned, particularly about guerrilla warfare. He also kept a diary covering
the period of consultations with African leaders. Mandela had brought the
notes and diary to Liliesleaf Farm, where they were seized in the raid.[17]
Other papers, dealing with topics from military training to the tactics of
the Chinese and pre-1948 Israeli undergrounds, all in Nelson Mandela's
meticulous handwriting, were found as well.[18] He also left a summary of
ideas expressed in the book *Guerrilla Warfare* by Fidel Castro lieutenant
Che Guevara,[19] whose name alone was enough to strike terror in the hearts
of not just white South Africans but governments around the world. One
of the documents seized in the raids was an ANC pamphlet that boasted:
"We have struck against the White State more than 70 times (boldly yet
methodically). We are trained and practised. We shall be more so."[20] The
indictment against Mandela listed 193 alleged acts of sabotage.[21] One
would have been enough for conviction.

There were other documents produced that appear to have been created by the Communist Party of South Africa. The writings expressed
strong approval of the actions of MK. Although these Communist Party
documents were enormously useful to Yutar—and the South African
government—as part of their propaganda efforts at the trial, de Wet was to
find them of lesser significance than the other exhibits in establishing the
guilt of the accused of the crimes of which they were charged.[22]

In addition to the documents were the state witnesses, who fell into
four categories. The largest group consisted of those who had had some
involvement in antigovernment activities, or who had had other contact
with either the accused or alleged coconspirators at Liliesleaf Farm. All
were black or Coloured, and all were under threat of prosecution; most had
been or were currently being held in detention. The second group consisted of police officers who had been present at the raids or otherwise
involved in the investigation. The third were individuals contacted by Denis
Goldberg in his attempts to secure materials to be used for sabotage or
guerrilla warfare. The fourth were people who had some knowledge of the
law practice that Harold Wolpe and the defendant Jimmy Kantor shared, or
who would testify to the circumstances surrounding the purchase of the
properties used by MK. In all there, were no fewer than 173 witnesses.

Black workers at Liliesleaf Farm were among the first witnesses
called. These men and women could detail only the comings and goings

of various defendants, but they were able to identify several on the scene at Liliesleaf, and that was all Yutar really needed from them. Bram Fischer was deliberately absent during most of this testimony. He claimed that an arbitration proceeding in Johannesburg conflicted with his presence at the Rivonia Trial. But any one of these witnesses, when asked to identify any-one in the courtroom they had seen at Liliesleaf, might well have pointed a finger at the lead defense counsel.[23]

One success for the defense in the early days of the trial was Arthur Chaskalson's cross-examination of Joseph Mashifane, a witness who had made a tentative identification of Bernstein as the man who had put up radio masts on the property.[24] Chaskalson pinned down the timing of the erection of the masts to a Saturday afternoon[25]—as later established, a day and time when Bernstein, under an order of house arrest, could not have been present.[26]

With varying amounts of truth, several other black or Coloured wit-nesses tied the other defendants—with the exception of Bernstein and Kantor—to acts of sabotage, meetings at which sabotage and other anti-government activities were discussed, and to the transport abroad of recruits for training in sabotage and guerrilla warfare.

A few witnesses had had only peripheral involvement in the illegal activities—taxi drivers who transported recruits to the borders—and others had attended meetings at which sabotage or recruitment of guerrillas had been discussed. Two witnesses, Alfred Jantjies and Isaac Rani, testified to their training in guerrilla warfare at Dabrazi, Ethiopia.[27] This course lasted three months and included "first aid, swimming, map reading, compass reading, hand grenades, bazookas, demotion, roadblocks, Molotov cocktails, ambush, rope-climbing, hand-combat, obstacle-crossing, Jerry-can bombs, mine-bombs, booby-traps, range-finding, use of pistols, light ma-chine-guns, carbines, sketch-drawing, broadcasting, construction of bridges, signals and use of bayonets."[28]

The testimony that most stood out, however, was given by those who had in fact played truly significant roles in antigovernment plans and actions. One was English Tolo Mashiloane. Mashiloane, although illiterate, was a successful businessman (an herbalist, he peddled remedies even while in detention). He was also a distant relative of the accused, Elias Motsoaledi.[29] His testimony firmly tied Motsoaledi and another defendant, Andrew Mlan-geni, to the transportation of guerrilla recruits and acts of sabotage.[30] His testimony was especially significant against these two defendants, neither of whom had been present at the time of the Rivonia raid. Mashiloane had been granted immunity for his own participation in the affairs of the ANC in exchange for his testimony. Judge de Wet asked Yutar to warn Mashiloane, in accordance with South African law and practice, that as an accomplice he must give his evidence satisfactorily or face prosecution. Yutar responded that he did not consider Mashiloane an accomplice. The judge ignored Yutar and himself warned the witness of his position.[31]

Even more significant was the testimony of two witnesses whom the press referred to as Mr. X[32] and Mr. Y.[33] Mr. X was Bruno Mtolo, who had been intimately involved in the planning of antigovernment activities by the ANC, the Communist Party, and Umkhonto we Sizwe in the Durban and Natal Province area. Mr. Y was Patrick "Abel" Mthembu, who was a principal of MK. As in the case of many witnesses, their testimony was partly true, partly embellished, and partly false. The defendants were the most troubled personally by the testimony of Mr. Y, Abel Mthembu, as he was the only person of any standing in the ANC who could be persuaded to testify for the state. Mthembu tied several of the accused—most specifically Elias Motsoaledi—to the planning of acts of sabotage and recruitment of guerrilla fighters.[34]

But Mr. X—who was addressed as "Bruno" by Yutar and "Mr. Mtolo" by the cross-examiner, Vernon Berrange—gave by far the most detailed testimony of the trial, the most useful testimony for the prosecution and the most devastating for the defense. Mtolo maintained that he had had been thoroughly instructed in Communist doctrine and had learned that the white man had robbed the blacks of their country.[35] He could outline the complex organizational structure of the ANC, the Communist Party, and MK. He had planned and participated in more than twenty acts of sabotage in the Durban area—all on behalf of MK—and could provide exacting details, such as about the theft of dynamite and the manufacture of petrol bombs. At one point, Judge de Wet, obviously fascinated by the specifics of bomb making, engaged in a direct discussion with Mtolo about the technique.

DE WET: And as you push the plunger down, the glycerin goes onto the potassium or permanganate?
MTOLO: . . . After you have poured the glycerin in, then you pull the plunger down, and then it closes the top.

To carry out the bombings, Mtolo had worked with the Natal Regional Command, whose activities were directed from above by the National

High Command. Mtolo named Sisulu and Mbeki as active leaders of the High Command. His activities were directed by others in the movement, including, among others, Harold Strachan, Jack Hodgson, and Joe Modise, representing the High Command, and Ronnie Kasrils and Billy Nair, leaders of the Natal Regional Command. All were named as unindicted coconspirators in the indictment.

Mtolo had recruited guerrilla fighters to be trained abroad and transported them to Johannesburg to be smuggled out. While in Johannesburg, he met some of the accused, including Sisulu, Mbeki, and Kathrada, at Liliesleaf Farm. He dealt with Mlangeni—whom he referred to as the "robot" because nothing deterred him from the completion of a task—and with Motsoaledi, who added to Mtolo's already substantial knowledge of sabotage and explosives. Mtolo described a speech given by Mandela in Natal—then the province of the city of Durban—in which he discussed his trips to secure aid in other parts of Africa. Mandela openly promoted resistance to the South African government by sabotage and, ultimately, guerrilla warfare. He spoke of support for their movement among other African leaders, including the infusion of 60,000 rand. He also, Mtolo testified, told of one person sent to Ethiopia who was "thrown away" there because he had "let out the fact that he was a Communist." "That was a very dangerous thing to do."

Mtolo's testimony on these points by itself would have been enough to convict most of the accused under the Sabotage Act—promoting acts of sabotage and fomenting guerrilla warfare. But he went further. Although he admitted that he had been instructed not to endanger human life, several of the acts of sabotage Mtolo described did involve danger to others. For example, he testified that a passenger train had been hit with Molotov cocktails, despite the fact that his instructions had been to go after a "goods" train. The train was left burning on the tracks.

Mtolo claimed that he lost faith in MK because it was under the control of the Communists. He became bitter about the influence of Communism and the affluence of people like Sisulu and Mlangeni. Mtolo claimed that Sisulu lived in a house far above the standards of other blacks in the townships, and that Mlangeni had an automobile, a luxury available to very few blacks.

There was very little the defense could do to challenge the basic thrust of Mtolo's testimony about acts of sabotage and the recruitment of guerrilla fighters—it was both true and corroborated by the documentary evidence. Indeed, the defense was expecting all of it.[36] But Mtolo could be challenged on his embellishments and falsehoods, and that tactic might be sufficient to blunt the impact of his words.

In one instance, the defense had to accept the basic truth of Mtolo's testimony involving Mandela and thus ensure that Mandela would be convicted. In his report of the speech given by Mandela to the Natal Regional Command, Mtolo said that Mandela had warned those going abroad not to broadcast their Communist affiliations. Mandela had given his lawyers a different version of his statements. He had said only that those sent abroad should not use their position in MK to advance Communist propaganda. Mandela authorized his lawyer, Vernon Berrange, to make this point on cross-examination, despite the fact that by doing so the defense was conceding the essence of the speech as described by Mtolo—the fostering of acts charged in the indictment.

With regard to acts of sabotage in which life was endangered, the defense's cross-examination of Mtolo succeeded in establishing that some of the acts were not committed under the mandate of the MK High Command. In other respects, defense could only soften the impact of Mtolo's testimony and refute his embellishments by exposing the motivations behind them. Mtolo was a career criminal who had served time for both theft and attempted murder, a crime that he admitted on cross-examination was not politically motivated. His descriptions of Sisulu's allegedly posh home were effectively debunked by a cross-examination that successfully called into question whether he had ever in fact visited the house. He hadn't. The leadership he had accused of fleeing and leaving underlings like him to bear the brunt of the fight was in fact in the prisoner's dock at this trial.

Berrange also destroyed Mtolo's attempt to blame the Communists for his disillusionment, given that he established that Mtolo himself was a member of the Party. Mtolo's distinction between the goals of the ANC and the Communists was based upon his supposed concern for the protection of private property—a concern that was challenged as hypocritical in light of the witness's conviction for theft.

Nonetheless, the essence of what Mtolo had said remained unchallenged before the court: all of the accused, with the exception of Bernstein and Kantor, were tied to acts of sabotage and other actions that were intended to result in the armed overthrow of the government of South Africa. No amount of cross-examination, no matter how effective, could change these facts. The defense left them unchallenged.

The testimony of police officers was essential to the prosecution's case, for it was the foundation for the introduction of the damning documents.

Officers testified that the raids on Liliesleaf Farm and the other properties—Travallyn and Mountain View—resulted in their discovery, and established their connection to the defendants either by their presence at the places where the writings were found, by handwriting analysis, or by the admission of the defendants themselves.

There was more to be gained from some of the officers' testimony. The state had enough evidence from the documents and testimony of witnesses—especially Bruno Mtolo—to tie the principal defendants to some acts of sabotage. But for propaganda purposes, as well as to beef up its case in court, they needed to tie them to as many of the 193 acts of sabotage laid out in the indictment as possible. The documents and the testimony of witnesses who had participated in those acts accounted for only a few. Furthermore, the prosecution had anticipated the defense strategy that it was the policy of MK not to engender human life. It was critical to Yutar that he establish that some of the acts traced directly to MK, the ANC, or the Communist Party involved injury to persons or at least the threat of injury.

Some of the officers identified those arrested and charged as affiliated with MK or the ANC. Two of the primary witnesses to the sabotage investigations were Sergeant Donald John Card of East London and Sergeant Jonathan du Preez of Port Elizabeth, two cities located in what is now the Eastern Cape Province. East London and Port Elizabeth were white enclaves amid largely Xhosa homelands. The area was the birthplace of Mandela, Sisulu, and Mbeki, as well as Stephen Biko, later a martyr to the struggle for rights when he died in police custody in 1977. Both Eastern Cape cities and their adjacent townships had experienced violence for which there were arrests, charges, and convictions.

Sergeant du Preez testified to the numerous acts of sabotage he had investigated, several of which involved vicious attacks on the homes of black constables or other pro-government blacks.[37] He also described the destruction of train tracks—damage that threatened both freight and passenger trains.[38] Du Preez described many of the persons arrested by what he said were their MK military ranks, such as "corporals," "line corporals," or "ordinary soldiers."[39]

Sergeant Card's testimony was similar: he, too, had investigated numerous acts of sabotage, some life-threatening, and arrested numerous people.[40] Card went a step further than du Preez, however. He could not only tell the court that those arrested were members of the ANC but also identify the particular "cell" to which he said they belonged. For example,

Mlambi William Ondale was a member of the ANC and the African Students Association—allegedly an ANC wing. He was also "a member of the Westbank cell."[41] Buyton Sikawu "was a member of the Zipunsana cell."[42] Tying these individuals to the ANC also tied them confidently to the ANC leadership—the men on trial.

Fischer and Berrange largely softened the impact of this testimony by effective cross-examination. As in an American courtroom, hearsay evidence—the out-of-court statements of others—is ordinarily inadmissible in a South African court. In a trial in which there is no jury, the judge may permit the witness to testify to hearsay but will disregard such evidence in his judgment. Fischer and Berrange successfully established that both du Preez and Card were testifying to the affiliations of those charged with sabotage based upon information received from others, the statements of those accused, and from police records.[43] Testimony demonstrating their prolific memories of those charged as ANC members—with military-sounding ranks and specific cell affiliations—was all hearsay. According to the rule, the judge was to ignore such evidence when reaching his decision as to whether the defendants' organizations were responsible for the actions attributed to them and whether these actions constituted a risk to life. The exclusion of this evidence as hearsay would not be sufficient to acquit Mandela and the other principal defendants, but it may have helped to save their lives.

Another aspect of the state's proof was testimony that the Operation Mayibuye document was found lying open on the table in the thatched cottage where most of the defendants were found on the day of the raid. The inference was obvious—the men had been discussing what it contained. Two witnesses present on the day of the raid, Sergeants Dirker and Kennedy, testified to finding the document in the middle of the table.[44] The defendants knew that this was false—the document had been stuffed in the soot box of the heating stove in the corner of the thatched cottage.[45] But rebuttal proof from the defendants would likely result in a swearing match between them and the police detectives—one that the judge was likely to resolve in favor of the detectives. The defense considered that such a resolution of the dispute might well adversely affect the judge's overall view of the defendants' credibility. In the end, counsel elected not to challenge the detectives' false testimony and to contest only those points where they could clearly win and, wherever possible, to promote the general character of their clients.[46] Disputing the discovery location of critical documents was deliberately ceded in favor of making a greater point.

Berrange challenged Sergeant Dirker on a point crucial to Rusty Bernstein's defense. If nothing else, this gave counsel the opportunity to attack a much-hated police officer. Dirker was a longtime nemesis of all of the defendants and the others with whom they worked. He was not very bright—he had never risen above the rank of sergeant when his cohorts were promoted to higher ranks. The defendants' hatred stemmed in part from his appearance. Joel Joffe described him, with his lock of black hair hanging down over one eye from a balding pate and his moustache, as a "gross, inflated version of the fanatical Adolf Hitler."[47] Dirker had been caught before in lies in other security police cases.

Dirker testified that he examined Bernstein's car after arresting the men in the thatched cottage at Liliesleaf at 3 p.m. He stated that when he lifted the hood of the car the engine was cold, suggesting that it had not been used recently and therefore that Bernstein had been at the meeting in the cottage for a long time. On cross-examination, Berrange confronted Dirker with the records of the Marshall Square Police Headquarters in Johannesburg, establishing that Bernstein had signed in there—witnessed by a policeman on duty—at 2 p.m. Dirker admitted that the trip from Marshall Square to Liliesleaf Farm would take at least thirty minutes. Bernstein could not have been at the farm for more than thirty minutes. In fact, according to all of the accused, he had not been there for more than ten minutes. To top it off, Berrange also established that Bernstein's car made no sound when Dirker lifted the hood. Defense counsel would later establish that this car had an alarm system.[48]

Other state witnesses were more effective. Several helped establish that Denis Goldberg had made extensive inquiries around the Johannesburg community regarding the purchase of material that might be useful in making explosives. Goldberg, under a couple of assumed names—Mr. Williams and Mr. Barnard—had, they said, made contact with various manufacturers or merchants, seeking castings suitable for hand grenades. He had also made inquiries for the purchase of wooden boxes of the sort that fitted a design for landmines. All of this was done in accordance with plans and sketches found at Travallyn.[49] Goldberg, in his testimony, readily admitted to all of these activities, thus assuring his conviction of the charges of conspiring to commit sabotage.[50]

Defense counsel seriously contested the testimony of only two witnesses against Goldberg. One, a man named Cyril Davids, testified that he had attended a camp at a site near Cape Town where young recruits—black and Coloured men—were trained in techniques useful in guerrilla warfare.[51] Davids himself had lectured the others on the use of a field telephone and on judo. Goldberg, said Davids, had been addressed as "Comrade Commandant," and another leader, Looksmart Nguldle (who had died in police custody), as "Comrade Sergeant." The camp had lasted only two days before it was broken up by the police. Davids testified that the campers were told not to give any information to the police except that the camp was for health and spiritual purposes.

On cross-examination, Berrange got Davids to admit that he had had little contact with Goldberg prior to being recruited to the camp and that most of the activities at the camp involved speeches about the history of racial oppression in South Africa, rather than instruction in military tactics. Berrange cast considerable doubt on Davids's story by establishing that his description of the camp had changed dramatically while Davids was in police detention, during which time he had endured regular Security Police interrogations and threats that his ninety days would turn into an infinite series of detentions without trial. During all this, Davids's recollection of the camp transformed from a place designed to assist with health and spiritual issues to one in which the campers were schooled in guerrilla techniques.

Goldberg himself later testified to the benign nature of the activities at the camp.[52] The defense had argued that it was highly unlikely that he would take thirty men he had never really met and announce to them that they were to be treated as guerrilla fighters. All had been interrogated during a raid on the camp; none had told the police that there was anything more going on than discussion of politics.

Nonetheless, another witness, Caswell Mboxela, gave substantially the same evidence as Davids, though his version contained even more contradictions.[53] Later, in his written judgment, Judge de Wet found the two state witnesses to be "substantially truthful."[54] Many years after the trial, Goldberg, in a private interview, admitted that the camp had indeed been for the purpose of guerrilla training.[55]

The evidence against Jimmy Kantor was circumstantial and weak. Nonetheless, Yutar apparently felt that letting up on Kantor would weaken the entire Rivonia case. He was the stand-in for his brother-in-law and partner, the escaped Harold Wolpe, who the state believed was key to the conspiracy. Yutar called a parade of witnesses in an attempt to tie Kantor to his brother-in law's involvement in the purchase of Liliesleaf Farm and other activities of MK.[56] The witnesses established Wolpe's involvement beyond a reasonable doubt. But they were completely unsuccessful in establishing that Kantor even knew of those activities, let alone was involved in them.

The law firm had represented several people who were allegedly involved in the subversive activities charged in the indictments and had held meetings at the firm's offices.[57] But there was no proof that Kantor himself was in any way connected to them. The partnership had participated in the purchase of Liliesleaf Farm, but there was nothing to indicate that Kantor had any knowledge of the activities to be conducted there.

Judge de Wet dismissed Kantor at the end of the prosecution's case. The court ruled that the prosecution had failed to make a *prima facie* (legally sufficient) case for his guilt. De Wet did not give reasons for his ruling at that time, but he elaborated on it at some length in his final judgment.[58]

The state argued that under South African law, when a partner has committed an offense while carrying out the business of a partnership, any other partner is deemed guilty of that offense—"unless it is proved that he did not take part in the commission of the offence, and that he could not have prevented it."[59] Despite this heavy onus and the fact that Kantor neither testified nor presented witnesses, the court found that he had met his burden. The proof of his innocence was "found in the evidence of the State's witnesses."[60] There was no proof that Kantor had participated in any wrongful activity or that he had had any knowledge of it. Judge de Wet noted that when "an accused person has no knowledge of an offence and cannot reasonably be expected to have such knowledge . . . it follows that he could not have prevented it."[61]

With the release of Kantor, nine defendants remained. Counsel would have five weeks to prepare its case. In their defense, they would try to both save the lives of the accused and justify their actions to a world audience.

Mandela at the Dock

THE MOST CRITICAL decision the defense needed to make is one familiar to criminal defense lawyers throughout the Anglo-American legal world: whether or not to have the accused testify as witnesses. The accused can elect not to testify; if they choose to remain silent the prosecution cannot require them to take the witness stand.

One effect of electing not to testify is that the court—or in some cases, the jury—will likely draw adverse inferences. Yet by refusing to testify, the witness can avoid making harmful admissions, either as part of his examination by his own lawyer or on cross-examination. The decision is sometimes an easy one, such as when the accused has a criminal record that otherwise would not be disclosed, or is for some other reason unlikely to be believed. The task then facing counsel is only to persuade the client that he ought not to exercise his right to testify. But if the client has an important story, it may be worth subjecting him to the inevitable cross-examination to get him to tell it to the world.

The decision facing the Rivonia defendants and their lawyers was even more complex than usual. If they testified truthfully, most would have to admit to enough charges to ensure their conviction. But if they failed to testify, they would lose the opportunity to make their case against apartheid.

An advantage of having the defendants testify at the Rivonia Trial would be the opportunity it gave them to expand on the reasons for their actions—testimony that would be even more effective if given in response to cross-examination by the prosecution. Should Yutar challenge them on their beliefs and motivations, they could articulate them without it seeming that their own lawyers were leading them through a scripted performance. But most of the defense team did not believe that Yutar would be foolish enough to engage in a political debate with the accused. They assumed he would stay with what he knew he could prove—the participation of the defendants in acts in violation of the law.

Defense advocate George Bizos strongly disagreed.[1] Yutar would not pass up the opportunity to try to make his own political case. Bizos persuaded the others that most of the accused should testify—not that the defendants resisted the idea; they welcomed the opportunity to rebut the distortions of many of the state witnesses. Nonetheless, the decision was made that Mandela would make a statement to the court rather than testify.[2] Mandela had made a similar decision at his 1962 trial, at which he had given a powerful speech, solidifying his stature as representing the philosophical core of antiapartheid resistance.[3]

Mandela would admit to many of the acts charged in the indictment, deny others and, most importantly, offer his justifications. Under South African law, he could make such a statement without being under oath and without enduring cross-examination. Theoretically, the statement would not count as evidence in the case. But he would be able to get his points across to both the judge and the court of public opinion. Mandela's statement would be followed by the testimony of most of the other defendants. Elias Motsoaledi and Andrew Mlangeni would make short nontestimonial statements. All agreed that testimony from these two men would not improve the odds for either of them. They had been involved in the activities with which they were charged, but at a rank-and-file level. Should they testify, their defense worried, they might make statements on cross-examination that would overstate their responsibility.

The defense's case began on Monday, April 20, 1964, with Bram Fischer's opening statement. Like Yutar's opening on the first day of the trial, some of the issues in Fischer's opening went beyond those before Judge de Wet. On trial were not merely the accused but the apartheid regime itself. The whole world was watching.

Nonetheless, Fischer began by making a more local distinction. The defense would show, he said, that MK was in fact not a section of the African National Congress but a separate organization.[4] The point was significant for other ANC members, who at some later trial would otherwise be criminally responsible for any acts attributed to MK. He also told the judge that the defense would show that the ANC was not a tool of the Communist Party. Although support from the Communist Party was welcome, the aims of the two organizations were very different. The ANC was "a broad national movement, embracing all classes of Africans within its ranks, and having the aim of achieving equal political rights for all South Africans."

In other parts of his opening, Fischer sought to diminish the involvement of some of the defendants in the overall antigovernment activity.

He said that defense evidence would show that Goldberg, Kathrada, and Bernstein, for example, were not members of MK at all, let alone members of its High Command. Even more significantly—although more likely to affect the sentence rather than the verdict—the defense would establish that Operation Mayibuye was never in fact adopted, and that it was hoped that the tactics it laid out could be avoided so long as there was some chance of achieving the objectives of MK by other means.

Fischer's opening was followed by the most dramatic moment in the trial—the moment that would come to symbolize South Africa's struggle against oppression in the eyes of the world for all time. Fischer paused when he finished his opening speech—ostensibly to let the judge finish making notes. He then announced, "The defence case, my Lord, will commence with a statement from the dock by Nelson Mandela who personally took part in the establishment of Umkhonto, and who will be able to inform the court of the beginnings of that organization and of its history up to August [1962], when he was arrested."

Joffe remembers Yutar "behaving as though he could not believe his ears." His voice rose to his now-familiar falsetto: "My Lord! I think you should warn the accused that what he says from the dock has far less weight than if he submitted himself to cross-examination." The judge replied, tartly, "I think, Mr. Yutar, that counsel for the defence have sufficient experience to be able to advise their clients without your assistance." Fischer responded in turn that he appreciated his learned friend's advice, but, he said, "Neither we, nor our clients are unaware of the provisions of the Criminal Code."[5] Mandela was, after all, himself a qualified attorney with enough experience to know the difference between a statement to the court and testimony subject to cross-examination.

But nothing said or done at this trial was more likely to have an effect on its outcome than what Mandela would say in the course of the next five hours.[6] It may have saved the lives of all of the defendants. A few minutes after beginning his oration, Mandela made an admission sufficient to condemn him to the gallows: "Some of the things so far told to the Court are true and some are untrue. I do not, however, deny that I planned sabotage." However, he argued, planning for it was "a result of a calm and sober assessment of the political situation that had arisen after many years of tyranny, exploitation, and oppression of my people by the Whites."

Mandela firmly denied some of the detailed evidence that had been presented by the state witnesses, especially with regard to activities involving risk to human life. As he well knew, Mandela's denials, even if they were believed by the court, were insufficient to gain his acquittal on any of the charges. They were important only as part of the battle for public opinion that was so much a part of this trial and, perhaps, in mitigation of punishment.

Much of his speech was intended as a lesson on the history of the ANC and its long-standing and deeply entrenched policy of nonviolence. From its formation in 1912 the ANC had sought political relief from the oppression of black people in South Africa until 1961. The government rebuffed all of its attempts. The organization's efforts were increasingly met with violence, including the killing of sixty-nine unarmed Africans at Sharpeville in 1960. After Sharpeville, the government proclaimed a state of emergency and the ANC was declared an unlawful organization. But the ANC did not disband. "I have no doubt that no self-respecting white political organization would disband itself if declared illegal by a government in which it had no say."

Peaceful demonstrations were met with new and harsher measures and "a massive show of force designed to intimidate the people." It was clear, Mandela said, that the government now intended to "rule by force alone," a decision that was, he added, "a milestone on the road to Umkhonto." "What were we, the leaders of our people, to do? Were we to give in to the show of force and the implied threat against future action, or were we to fight it out and, if so, how?"

A few minutes later, Mandela answered his own questions. He and his colleagues concluded that because violence in the country was inevitable, it would be unrealistic and even wrong for African leaders to continue preaching peace and nonviolence. "The conclusion, my lord, was not easily arrived at. It was only when all else had failed, when all channels of peaceful protest had been barred to us, that the decision was made to embark on violent forms of political struggle, and to form Umkhonto we Sizwe."

The leadership recognized that there were four forms of violence available—ascending in order by degree of violence: sabotage, guerrilla warfare, terrorism, and open revolution. The decision was made for sabotage, which, Mandela said, did not "involve loss of life and . . . offered the best hope for future race relations." Plans were made to damage power plants and hinder rail and telephone communications. These would deter investment, make it more difficult for goods from the industrial areas to reach the seaports, and eventually drain the economic life of the country. Government buildings that were symbols of apartheid would also be sabotaged. "These attacks would serve as a source of inspiration to our people" and, as he put it, provide an "outlet" for those in the resistance organizations calling for action. If the government responded with mass reprisals, they would provoke sympathy for their cause in other countries.

Mandela went on to describe in detail the management of the affairs of MK—including the existence of the National High Command, which—contrary to the allegation in the first indictment—was not an entity in itself but rather the designation given to the MK leadership. Beginning in December 1961, attacks were carried out but confined to empty buildings and power stations. In pointed rebuttal of Bruno Mtolo's testimony, Mandela disclaimed involvement in attacks before that date and later attacks involving risk of injury to anyone. The government reacted with force to MK's actions. He added, "The Whites failed to respond by suggesting changes: they responded to our call by retreating behind the *laager* [circled wagons]."

Although MK had decided to engage only in sabotage at this point, plans were made to step up the violence to the next level—guerrilla warfare. The idea was to build up a nucleus of trained men who would be able to provide the leadership required if guerrilla warfare started. Mandela said that this was why he left the country in early 1962. His goal was to tour other African states, to locate training facilities and to solicit funds. He met with African leaders and began to school himself in the art of war and revolution, including undergoing a course in military training. "If there was to be guerrilla warfare, I wanted to be able to stand and fight with my people and to share the hazards of war with them."

Mandela then carefully outlined the distinctions between the ANC and MK—recognizing that they had overlapping membership but maintaining that the organizations were separate. He also took pains to distinguish the ANC from the Communist Party—a connection made virtually every time Yutar addressed the court or the public. The ANC stood for African nationalism—freedom and rights for people living in their own land. It relied on the "Freedom Charter," a document signed in 1955 by a broad range of antiapartheid groups. Mandela maintained that the charter was "by no means a blueprint for a socialist state." It called for redistribution, not nationalization—although mines, banks, and monopolistic industries would be nationalized to end domination by one race. The idea was to build an economy based on private enterprise rather than Marxism. The economic result of apartheid was that most Africans were impoverished by low incomes and high cost of living. There was widespread poverty and a breakdown of family life. "Africans want to be paid a living wage," he said toward the end of his statement. "Africans want to perform work which they are capable of doing, and not work which the Government declares them to be capable of."

The relationship between the Communist Party and the ANC was one of cooperation—not unlike, he pointed out, the alliance of Great Britain, the United States, and the Soviet Union in the fight against Hitler. There were theoretical differences between the ANC and the Communists, but "theoretical differences amongst those fighting against oppression are a luxury we cannot afford at this stage." "What is more," he added, "for many decades Communists were the only political group in South Africa who were prepared to treat Africans as human beings and their equals: who were prepared to talk with us; eat with us, live with us and work with us."

In a statement that must have sent shudders down the spines of most white South Africans—just as it would have most whites in the United States or Great Britain—Mandela referred to the support of the Communist bloc in the United Nations and other international bodies in the struggle against colonialism. "Although there is a universal condemnation of apartheid, the Communist bloc speaks out against it with a louder voice than most of the Western world."

In outlining his own role as an "African patriot," Mandela noted his broad range of sources of inspiration, including not only Communist literature but also British and American political institutions. "Our fight is against real, and not imaginary hardships, or to use the language of the State Prosecutor, 'so-called hardships.'" "Basically, my lord," he told de Wet, "we fight against two features which are the hallmarks of African life in South Africa and which are entrenched by legislation which we seek to have repealed." These "features" were poverty and the absence of human dignity, and, he said, "we do not need Communists or so-called 'agitators' to teach us about these things."

The courtroom had grown quieter as Mandela's speech went on. As he began to close, the silence became even more profound.

Above all, my lord, we want equal political rights, because without them our disabilities will be permanent. I know this sounds revolutionary to the whites in this country, because the majority of the voters will be Africans. This makes the white man fear democracy.

But this fear cannot be allowed to stand in the way of the only solution which will guarantee racial harmony and freedom for all. It is not true that the enfranchisement of all will result in racial domination. Political division, based on color, is entirely artificial and, when it disappears, so will the domination of one color group by another. The ANC has spent half a century fighting against racialism. When it triumphs, as it certainly must, it will not change that policy.

This then is what the ANC is fighting. Our struggle is a truly national one. It is a struggle of the African people, inspired by our own suffering and our own experience. It is a struggle for the right to live.

At this point, Mandela put down the papers from which he had been reading and spoke from memory, ending his speech with the words that remain his most famous (and which today adorn the wall of the new Constitutional Court in Johannesburg):

During my lifetime I have dedicated myself to this struggle of the African People. I have fought against white domination, and I have fought against black domination. I have cherished the ideal of a democratic and free society in which all persons live together in harmony and with equal opportunities. It is an ideal which I hope to live for, and see realized. But if needs be, it is an ideal for which I am prepared to die.

The words "if needs be" had been added at the insistence of George Bizos, who felt that without them the invitation to sentence Mandela to death was simply too patent.[7] Mandela consented to the editing but in later years would have a different view of his invitation to the court. Forty-five years later, Denis Goldberg would ask Mandela why he thought de Wet had not sentenced him to die. "Because I dared him to do so," he replied.[8] Those who were there said that the silence was complete. There were deep sighs from the public benches; some women in the gallery burst into tears.[9] After a pause, de Wet turned to Bram Fischer and said, "You may call your next witness."

The trial was largely over for Nelson Mandela. He had admitted to enough to be found guilty of all charges against him. What remained was whether the judge would respond to what seemed to be a challenge to render a death sentence. He joined the other prisoners in the dock and waited to see what would unfold as the other defendants gave evidence. For his part, he had said what he wanted to say.

9

Others Make Their Case

WALTER SISULU WAS the first defense witness. His testimony was crucial for the defense. Other than Mandela, Sisulu was the defendant best known to the outside world. The *New York Times* carried his photograph rather than Mandela's in its story about the beginning of the trial.[1] Aside from Govan Mbeki, he was also the figure most familiar with the activities of the ANC and MK leading up to the Rivonia raid. Powerful though it was, Mandela's statement was nontestimonial. Judge de Wet would have to be given something in the form of admissible evidence in order even to consider mitigating punishment.

Most importantly, the court needed to be persuaded that Operation Mayibuye had not been adopted. A finding that the defendants had decided on guerrilla warfare could lead them to the gallows. For purposes of both the trial and the protection of other ANC members who would likely be prosecuted in the future, Sisulu's testimony would also have to separate the ANC from both MK and the Communist Party. To make these points effectively, Sisulu would have to withstand Yutar's cross-examination.

Unlike Mandela, Sisulu was not a lawyer. Fifty-one years old, he had spent much of his life as an ANC activist, He and Nelson Mandela had transformed the ANC Youth League into the driving force for confrontation with the government. Sisulu had little formal education, having left school at age fifteen, and then working in the mines and as a salesman and clerical worker. He had served as secretary general of the ANC from 1949 until 1954, when the government restricted his involvement in political activities through banning orders that effectively prevented him from attending public gatherings.[2] Some of the defense lawyers feared that Sisulu would be no match for Yutar, who after all had a doctorate in law and years of experience sparring with witnesses.

Sisulu's codefendants believed otherwise. They trusted not only his thorough knowledge of the inner workings of the ANC and MK but his intellect. George Bizos predicted that Yutar would try and argue

Palace of Justice, Pretoria today. *Photograph by the author, 2009.*

Main house, Liliesleaf Farm today, part of the Liliesleaf Farm Museum. *Photograph by the author, 2009.*

Thatched Cottage, Liliesleaf Farm today, Liliesleaf Farm Museum. *Photograph by the author, 2009.*

Items seized in the July 11, 1963 raid on Liliesleaf Farm. *National Archives of South Africa.*

Aerial view of Liliesleaf Farm, 1963. *National Archives of South Africa.*

Security Police search Liliesleaf Farm Main House. *National Archives of South Africa.*

Security police search outside Liliesleaf Farm, July, 1963; Arthur Goldreich (front) and Lieutenant Willem Petrus van Wyk (at rear) observe. *National Archives of South Africa.*

Thatched cottage at Liliesleaf Farm, 1963. *National Archives of South Africa.*

Photos on this page and the following, with the exception of Nelson Mandela's, were taken at the time of the individual's July 1963 arrest. Mandela's arrest was in 1962. *National Archives of South Africa.*

Ahmed Kathrada

Andrew Mlangeni

Denis Goldberg

Elias Motsoaledi

Govan Mbeki

James Kantor

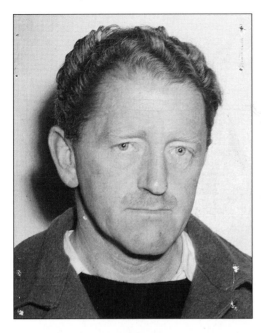

Lionel (Rusty) Bernstein

Nelson Mandela

Raymond Mhlaba

Walter Sisulu

politics with this seemingly outmatched and, in the eyes of almost all white South Africans, inferior individual.

Two things made Sisulu's time on the stand even more difficult for him than for other witnesses. First, although he could testify fully about his own actions, he had to be careful not to answer any questions that might lead to the prosecution of others. Even if it would weaken his position, he was determined not be an informer. The other defendants who testified followed his lead. Secondly, South African practice dictated that a witness could not discuss his testimony with his lawyer until his evidence was fully given. The prosecution in this case went one step further than usual and isolated Sisulu from his codefendants as well.[3] The defense lawyers at first sought to challenge this added limitation, but Mandela persuaded them that Sisulu could handle the situation.[4] The defense later successfully protested the isolation for other defendants.[5]

The procedure in South Africa is the same as in other nations drawing on English courtroom procedure. There is an "examination-in-chief"— usually called "direct examination" in the United States—conducted by the lawyer for the party calling the witness, in this case his own counsel. Cross-examination by opposing counsel follows. The direct examiner then has an opportunity to question the witness again—"redirect examination" in the United States and "reexamination" in South Africa.

In his examination-in-chief, conducted by Bram Fischer, Sisulu confirmed much of what Nelson Mandela had said about the history of the ANC, the formation of MK, and the decision to engage in sabotage. Just as Mandela had said, Sisulu insisted that for most of its history, the ANC committed to nonviolent protest. The government's actions, especially after the 1960 Sharpeville Massacre, left it no choice but to engage in controlled violence in the form of sabotage. Although not a member of the Umkhonto High Command, Sisulu attended some of its meetings as an ANC representative. He stressed that Operation Mayibuye had not been adopted. At least at this time, he and other ANC leaders were opposed to the adoption and implementation of the plan. Sisulu was also careful to distinguish the views of the ANC, which he described as an organization reflecting the aspirations of the African people, from those of the Communist Party.

But while making these points, which were crucial to the defense, Sisulu confirmed the principal allegations of the indictment: he had been involved in the planning for sabotage and the recruitment and sponsorship of young men to be trained abroad for eventual involvement in guerrilla warfare. At the end of Sisulu's examination-in-chief, Fischer asked him if should have acted otherwise than he did. "I can't see how I could have done otherwise," Sisulu responded, "other than what I have done. Because even if I myself did not play the role I did, others would have done what I have done instead."

Sisulu then prepared to face cross-examination. Judges in an adversary system—such as in South Africa, Great Britain, and the United States—do not generally ask questions of the witnesses, although they may step in to clarify an answer. In the Rivonia Trial, however, Sisulu often faced two cross-examiners—Yutar, who brought all of his experience, thoroughness, and sarcasm to bear on Sisulu, and Judge de Wet, whose interventions suggested where he stood on both to the criminal prosecution before him and the racial issues facing the country. Both the prosecutor and Judge de Wet appeared more interested in debating politics than in establishing the acts with which Sisulu was charged. Sisulu had already admitted to enough of those acts to ensure his conviction. The judge's active participation in Sisulu's cross-examination concerned defendants and their counsel because of what it might portend regarding his final judgment and sentencing.

Yutar sought to minimize support for the ANC, which had a membership of 120,000 out of a total African population of more than 12 million. It was a point he would make in his cross-examination of other defendants as well. Sisulu responded by noting the government's intimidation of the ANC and stated that he believed that the organization still represented the "aspirations of the people." He added that the masses would rise up in an armed struggle if there were a real possibility of success, because "the people do want to have a vote in this country." At this point, de Wet interrupted. "How do you know that the ordinary Bantu-around-town wants the vote?" Sisulu responded, "Well, I have not come across meetings where I have heard people saying, 'No, we don't want the vote!' People always support the idea of the vote."

The prosecutor referred to ANC radio broadcasts that were made by Sisulu at locations other than the Rivonia farm. Sisulu testified that the broadcasts were made from other locations so that, if the broadcasts were traced, they would not lead to the leadership at Liliesleaf Farm. Judge de Wet noted that others involved in the broadcasts might in fact be arrested even though the leadership was not. The judge interjected that politicians were "always prepared to let the rank and file take the risk, and see that they don't put themselves to danger." Sisulu responded that the judge's interpretation was not correct, comparing the leadership's role to that of generals in a war, who were less exposed to danger. The judge retorted, "But exactly the same thing happens with people who are plotting a rebellion or a revolution. They look forward to being the government in due course. And they see to it that they preserve their own skins, not so?" "My understanding, My Lord," responded Sisulu, "is that we, to the best of our ability, want to preserve everyone." The judge's attitude toward the leadership of revolutionary movements would surface again when the defendants were sentenced.

Still another instance of the judge's intervention and attitude involved a point particularly critical to the defense—the lack of intent to harm human life during the sabotage actions. He asked Sisulu whether it was his argument that "as long as you have not got the intention to kill people, it does not matter if you kill people." Sisulu answered that everything had been done to prevent injury. "I am not saying that it can't happen," he replied to de Wet. "But I am saying that precautions are taken that it should not happen."

The witness, the prosecutor, and the judge also sparred over who would control the country if blacks were given the right to vote—another point irrelevant to the acts with which Sisulu was charged. Sisulu insisted that full voting rights would not mean black domination.

JUDGE DE WET: No, but black control! Won't it mean black control?
SISULU: Only in the sense that the majority of rulers will be black.
JUDGE: That necessarily involves control, not so?
SISULU: Well it might be that control can be exercised by both races, elected together.

This interchange is from the official transcript of the trial, in which the defendant was referred to merely as "Sisulu." Up to this point, Yutar had used first names in his interrogation of all black witnesses, a common practice in South Africa when whites addressed blacks. This practice, of course, emphasized the white perception of the blacks as inferior. However, by the time Sisulu testified, the prosecutor shifted into a more clearly hostile use of only his last name.

Joffe believed that Walter Sisulu was a "triumph" in the witness box.[6] Bram Fischer's biographer Stephen Clingman refers to Sisulu's performance as one of the most remarkable ever seen in a South African courtroom.[7] Certainly, Sisulu more than held his own in sparring both with

Yutar and Judge de Wet. The picture that the defense wanted to emerge about the defendants' idealism and greater sense of purpose largely came through in the course of a grueling five days of examination.

Sisulu and colleagues had planned sabotage, but they were driven to it by the policies of the government that denied them their basic political, social, and economic rights. Black South Africans believed that there was no choice other than to respond with violence of their own. The form chosen—sabotage of public buildings and communications facilities—was the least threatening to human life. Further and escalating violence was certainly foreseeable but it had not yet been agreed upon. Perhaps even more importantly, and despite de Wet's seeming hostility, George Bizos observed that the judge "was bemused by Walter's manner, memory and directness in answering the questions."[8] Joffe added that the judge had come to understand that in Sisulu he was dealing with someone of intellect and reflection. "To sentence such a man to death would not be easy for any judge."[9] De Wet's active participation in the cross-examination had at least had that effect.

But Yutar also accomplished much of what he had set out to do. At several points in his examination, he confronted Sisulu with damning statements found in the seized documents—including threats of further violence, threats that were ominous whether or not they involved a specific plan for guerrilla warfare. Yutar was also able to demonstrate that, whatever the intentions of the Umkhonto and ANC leadership, acts of sabotage could nonetheless lead to injury or death. And, although Sisulu did not concede that the ANC was controlled by the Communist Party, he had admitted that the aims of the two coincided. None of this was necessary for conviction but, again, all of it could factor into the judge's ultimate decision on sentencing.

An experienced trial lawyer knows that the order in which witnesses are called is an important tactical decision. In some ways, therefore, the defense's choice of Ahmed Kathrada as the next witness was an odd one. As the defendants were listed in the indictment, Mandela was accused Number. 1; Sisulu, Number 2; Denis Goldberg, Number 3; Govan Mbeki, Number 4; and Kathrada, Number 5.[10] That order would have suggested calling Goldberg next. Another would have been to call Mbeki after Sisulu. Next to Mandela and Sisulu, Mbeki was the most knowledgeable about the inner workings of both the ANC and MK and could best make the political points so important in this case.

Yet calling Kathrada at this point made tactical sense in other ways. Of all the defendants, Goldberg was perhaps the most likely both to be found guilty and to hang. The evidence that he actually purchased material to be used in sabotage and potentially in warfare was simply overwhelming. Yet despite Goldberg's clear involvement in the acts most frightening to both the government and the white population, he had not been involved in decision making. Calling him at this point might have detracted from the defense's efforts to make its political case. Indeed, calling him at all presented risks, both for Goldberg himself and the defense as a whole. The decision would later be made to call him near the end.

Calling Mbeki after Sisulu would have made more sense for the defense to explain to South Africa and the world the defendants' motives and actions. But like Mandela and Sisulu, Mbeki would clearly admit enough for him to be found guilty on all counts. Tactically, it was useful to intersperse a defendant for whom there was at least the possibility of a not-guilty verdict. Kathrada fit that bill. He had clearly been involved in some way in the activities at Rivonia because he was there on the day of the raid. However, it would be much more difficult to pin Kathrada either to the planning or the carrying out of the acts charged.

Kathrada and Goldberg presented a common problem for defense counsel. Kathrada, aged thirty-four, and Goldberg, thirty-three, were the youngest of the accused, and the ones most given to flippant, irreverent responses. Kathrada could pepper his conversation with sarcasm and humor.[11] Goldberg had a tendency to "wise-crack."[12] Neither man's attitude was likely to sit well with Justice de Wet. Nonetheless, for the most part, both behaved themselves on the witness stand.

As was the case with all of the defendants, Kathrada's testimony was his opportunity to present himself as someone with real grievances and sincere belief in his cause. If not enough to achieve acquittal, the defense believed that his presentation might be enough to lead the judge to spare his life.

Unlike Mandela's statement to the court and Sisulu's testimony, Kathrada's examination-in-chief contained no admissions of the charges in the indictment. Instead, advocate Vernon Berrange led him through his life dedicated to the liberation struggle. He had begun his activist career at age twelve and from that age devoted virtually all of his energies to the cause in which he believed. On the witness stand, Kathrada told his story from the perspective of an Indian in South Africa—a separate classification of persons with limited rights. He told of his many arrests,[13] banning orders (a form of house arrest limiting contact with other persons), and convictions that kept him from pursuing legitimate, peaceful protests against the government. One of his convictions was for being outside his home province without a permit; all Indians had to have a permit to travel between provinces. Other convictions stemmed from his entry into an African residential area (an area prohibited to Indians) and for visiting his mother in violation of a banning order.

When the ninety-day-detention law went into effect, Kathrada decided to go "underground." It was that decision that caused him to be at Rivonia disguised as the Portuguese Pedro Perreira. He had been at the Mountain View retreat for several days and moved back to Rivonia on the night before the raid, July 10. Kathrada admitted that he was working on a speech at the time of the raid, a speech that was to decry the oppression of Indian people. A draft of the speech was found in the raid.

Most critically for the defense, Kathrada firmly denied the one piece of testimony directly tying him into an act in violation of law. A state witness, Essop Suliman, said that Kathrada hired him to take recruits to the Bechuanaland border for transport to training camps out of the country.[14] Kathrada testified that he did not hire Suliman for any illegal purpose.

Yutar immediately went on the political offensive in his cross-examination, describing Kathrada's draft of the speech on the rights of Indians as "vicious." Kathrada would only admit that the language may have been "immoderate."

The debate over Kathrada's speech was only a sample of the political sparring that dominated Yutar's questioning and the witness's response. The antagonists debated the welfare of Indians in India and detentions in Ghana, as well as the South African government's schemes to remove Africans and others from sections of cities into special areas reserved for them. As part of the apartheid scheme, well-known sections of Johannesburg (Sophiatown) and Cape Town (District Six) that had historically housed people of all races were systematically razed and replaced with housing for whites only.

More germane to the charges against him, Yutar also cross-examined Kathrada about his view of sabotage. The witness testified that he had opposed sabotage unless it was directly related to a specific campaign, such as a protest against the passes Africans were required to carry. But Kathrada also said that he respected the decision to engage in such action. He admitted that he was a member of the Communist Party and a follower of its aim to secure freedom for the oppressed people of South Africa by force and violence "if necessary."

Kathrada kept his sarcasm in check for most of the examination. However, at one point, he couldn't help himself. One of the Mandela diaries put into evidence contained entries referring to a "K." Yutar, not surprisingly, was anxious to show that the "K" was Kathrada.

KATHRADA: I am not referred to as K.

YUTAR: Never?

KATHRADA: I don't know of anybody who refers to me as K.

YUTAR: Do you know anybody else who goes under the initial of K?

KATHRADA: Yes.

YUTAR: Who?

KATHRADA: Mr. Kroestchef [the court reporter uses this spelling; the standard transliteration is Khruschev].

[*Laughter in the court*]

YUTAR: [. . .] So you were just trying to be funny at my expense?

KATHRADA: I wasn't. You asked me if I know of any Mr. "K" and I told you.

But Yutar's cross-examination of Kathrada was not all political debate and laughter. The prosecutor methodically went through Kathrada's close involvement with the activities of the other defendants and their causes. Kathrada associated with the defendants and others who had planned violent actions against the state. He was present for significant amounts of time at the place where such planning took place—Liliesleaf Farm. What turned out to be the most damning evidence was Kathrada's admission that he helped prepare an ANC leaflet about the worldwide observation of a Freedom Day to support the plight of the oppressed in South Africa. The leaflet referred to "freedom fighters" struggling to free South Africa from the racial domination by a "ruthless white minority." The leaflet also noted that the prime minister of Algeria had called for a "Blood Bank" to aid the struggle, no longer supporting them with words alone but with deeds. Yutar's questioning explored the cryptic reference to the "blood bank," with little success. Nonetheless the point was made, and it was to be a critical factor in the court's decision. Kathrada made an overall favorable impression on the court. But there was possibly enough evidence to justify conviction, at least on the conspiracy count.

The next witness—also called out of his order in the indictment listing—was Raymond Mhlaba, Accused Number 7. Mhlaba was an active trade unionist and a member of the Communist Party. He was forty-three at the time of the Rivonia Trial. His friends and associates called him "Oom Ray" ("Uncle Ray" in Afrikaans) for his kindly manner. Mhlaba's time on the witness stand was the shortest of all the accused and, in Joffe's opinion, the least effective. Joffe commented that Mhlaba was a "slow-moving man," and that his "sincerity, his honesty and his simplicity did not come across from the witness box."[15]

The evidence against him was weak, however. Most damning was testimony that he had taken part in acts of sabotage in the Port Elizabeth area on December 16, 1961—the day the sabotage campaign was said to have begun.[16] Whether or not he had ever engaged in sabotage in 1961 or at any other time, he had in fact been on an ANC mission abroad—to Leipzig, East Germany—in December 1961. However, he could not admit to being abroad without also confessing to the crime of being out of the country without a passport. Yutar offered him immunity from prosecution for that crime if he would answer the question as to his whereabouts. As Rusty Bernstein would later in the trial, Mhlaba refused the offer of immunity. Yutar was bound by his offer, but his superior—the minister of justice— was not, and this was well known.

Like the other accused, Mhlaba refused to incriminate others involved in antigovernment activity. Yutar asked him who the members of the ANC in Port Elizabeth were. Mhlaba responded, "I'm afraid I can't assist you there."

YUTAR: Why not?
MHLABA: It is not my duty to tell you about that.
YUTAR: Who gave you instructions not to divulge their names?
MHLABA: Nobody gave us instructions.
YUTAR: But you [the defendants in this case] are all acting alike?
MHLABA: We are acting alike, because we feel that is it not in the interest of the organisation, it is not in the interest of the oppressed people in this country.

In the end, Mhlaba was tied by his own testimony to little more than general involvement in ANC activities. But the unfavorable impression he made on the court, as well as his refusal to say where he had been at the time that, according to a state witness, he participated in acts of sabotage would be enough to convict him.

Before the next accused, Lionel "Rusty" Bernstein, was to be called, the defense asked the court to hear the testimony of two psychologists. The witnesses were to testify about the effect of solitary confinement on prisoners, and more specifically about the possibility that such confinement would lead to brain damages and marked abnormalities. Any evidence these former prisoners gave would be highly suspect; they could not distinguish truth from fantasy. Those suffering from this might believe that what they were saying was true when it in fact had been suggested by the police. Judge de Wet refused to hear the testimony. No doctor was needed to tell him the weight that should be attached to the evidence. But the point was made to the court through the offer of proof.[17]

The timing of the psychologists' testimony—immediately before Bernstein was called—was a little puzzling. The defense clearly wanted the court to believe everything that Bernstein would say, yet more than any of the other accused he had been clearly physically and mentally affected by his confinement. If solitary imprisonment affected one's perception of the truth, Bernstein's testimony became less, rather than more, believable. But the juxtaposition of the proposed psychological evidence was likely intended to have another and more favorable impact on the judge. Bernstein was a human being—and white, moreover—who had already suffered dearly for his politics.

Together with James Kantor and Denis Goldberg, Rusty—nicknamed for his bright red hair—Bernstein, aged forty-three, was one of the three whites on trial. All were Jewish. Unlike Goldberg, Bernstein had not been involved in any of Umkhonto's sabotage or recruitment activities. But he was very much a part of the intellectual movement for change in the country through his associations and writings. Although he was an architect by profession, most of Bernstein's work on behalf of the antiapartheid movement had been as a writer of publicity and propaganda. He had written or participated in the writing of pamphlets and leaflets protesting government policies. No publication with which he was shown to be involved promoted violence.

Bernstein had served in the South African army in World War II, as a gunner in North Africa and Italy. After the war, and until the time of the trial, he was active in veterans' organizations.

Being white gave Bernstein both advantages and disadvantages. The judge's racial biases of course would count in his favor. The court's interventions indeed seemed gentler. For example, early in his examination, Bernstein referred to his work on behalf of the National Liberation Movement. Judge de Wet intervened by noting: "It is a reference to a particular ideology, really that is all it is?" Bernstein agreed. The National Liberation Movement was more accurately a description of "the currents of opinion which stand for the abolition of the color bar."[18] There were fewer and less hostile interventions by the court during cross-examination.

In contrast, Yutar's hostility was patent throughout his cross-examination of Bernstein. The prosecutor was clearly working hard to distinguish himself and other Jews from Communists like Bernstein. But even Yutar favorably distinguished Bernstein on the basis of his whiteness. As we've seen, the prosecutor addressed black witnesses either by their first names or, in the case of the accused, simply by their last. Bernstein was "Mr. Bernstein" throughout.

All of the defendants had followed Sisulu's lead in refusing to answer any question that might incriminate another person not before the court. Interestingly, Judge de Wet never challenged any of the defendants' refusals to answer some of Yutar's questions, most particularly when an answer might incriminate another person. Such refusals were unprotected by any evidentiary privilege and could have subjected him to imprisonment for contempt. The judge's thinking became apparent in connection with Bernstein's refusal to answer a question. After Yutar threatened Bernstein with imprisonment, a smile crossed Judge de Wet's face. "I don't suspect that will make much difference to you under present circumstances." "No, sir, I am afraid not." Bernstein, and all of the others, had already been in jail for more than nine months.

At one point, he protected Bram Fischer by refusing to authenticate a copy of a magazine called *Fighting Talk*, which contained an article pertaining to Fischer's activities on behalf of the Communist Party and identifying him as a member of the party's Central Committee.

Bernstein's examination-in-chief was largely a political statement. Through questioning by Vernon Berrange, he described the oppression that he saw in South Africa and the efforts of organizations with which he associated to combat that oppression in a nonviolent way. He was an active Communist until the Party was banned in 1950. He continued to promote its policies against racism through other organizations, including the Springbok Legion, a veterans' organization. He was active in the South African Congress of Democrats and in its work in creating the doctrinal foundation for a nonracist South Africa—the Freedom Charter. His political activities led to his arrest on several occasions. At the time of the Rivonia raid, Bernstein was under a banning order, which severely limited his movements outside his home and required him to report daily to Marshall Square—the Johannesburg headquarters of the security police.

Bernstein worked as an architect in the renovation of Liliesleaf Farm. He knew that the farm was used for political purposes but not the precise nature of the activities there. He knew of the formation of MK and had read its manifesto, but he was not, he maintained, involved in any way with it. Bernstein visited Liliesleaf Farm several times, including the four or five visits he made there in 1963 to discuss political questions, such as the dispute between the Soviet and Chinese Communist Parties. He met both Nelson Mandela and Govan Mbeki there.

On the day of the raid, he had gone to the Farm to discuss the ninety-day-detention controversy. He knew nothing of Operation Mayibuye until the beginning of the trial. On the day of the raid, he reported to Marshall Square at 1:55 p.m., conducted some other business in Johannesburg, and came to the farm shortly before 3 p.m.—just before the police arrived. The earlier testimony of Sergeant Dirker, testifying for the state, that he had opened the hood of Bernstein's car at the time of the raid and found it to be cold, was successfully rebutted.

Contrary to the testimony of a Liliesleaf Farm worker testifying for the state, Bernstein also unequivocally denied that he helped put up a radio antenna on a building at the farm. The laborer testified that he had seen Bernstein on the roof of the building on a Saturday afternoon. The terms of Bernstein's house arrest would not have permitted him to be outside his home at that time. There was no need even to rebut Bruno Mtolo's testimony that he had been told by someone that a certain "Rusty Bernsteam or Bunstead" had been in Durban to start an MK branch. The testimony was vague and, at best, hearsay, which would be disregarded by the court.

Yutar's cross-examination continued the political thread of the examination-in-chief but, not surprisingly, with an entirely different tone. Rather than focusing on Bernstein's involvement in the acts charged in the indictment, Yutar's cross-examination generally set out to prove that the activities of the ANC, as well as virtually all antigovernment violence, were in fact inspired and controlled by the Communist Party. According to Yutar, Bernstein was an ardent Communist—a loyal disciple of Karl Marx—whether or not he was still a member of the Party. The witness admitted that there was cooperation between the Communist Party and the African National Congress but denied that the Party used the ANC to propagate its aims. This seemed absurd. "I don't think the leaders of the African National Congress are people of a caliber who allow themselves to be used by just anybody who wants to make use of them."

Bernstein was asked to comment on numerous documents found in the raids dealing with Communism, though there was no allegation that he had written them or knew of them before the trial. Yutar argued with the witness with regard to matters such as whether the police and government had undertaken adequate investigations of incidents in which black people had been killed.

The prosecutor's sensitivity to allegations that the state had in any way been involved in wrongdoing were dramatically emphasized in his extensive questioning of Bernstein with regard to a statement made in a letter to his sister that was intercepted by the prison authorities and turned over to the security police. The letter accused the state of coaching witnesses who had been detainees. It stated that all of the substantial witnesses against the accused were detainees "who made statements under pressure and while subject to detention and solitary confinement, and subject certainly to threats of either indefinite detention or prosecution or both." Elsewhere in the letter, Bernstein had added that Vernon [Berrange] had done a "great job exposing . . . patent, or blatant coaching of witnesses." Yutar went through the testimony of various witnesses who he claimed had given testimony admitted to by the accused. Bernstein's response, aided by objections from Berrange, demonstrated that these witnesses had in fact given different versions of their stories—differences that were exposed on cross-examination. Yutar confronted Bernstein with a particular passage from the letter: "The whole thing disgusts me, the unprincipled timidity of people and even the more unprincipled willingness, eagerness, of the authorities to use them."

YUTAR: You adhere to that?

BERNSTEIN: I adhere to that.

YUTAR: That is a condemnation of course of not only the investigating officer but also of the State prosecutors in this case?

BERNSTEIN: It is a condemnation of the State, sir, which has provided facilities for witness statements to be taken from them under duress.

YUTAR: Have you told your friends overseas, to whom . . . information this was, [sic; ellipsis in original] most probably for publication?

BERNSTEIN: It was not at all for publication my lord, and there is no possible suggestion that it was.

YUTAR: No?

BERNSTEIN: Not at all sir.

YUTAR: Did you tell your good friends across the border that the defence have in fact admitted the major part of the State case in this case?

BERNSTEIN: My lord . . .

YUTAR: Have you done that?

BERNSTEIN: I have only written one letter dealing with this case at all, my lord, and that is the one, and it has been stopped by the gaol authorities. I have not written anything else about this case.

The exchange between prosecutor and witness in many ways revealed each side's agenda. Well aware of the international criticism surrounding the South African government generally and this trial in particular, Yutar had justifiable concerns that statements such as Bernstein's to his sister might well be leaked to the press. Like the defendants, he and his government were trying this case not only for the people of South Africa but for those abroad as well. The apartheid administration was anxious to show that, regardless of their racial policies—which were impossible to deny— the South African judiciary was independent and fair. From the defense standpoint, it was just as important to get the word out that the formal façade of this trial did not reflect the brutality of the regime. Both the defendants and their counsel thought that those points had been made in their cross-examination of the state witnesses, and through the statements and testimony of the accused. Yutar's persistent questioning about the prison letter presented an opportunity for Bernstein to make the point more specifically.

Toward the end of a brief redirect examination, Bram Fischer asked about the impact that detention and solitary confinement had on Bernstein. He asked whether it had affected his memory. Bernstein responded:

I can only speak about the symptoms I observed in myself, and I don't know if I have got a record of them. I developed an extremely severe handshake after about 60 days, a tremble in my hands, which lasted for some weeks after the end of my detention. I found at the end of my detention, sir, that I was utterly unable to concentrate. If I sat down to write a letter, I could write two sentences, and then I would have to get up and walk around for 5 or 10 minutes before I could write a third. Extreme anxiety, my lord, about absolutely ridiculous things which a normal person would not feel the least anxiety about at all, I found making me extremely anxious and reducing me to a state of nerves under certain conditions. These things I observed."

Shortly after this statement, Judge de Wet intervened, asking Fischer the relevance of this line of testimony and adding, "You are now trying to get evidence in at the back door which I excluded from the front door"—an obvious reference to the court's rejection of expert testimony on the effects of solitary confinement.

FISCHER: Well, this is personal experience, my lord.

[. . .]

THE COURT: Are you suggesting I should not believe any of his evidence, because he has been . . . at one time was confined?

FISCHER: No my lord. This witness did not make a statement.

But even without the psychologists, Fischer made the point that solitary confinement produced effects that undermined the testimony of certain state witnesses. Bernstein said the same thing—more powerfully—through personal testimony. The point was not lost on de Wet.

It was finally Govan Mbeki's turn to take the witness stand. The timing of his appearance on the witness stand was deliberate. His knowledge of the workings of both the ANC and MK was the most complete, and he had been at the center of activities during the period covered by the indictment, as well as in earlier years. Now that the defense had heard Yutar's examination of the other accused, especially the political nature of the questions asked of Walter Sisulu, Mbeki could give a comprehensive response. Unlike Sisulu, Mbeki was an educated man who held degrees in the humanities and economics. He was fifty-three years old—the oldest of the defendants.[19] In the years immediately preceding the trial, he had been a journalist, writing for a liberation publication, *New Age*, until it was banned in 1962. After its banning, Mbeki wrote for other publications, which were also closed by the government but which rose up again under other names.

Mbeki also had the advantage of a calm manner. Indeed, his demeanor became a subject of Yutar's cross-examination of him, such as when, during questioning about a speech broadcast illegally, he was asked if he could raise his voice and speak faster. Mbeki agreed that he could if he must.

YUTAR: And not so sanctimoniously as you have tried to speak here.

MBEKI: That is your own affair [sic].

Yutar then read from a newspaper account that noted that beneath his quiet charm and gentle smile Mbeki had a ruthless determination to reach his goal—the emancipation of his people. Yutar asked if that was a fair description.

MBEKI: I think so.

YUTAR: A ruthless determination. And in some of your speeches you
could be ruthless, not so?

MBEKI: What speeches?

YUTAR: In some of your speeches.

MBEKI: Which speeches?

YUTAR: That you addressed when you attended meetings throughout the
country. Do you deny that?

MBEKI: I exposed the truth and exposed what was the hardship of
the Africans. If you call that ruthless—speaking the truth—then I
was ruthless.

YUTAR: No. I am just trying to convey, not the subject matter, but the way
in which you put it across. You were not the gentle, quiet, sanctimoni-
ous human being that you are now showing in this witness box up
to now.

MBEKI: Well, that would have to be the opinion of whoever was listening
to me.

Mbeki's examination-in-chief was a history lesson for the court, and by
extension the world outside, tracing the roots of the ANC and its struggle
against oppression as well as his own involvement. The banning of the ANC
had forced the organization to carry on its activities illegally. The problems
of black people resulted from the basic premise of the government
as expressed by former prime minister J. G. Strydom—one of the archi-
tects of apartheid—in the mid-1950s: "*Die wit man moet altyd baas wees*"—
the white man must always remain the boss.

Mbeki's testimony covered not only political oppression but the resulting social and economic conditions. He traced the roots of economic oppression against Africans into the 1920s, decades before the current
Nationalist government with its apartheid policy took office in 1948. His
own situation typified that of many. His wife and children could never
accompany him to his work in Port Elizabeth, for example, because he had
not worked there continuously for one employer for ten years and could
therefore not be a permanent resident.

Yutar started his cross-examination, promising that he would stick to
the allegations of the indictment rather than the "grievances of the Bantu."
But he immediately launched into political sparring. If things were so bad
for Africans in South Africa, he asked, why did so many foreign Africans
flock here for work? For the most part, Mbeki simply refused to be drawn

into the argument. He suggested only that the influx of immigrants from other African countries was not explained by the benevolence of the South African government.

In the end, however, Yutar did all that he needed to do for purposes of this trial. He put to Mbeki the four charges in the indictment in the form of questions. At the end of each, Yutar asked, "Did you do this?" To each Mbeki replied, "Yes."

YUTAR: Well, Mbeki, I will put it to you in very brief form. Four charges against you, and you have replied to all of them. You have replied "yes" to all of them. Can you tell his Lordship why you have pleaded not guilty to the four counts?"

MBEKI: Yes, I did not plead guilty to the four counts for the simple reason, that firstly, I felt that I should come and explain from here under oath some of the reasons that led my to joining Umkhonto we Sizwe. And secondly, for the simple reason that to plead guilty would in my mind indicate that there was a sense of moral guilt to it and I do not accept that there is any moral guilt attached to my actions.

That exchange effectively ended Mbeki's testimony, although more questions about specific documents and acts followed. His testimony was successful at least in getting across that the ANC and MK were separate organizations, that neither was dominated by the Communist Party, and that guerrilla warfare had not yet been decided upon. Mbeki admitted his guilt and gave his reasons. He would be convicted. Whether his testimony helped the cause for which he had lived his life and whether it would help save that life remained to be seen.

Denis Goldberg was the last defendant to testify. He was a civil engineer by training and had worked in that capacity for several years. But his passion was for the liberation struggle. His career was laced with activism on behalf of the Communist Party as well as engineering. He had frequent encounters with the security police.

Goldberg presented a tough problem for defense counsel. As with Bernstein, the evidence against him was overwhelming. Using false names, he made inquiries all over the Johannesburg area in the weeks immediately preceding the Rivonia raid, exploring the possibilities of the purchase of basic materials for explosives. He was present at Rivonia at the time of the raid, although not in the room where the others were meeting. He was also a joker, and his flippant attitude risked irritating de

Wet, who had referred during Sisulu's testimony to "clever colleagues like Goldberg." But Goldberg wanted to testify. Indeed, at one point, he offered to take the blame on himself, an offer—as noted earlier—that his codefendants rejected out of hand.[20] And, as with the others, his testimony could present his case in sympathetic terms. Goldberg was a man with deep convictions who cared about oppression. He couldn't avoid conviction, but he could tell his story and perhaps avoid being hanged.

Thus, with stern warnings from counsel to behave himself on the witness stand, he testified. Joffe believed that he accomplished his purpose. In his view Goldberg was "an outstanding witness, articulate and clear." For the most part, he avoided smart-aleck responses. On one occasion, during cross-examination (interestingly, mentioned but unspecified by Joffe and unremembered by Goldberg himself), he lapsed into sarcasm and received a "cold terrifying stare" from Vernon Berrange. He did not stray after that.[21]

His examination-in-chief described the camp outside of Cape Town about which the state witnesses had testified was a training facility for guerrilla fighters. As we have seen (chapter 7), Goldberg's description of it was far more benign. There was talk of political change and violent change elsewhere in the world. He firmly denied that there was any training directed at guerrilla warfare—and indeed that there was any mention of guerrilla warfare.[22]

Goldberg described harassment from security police, including the placement of a bomb that exploded in his yard in December 1962. He testified that when he reported the incident to the police, they argued that they did not know how to make such a bomb. What brought him to Johannesburg shortly before his arrest was his plan to leave South Africa once and for all.[23] But before his departure, Arthur Goldreich had asked him to investigate the accessibility of raw materials and the components of weapons for use in guerrilla warfare. Goldberg was a trained engineer and would be able to give a realistic assessment of the possibility of obtaining such material. The investigation was made and completed during the month of June 1963. The materials and means to develop them were simply not available.[24]

Goldberg's cross-examination was conducted not by Yutar but, for some unexplained reason, by his colleague A. B. Krog. Krog was known as an effective cross-examiner and was not easily sidetracked by political discussions. Nonetheless, according to Joffe's account, Krog abandoned his usual straightforward style and resorted to Yutar's. According to Joffe, the result was not impressive. "What in Yutar was dramatic if irritating, in Krog was merely pathetic."[25] He lacked Yutar's righteous indignation. His cross-examination was largely an attack on the credibility of Goldberg, who had, after all, used several false names in his inquiries about explosive materials.

In the end, Goldberg, like the others before him in the dock, admitted enough to ensure his conviction. But he had hurt no one else. And perhaps he, like the others, had said enough about his motives for the judge to view him with some sympathy.

All that remained for the defense were the cases against Elias Motsoaledi and Andrew Mlangeni. Both made unsworn statements to the court.[26] Motsoaledi, aged thirty-nine, and Mlangeni, thirty-seven, had both been active in the trade union movement. They participated in MK activities but were not part of the command structure; they were from the rank and file. There was enough evidence of their activities to convict them. Moreover, if they had testified, they might have been trapped into statements that would have made them seem more important than was in fact the case. Their statements, as with the testimony of the others, outlined their struggles and work to end the oppression of their people. There was no denial, only explanation.

Mlangeni and Motsoaledi's statements effectively ended the defense case. Mlangeni and most of his colleagues were going to be convicted. The question now was their punishment.

10

Closing Arguments

PERCY YUTAR AND his staff strode into the Pretoria court on May 20, 1964, carrying several sets of large, neatly bound tomes with gold-lettered titles. There were four volumes in each set. Three of the volumes summarized the state's case in English; the fourth did the same in Afrikaans. One set was handed to the court; the others were distributed to the press. The defense was given one unbound copy.[1]

Yutar's closing argument consisted largely of his reading the three English language volumes from cover to cover. He made no attempt at the Afrikaans; he spoke the language poorly. The volumes simply restated the evidence. In Joffe's words, they were "a garbled summary."[2] The testimony of every witness was included, as were all of the incriminating documents.

Unlike the typical closing argument in South Africa—or that given before any judge or jury in the common law tradition—there was no attempt to analyze the evidence. But Yutar did intersperse his hours-long summary with some telling comments and asides. "Although the State has charged the accused of sabotage," he noted in his introduction to the reading of the volumes, "this is nevertheless a case of High Treason *par excellence*. It is a classic case of the intended overthrow of the government by force and violence with military and other assistance of foreign countries."[3]

At the close of his long oration, Yutar repeated his reference to "treason *par excellence*" and added, "Because of the people who have lost their lives and suffered injury as a result of the activities of the accused it is apparent that this case is now one of murder and attempted murder as well."[4]

The prosecutor's equating of the defendant's acts with High Treason and murder were not his only argumentative asides. There were other flourishes, directed at the public as much as the court. At one point, Yutar restated a point he had made during the cross-examination of several of the defendants. The ANC had a membership of only slightly more that 100,000—about 1 percent of the African population. He portrayed the defendants as operating behind the scenes to avoid personal risk. He ignored his own state's evidence that at least Govan Mbeki had been personally engaged in acts of sabotage. The image presented to the court and public was that of a conspiracy fostered largely by the Communist Party but carried out unwittingly by the law-abiding "Bantu" population of the country. The argument was interlaced with references, dripping with sarcasm, to Communist leaders who had fled the country, including Arthur Goldreich and Harold Wolpe.[5]

Yutar embellished his evidentiary summary by evoking a "shadow cabinet for the provisional revolutionary government." Who would rule South Africa in the event of a revolution was of course irrelevant to the charges against the defendants. But a recurring nightmare of many white South Africans must have been that a government run by blacks and Communists would rule one day. Despite the preposterous irrelevance of Yutar's speculation, the court made no effort to stop the exercise. And so he went full throttle. The ANC leader and 1960 Nobel Peace Prize winner Albert Luthuli was to be the president of the revolutionary government, according to Yutar. Although the prosecution had attempted to link him to the conspiracy, Luthuli was neither a defendant nor named in the indictment as an accomplice or coconspirator. Nelson Mandela would be minister of defense and deputy prime minister. Walter Sisulu was to be minister of the interior. Denis Goldberg, whose defense had been that the camp he had run was for spiritual and health purposes, was to be minister of health. Kathrada would be minister of Indian affairs; Mbeki, minister of European affairs; Bernstein, minister of information; Mhlaba, minister of foreign affairs. The other defendants were all given positions in the cabinet, as were several other ANC and Communist Party leaders named in the indictment or mentioned in the evidence.[6]

The nightmare scenario not only gave Yutar much self-amusement, it was enormously entertaining to the police contingent surrounding the prosecution team. He ended his exercise on a more serious note. "I have not been able to find portfolios for all the men involved. But if they run true to form, then if and when they come to power, there will be a lot of internal strife resulting in many casualties, and they will be able to fill the vacancies which will inevitably arise."[7]

Yutar's sarcasm was uncannily prescient. Mandela and not Albert Luthuli—who died in 1967—would someday be president of South Africa. None of the others filled the exact roles Yutar had imagined for them, but those roles were ultimately filled by persons very much like them.

And, as he certainly intended, Yutar's speculation was not lost on the South African press covering the event. The headline in the *Johannesburg Star* the next day read "Yutar Names Luthuli 'Revolution' Leader";[8] the *Pretoria News* announced: "Yutar Names the Rivonia Cabinet."[9]

Judge de Wet sat impassively through much of Yutar's performance. But he was not entirely silent, and the comments he did make gave the defense considerable hope for the court's ultimate decision. At one point, Yutar told the court that "the day of the mass uprising in connection with the launching of guerrilla warfare was to have been the 26th May 1963." De Wet intervened, inquiring, "You do concede," he informed Yutar, "that you failed to prove guerrilla warfare was ever decided upon." A stunned Yutar replied that preparations were being made. "Yes, I know that," replied the judge, "The defence concedes that. What they say is that preparations were made in case one day they found it necessary to resort to guerrilla warfare. But they say that prior to their arrest they never considered it necessary, and took no decision to engage in guerrilla warfare. I take it that you have no evidence contradicting that, and that you accept it." Yutar could only respond, "As your Lordship pleases."[10]

Other comments that were encouraging for the accused followed once defense counsel began its arguments. The first lawyer to argue was the young Arthur Chaskalson, who painstakingly analyzed the evidence of sabotage. There were 193 acts of sabotage alleged. As he began his careful, fully documented argument, he stated, "The defence concedes that Umkhonto we Sizwe recruited men for military training and that members of Umkhonto committed acts of sabotage. The defence denies, however, that they committed all the acts of sabotage with which they are charged. I will demonstrate to your Lordship, from the evidence, that there were other organisations in South Africa committing acts of sabotage at the time in question."

Judge de Wet interrupted him: "Mr. Chaskalson, there is no need to pursue your argument on this aspect. I accept that there were other organisations committing sabotage at the same time, and choosing the same targets."[11]

De Wet obviously had been listening to at least some of the defense's case. His recognition that others could have been responsible for individual acts of sabotage was significant—especially on the issue of sentence. Even the key state witnesses, such as Bruno Mtolo and Abel Mthembu, testified that Umkhonto had sought to act in a way that would not endanger human life. Nonetheless, some of its actions created real danger. It was critically important that they not be automatically attributed to the defendants. In the end, Chaskalson's thorough analysis reduced the number of acts of sabotage from 193 to 13—not one of which involved any danger to human life.

Next to argue for the defense was its leader, Bram Fischer. Fischer took responsibility for establishing two crucial aspects of his case: first, that guerrilla warfare had never been decided upon; and second, that the African National Congress was indeed separate from MK, which was a critically important point for any ANC member who might later be charged by the police.

The court saved Fischer the trouble of arguing. De Wet had already challenged Yutar with the comment that he failed to prove that guerrilla warfare had yet been decided upon. He did the same for Fischer, noting, "I thought I made my attitude clear. I accept that no decision or date was fixed upon for guerrilla warfare."[12] Similar assurances were given to Fischer on the second point. Judge de Wet told him that that it had been clearly established that the two organizations were in fact separate though they overlapped.[13]

Fischer had made his most important points without needing to argue. The careful presentation by the defense throughout the trial had made them more effectively than any oral argument by Fischer, however brilliant he was.

Vernon Berrange was the last of the defenders to argue. His job was to concentrate on the three defendants for whom a chance of acquittal remained—Bernstein, Kathrada, and Mhlaba. He began his argument with a reference to Yutar's interspersed "observations" on the accused, "On the assumption that these so-called observations, which consisted of a sarcastic and satirical attack on the accused, are relevant, we have consulted with our clients for the purpose of replying thereto. With the dignity that has characterized the accused throughout this trial, they have instructed us to ignore these remarks."[14]

Berrange's task was easiest with regard to Bernstein, although he carried out his argument with characteristically concise effectiveness. Nothing that Bernstein had testified to in his examination-in-chief had been rebutted in 153 pages of cross-examination. Berrange disposed of the only substantive evidence that Bernstein had been involved in the acts charged in the indictment—the erection of radio masts at Rivonia. As described in chapter 7, the evidence had been effectively rebutted both by showing that witness against Bernstein had been in ninety-day detention at the time of his testimony and that Bernstein, because of his house arrest and reporting obligations, could not have been at Rivonia on the day he allegedly put up the masts.[15]

Berrange continued his argument by dissecting the cases against Kathrada and Mhlaba. One witness testified that Kathrada had been involved in transportation of recruits out of the country. Berrange challenged the credibility of this witness, who had given several different accounts of the same events.[16] Other evidence against Kathrada, though it did not tie him directly into antigovernment acts, was not so easy to argue away. He had lived at Rivonia for a time and had written pamphlets, as well as a draft speech to be given in an illegal radio broadcast. However, nothing proved that he had had anything to do with sabotage or guerrilla warfare. The issue would be whether there was enough evidence to tie him to the conspiracy count.

Mhlaba presented more difficult challenges.[17] He had been a poor witness. There was little evidence against him, but probably at least enough to show that he had been involved in the recruitment and transportation of potential guerrilla fighters abroad.

Under South African practice, rebuttal arguments are limited to questions of law. Yutar tried to bolster his case against Bernstein. Judge de Wet quickly rebuffed him, reminding him of the limitations on rebuttal argument. Yutar backed off.[18] Instead, he sought to take advantage of a government proclamation issued during the course of the trial. The proclamation, which had the force of law, declared the African National Congress and MK to be the same thing. Yutar had earlier told the court that he would not rely on these presumptions. His change of heart in his rebuttal argument was expressly intended to tie Kathrada to the work of MK. Kathrada had admitted his involvement in the ANC; therefore he was involved in MK.

De Wet would have none of it. He asked Yutar whether he expected the whole case to be reopened to allow the defense to argue its case in light of his reliance on this presumption. Yutar retreated to the position that his case was already so strong that he did not need the presumption.[19]

The trial was over. The court adjourned for three weeks for the judge to consider his verdict and sentencing.

Outside Pressures

AS THE DRAMA inside the Palace of Justice moved toward judgment and sentencing, the battle for the high ground of public opinion continued in South Africa and abroad.

Percy Yutar and the South African government had won the battle for white South African opinion. The proof introduced at the Rivonia Trial demonstrated beyond doubt that the defendants and their compatriots were planning—and capable of inflicting—serious damage to people and property. To most white South Africans, they represented a threat to their way of life. The South African press—English and Afrikaans—had continued to run front-page stories each morning after a day of trial. The disclosures of the documents during the prosecution's case—especially the links to Communism—were, as we've seen, front-page news with banner headlines.

Yutar's dramatic opening statement was trumpeted in the *Johannesburg Star*, the country's leading newspaper, with the banner "War of Liberation Plot Unmasked." A photograph of Yutar—with his characteristic smirk—appeared below.[1] Even the more liberal *Rand Daily Mail* carried a headline on Yutar's speech reading "Reds Backed Revolt Plan."[2] The same paper reported the testimony of "Mr. X"—Bruno Mtolo—under the heading "Saboteur Tells How He Got Orders,"[3] and ran another story labeled "North Promised to Back Us," a reference to Mtolo's testimony that the prime minister of Algeria and the emperor of Ethiopia had pledged their support for the ANC cause.[4] The *Rand Daily Mail* headline accompanying the story on Yutar's closing argument read "Bloody Revolt Faced S.A."—the banner above was "Police Saved Us—Yutar."[5] The Afrikaans language newspaper *Die Burger* carried a headline reporting the closing reading "Rivonia Case Is Extreme High Treason."[6]

Yutar timed his disclosures in court to maximize their political impact—showing savvy in using news cycles. He was going to win his case, but he also desperately wanted to sway public opinion for the prosecution, both for the benefit of the government he served and for his own advancement. Yutar's insistence that prosecution witnesses were constantly under threat of violence from those associated with the defense was clearly intended for the public's benefit and did not reflect upon the conduct of the trial or the actual safety of the witnesses. Most of the witnesses whose testimony was critical to the state's case were either police officers or in detention. Yutar's theatrical labeling of the key prosecution witnesses Bruno Mtolo and Abel Mthembu as "Mr. X" and "Mr. Y," respectively, was directed to the same public purpose. The accused and their followers knew who both men were and where they lived. Yutar had maintained that Bob Hepple—his intended first witness—"had been threatened by the accused or their supporters and fled the country."[7] He added that the government was aware of plans for a mass escape of all prisoners.[8] Hepple was later to state unequivocally that his greatest fear had been of the police and prosecuting authorities,[9] but the point had been made for the white South African population.

At least in its public pronouncements, the South African government seemed adamant in its determination to seek the maximum penalty. Their goal was to demonstrate that this was a trial against Communist subversion and that the accused were dangerous terrorists. Nonetheless, South Africa's independent judiciary would deal with the issue—fairly but firmly.

The only perceptible shift in South African opinion—and it was a small one—came after Nelson Mandela's speech. The *Rand Daily Mail* printed his statement in full, despite a prohibition against quoting "restricted" persons.[10] From that point on—at least in the moderately more sympathetic English language press—there seemed to be a growing respect for the defendants, despite their guilt. Joel Joffe believed that the world had been made aware of the personality, attitudes, and integrity of the accused.[11] Yutar's vicious attack on the popular writer Alan Paton—described in the next chapter—was to further alienate at least a segment of the population. A small segment of South African whites were willing to entertain the thought that there was something wrong with the country and that these men were trying to fix it.

The international community almost unanimously supported the defendants, despite the concerted efforts of white South Africans to paint them as Communist stooges. The plight of the Rivonia accused would provide ammunition for opposition to the South African regime far into the future, irrespective of any declared—or actual—guilt of the defendants.

World media coverage continued throughout the months of testimony and argument. Although usually not front-page news, the Rivonia Trial appeared frequently in the major American and British papers, whose readers were kept up to date of the courtroom developments from beginning to end. The *New York Times* covered the beginning of the trial with a two-column headline on page 3: "South Africa Begins Trial of 11; Defendants Face Death Penalty."[12] The UK *Guardian*'s headline for its article on the beginning of the trial was "S. African prisoners 'drawn and haggard.'"[13] During the course of the trial—two months before the judgments and sentence—the *New York Times Magazine* carried a lengthy piece on the political situation in South Africa written by the British journalist and writer Anthony Sampson. Sampson was sympathetic to the defense and would later write an important biography of Mandela. His piece in the *Times Magazine* contained an analysis of the Rivonia Trial, noting that "whatever the substance of the charge, it is clear that the police have captured a formidable quantity of information. The chief of the Special Branch may well be justified in his boast that the African opposition has been effectively put out of action."[14]

Much of the press attention was devoted to United Nations debates and actions arising from the trial. The Afro-Asian bloc kept the pressure on both the South African government and on the Western powers that had frequently protected Pretoria from condemnations—due to its unambiguous anti-Communist stance. A key moment came on October 11, 1963, when the General Assembly passed a resolution 106 to 1 requesting the abandonment of the "arbitrary [Rivonia] trial" and the granting of unconditional release to all political prisoners—the resolution that had so heartened Bram Fischer. Pressure on the United States and Great Britain had forced both to vote for the resolution as a whole; nonetheless, both abstained from the portion calling specifically for abandonment of the Rivonia Trial. The African delegates supported the resolution in terms condemning not only the apartheid policies but the South African judicial system.

Some overstated the lack of fairness in the proceedings, but the tone reflected the sentiment of many on the African continent. The Guinean delegate, for example, referred to the "bogus trial, staged under arbitrary legislation, which deprives the accused of any possibility of legal defence and exposes them, without protection or safeguard, to the bloodthirsty executioners who control the country."[15] The Ghanaian representative went even further. Arguing that Rivonia was no trial, he said, "The so-called courts of South Africa are nothing but sanctuaries of apartheid. The judges are functioning under a misnomer, for in real fact they are only high priests of apartheid who read ritual incantations of a negation of God erected into a system of apartheid which is the policy of the Government of South Africa."[16]

The Nigerian delegate was somewhat more restrained. He didn't question the character or the ability of the judges, only the law they were administering. The "Sabotage Act is not law in the finest tradition of legislation as it is known everywhere else," he said. "It is just arbitrary, brutal justice put in the form of law, and people are put on the bench to administer it."[17]

As the trial progressed, the United Nations became a forum in which the opponents of apartheid continued to hammer away at the South African government and its prosecution of the trial. Rivonia had become a symbol of the evils of apartheid, and an opportunity to pressure the two nations commonly viewed as its allies, the United States and the United Kingdom.

Oliver Tambo, the leader of the ANC in exile, was twice invited to address the Special Political Committee of the General Assembly in October 1963—just as the trial was getting under way. His first speech, on October 8, was given immediately before the defendants' first appearance in court. At that point, he knew only of the detention of dozens of antigovernment activists. He predicted that "some thirty persons" would be brought to trial. He added, "[The trial] will be conducted in circumstances that have no parallel in South African history, and which, if the Government has its way, will seal the doom of that country and entrench the feelings of bitterness which years of sustained persecution have already engendered among the African people." Tambo called on the United Nations not to stand by calmly "watching . . . genocide masquerading under the guise of a civilised dispensation of justice."[18]

Tambo spoke again a few weeks later, on October 29, shortly before the dismissal of the first indictment and the rearrest of the defendants. He called the trial "largely farcical"—the defendants came to trial "after going through a phase of persecution, ill-treatment and torture that is new in the South African situation." The trial was simply his Exhibit No. 1 in the court of world opinion, the launching point for his primary goal—sanctions against South Africa. His speech thanked those who supported such sanctions and chided the Western powers—especially Great Britain—for their continuing trade and investment in South Africa. While the accused were prepared to suffer for their cause, the rest of the world could not simply stand on the sidelines.[19]

The United Nations Security Council followed up the almost unanimous October 11 General Assembly Resolution with two other resolutions pertinent to the trial. The first, Security Council Resolution 182, proposed in December 1963, reasserted demands for an arms embargo. It also called on South Africa to "liberate all persons imprisoned, interned or subjected to other restrictions for having opposed the policy of apartheid." It was passed unanimously.[20]

The second, Resolution 190, passed on June 9, 1964, shortly before judgment in the trial, was pointed directly at Rivonia. A special meeting of the council had been requested by fifty-seven countries—mostly African and Asian. The *New York Times* reported that seven had sent their foreign ministers to take part in the debate.[21] The resolution passed by the council called on Pretoria "to end forthwith the trial in progress, instituted within the framework of the arbitrary law of apartheid." It also called for a renunciation of the death sentences handed down in connection with antiapartheid activities and for amnesty for others imprisoned, interned, or subjected to other restrictions for opposing apartheid "and particularly to the defendants in the Rivonia trial." The death penalty references were likely directed at the March sentencing of three men convicted of the murder of a state informant. All three were executed a few months later. The reference to those "interned" or "subject to other restrictions" referred to the thousands of activists detained under the ninety-day law or subject to various forms of house arrest. Resolution 190 passed 7 to 0; the United States, United Kingdom, France, and Brazil abstained.[22] Even though they did not vote yes on this resolution, the Western powers were feeling growing pressure. They could no longer use the veto or threat of veto to protect their trading partner and ally against the Communists. The Rivonia Trial had provided substantial fodder for the antiapartheid forces in the international community.

The international attention to Rivonia was not confined to the halls of the United Nations Headquarters in New York. Various other groups protested against the prosecution. In particular, the trial drew the attention of the prestigious International Commission of Jurists (ICJ), which had begun to monitor the rule of law throughout the world. On October 17, 1963, before the beginning of the trial, the group sent a telegram to the South African minister of foreign affairs requesting permission for an observer to attend the trial.[23] The minister, Eric Louw, responded, also by cable, that he had forwarded the request to the minister of justice, future South African president John Vorster, who promptly rejected the request with a strongly worded response. "In the past you sent so called observers on a number of occasions without requesting permission," he wrote.

"These observers did not show elementary courtesy of paying their respects to South African Bar Council and other authorities." Vorster added that he found the request "tantamount to a suggestion that the trial will not be a fair one and appears to be motivated by the recent resolution of the United Nations." The opposite would be the case, given that South Africa's courts were "at all times open to everyone and our system of justice and our independent judiciary comparable with best in the world."[24] The response to the request was not a private one. The headline in Johannesburg's *Sunday Times* read "Vorster Attacks World Society of Jurists," with a smaller banner above reading, "Application to Attend S.A. Trial 'An Insult.'"[25]

The commission was undeterred. In December, 1963, the distinguished British barrister John Arnold, QC, attended the trial on behalf of the commission and observed a portion of the prosecution's evidence. He met with several defense counsel and others connected with the defendants, including Nelson Mandela and Oliver Tambo's former law partner, Godfrey Pitje. He also met with Yutar, Transvaal attorney general Rein, and—surprisingly—Justice Minister Vorster. Vorster told Arnold that he would not have met with him had he not visited Yutar and Rein the day before. Arnold described Vorster to officials at the British embassy as "cold and unsmiling." Although initially referring to the International Commission of Jurists as a "leftist Communist front organisation," Vorster relaxed some when he learned that Arnold was in fact an active member of the Conservative Party, and that the ICJ had originally devoted itself to exposing the injustices committed behind the Iron Curtain. Nevertheless, Vorster attempted to engage Arnold in a discussion of the severity of British action in Northern Ireland and the concerns of combating worldwide Communism. He repeated the gist of his earlier charge that the application to observe the trial was an "insult to the South African Courts and to the South Africa's legal system." Asked whether he had any message that Arnold should give to the ICJ, Vorster replied, "Tell them that I mind my own business and I suggest that they do the same."[26]

At his press conference on his return from South Africa, Arnold offered a mixed report. He stated there was a "substantial case to be tried" and that the evidence presented "should have resulted in the formulation of very serious criminal charges." "Nor, in my opinion can it reasonably be stated," he added, "that the conduct of the trial by the Judge President of the Transvaal is open to objection on any ground of want of fairness or impartiality." However, Arnold went on to criticize the statute under which the Rivonia charges were brought.[27] The Sabotage Act was based in part upon the "extraordinarily wide terms under which the definition of sabotage is drafted." Its language was broad enough to make the painting of antigovernment slogans on a wall a capital offense. The commission's statement also criticized the procedural aspects of the act—especially the placement of the burden of proof on the accused and the elimination of double jeopardy protection—and the possibility of a death sentence. The report concluded: "The world legal community is profoundly and deeply disturbed over the Sabotage Bill and other steps being taken by the South African Government which will lead inevitably to the annihilation of human rights in South Africa."[28]

Arnold and Tom Kellock, another British barrister, observing the trial under the auspices of the human rights group Christian Action, met in private with representatives of the British Embassy. Arnold told the representatives that he had a favorable impression of the lawyers on the defense side he had met, especially Vernon Berrange—whose cross-examination of a witness he described as "masterly"—and the Mandela and Tambo partner, Godfrey Pitje. The defense was a skillful team under the "Communist lawyer" Fischer. He described Yutar as a "fairly nasty piece of work," whose method of prosecution would certainly be very counterproductive in a British court. But both Arnold and Kellock concluded that the state had an unassailable case and that heavy sentences would likely be handed out. The accused, "whom they regretfully accept are either Communists or heavily Communist influenced," were "guilty as hell" of the main charges against them. If the death penalty were awarded—which Arnold saw as a real possibility—the British government might want to make an approach to the South Africans to warn them of seriously adverse consequent effect on public opinion in Britain and elsewhere in the West.[29]

Despite the negative publicity, the South African government seemed to believe that a truly impartial observer would see Rivonia as a straightforward criminal case conducted in a setting that would appear consistent with a fairly conducted case in any democratic country. The procedural and evidentiary rules followed by the court would be familiar to an American or English lawyer. To make the point that this was a fairly conducted proceeding, the prosecution invited representatives of foreign governments to attend the proceedings in a special box set up at the front of the courtroom.

This campaign met an abrupt end. During the prosecution's case, two of those sitting in that box were prominent American academics, Gwendolyn

Carter and Thomas Karis, both severe and very vocal critics of the South African regime. Carter had published a book in 1958 called *The Politics of Inequality*, based on her visits to South Africa starting in 1948. Karis, who had been assigned to the American Embassy in Pretoria, had observed the Treason Trial and published a book of documents about it. Given all this, it was a little odd that the government expected them to be sympathetic observers, but it is evidence of the confidence that South Africans had in the prosecution case and the regularity of the proceedings. The government sought to enhance its position by having police and prosecution officials spend the morning with Carter and Karis, seeking to convince them of the strength of their case.

The tactic backfired. On a day when Carter and Karis were sitting in the box, the defense unequivocally exposed a state witness as a liar. The witness, Peter Nbomvo, had testified that he had participated in the burning of the occupied house of an African supporter of the government. The defense established that Nbomvo had testified at an earlier trial that he knew nothing of the burning. Now he responded by maintaining that he had been told by his lawyer to deny knowledge of the attack. On further cross-examination, Nbomvo admitted that he had made two statements denying the attacks, one before he had ever even consulted with his lawyer in question, and the second after that lawyer had withdrawn from the case. From the expressions on their faces, it was obvious that Carter and Karis had absorbed every minute of the proceedings that day. After it was over, Yutar was furious. Orders were immediately issued that the special box for foreign visitors was no longer to be occupied. The next day, observers from the American and Dutch embassies were told—as result of "what had happened yesterday"—to sit in the public gallery.[30]

One gesture in support of the defendants was seemingly symbolic but actually important to the accused and their lawyers. During the trial, Mandela was elected president of the Students' Union of London University.[31] Mandela's sole contact with the school was his attempt to obtain a law degree from that institution—via correspondence from his Robben Island prison cell.

Not all the international reaction was as benign and well intended. Both Percy Yutar and Justice de Wet received death threats during the course of the trial.[32] One written threat in particular seemed especially significant to Yutar—enough so that he kept a copy in his private papers (which were ultimately sold to the Brenthurst Library in Johannesburg). The prosecutor and his family received death threats that purportedly

came from a radical Israeli group calling itself Sherut Habitachon Hazair—
"the young security service." (The existing Israeli security service is Sherut
Habitachon.) One threat was sent to Yutar's wife: "We wish to warn you
that if any of the accused in the Rivonia Trial is executed, we will avenge
their death by having nitric acid thrown at your face and at your son's
face." Their aim, they said, was to get the African states at the United
Nations to support Israel. Another letter, to Yutar himself, warned him
that if any of the accused were executed, they would get him and his family
"wherever you go, and certainly the last place for you to go is Israel." The
letter was signed with the Hebrew words *mavet labogdim*—"death to the
traitors."[33]

Based upon these threats, the government provided Yutar and his
family with special protection. Indeed, a man was later prosecuted in connection with an alleged plot to blow up de Wet and Yutar's homes.[34] No
actual attempts on Yutar or his family were ever reported.

The United States and the United Kingdom were in a quandary. The
pressure from the Afro-Asian bloc in the United Nations was an irritant,
as was the propaganda value the Communist world gained from the Western powers' continuing efforts to protect South Africa from the most
severe sanctions. There was little sentiment in favor of apartheid within
the governments of either nation, but there was considerable and ongoing
support for South Africa as an anti-Communist bulwark, a reliable military ally, and a significant trading partner. The trial and especially the possibility that it might result in a death sentence was cause for concern in
both London and Washington.

Diplomatic personnel on the scene confirmed that there was little
doubt as to the guilt of the defendants—not just of technical violations of
a vague statute but of acts that would be deemed criminal under the laws
of any democracy. The sabotage of public property in order to effect change
in government policy and the training of guerrilla warriors—even without
a definitive plan for launching such a war—would be punishable by long-
term imprisonment and possibly death under the laws of both the United
States and Great Britain. Contrary to the accusations of the African representatives to the United Nations, the trial itself was conducted in general
accord with the rule of law. The International Commission of Jurists criticized the law under which the prosecution took place, not the trial procedure. Placing the burden of proof on the defendants with regard to their
motivation was contrary to the norm. However, the allocation of the burden
was less significant when both the acts and their motivation were

admitted. These defendants had conceded that they had done far more than simply paint antigovernment slogans on a wall.

Yet there was a meaningful difference between the acts and motivations of the Rivonia defendants and acts of rebellion, especially Communist-inspired rebellion, in other places. There was general sympathy for the defendants' cause. They were fighting an abhorrent system. They had suffered greatly under the regime merely for expressing opposition to government policy or for their race, or both. As Mandela had so eloquently insisted in his statement to the court, they turned to violence only as a last resort.

Foreign observers therefore concluded early on that there was little to no possibility of an acquittal—at least not for Mandela, Sisulu, or Mbeki—the ANC's leaders.[35] The only hope was to save their lives. Their execution would be a propaganda disaster for the Western powers, who would be pilloried in the United Nations and other world forums by both the Afro-Asian bloc and the Communist nations. The issues facing the British Foreign Office and the American State Department were whether to make their views on the possibility of capital punishment known in Pretoria and, if so, when and how.

Both decided to tread cautiously and gently, resisting pressures from within and without government for direct intervention with Pretoria. In Britain, letters and delegations from prominent individuals seeking action were met with the response that any pressure would be counterproductive. Hundreds of letters about the Rivonia Trial—almost all in support of the accused—appear in the preserved official records.[36] The archbishop of Canterbury asked the Foreign Office to quietly persuade the South African government not to carry out any death sentence that may be passed.[37] A group of influential Conservative Party businessmen known as the Bow Group, led by Leon Brittan and Anthony Mitton, made the same request.[38] The very vocal Anti-Apartheid Movement, led by its president, Barbara Castle, MP, met with the minister of state with pointed requests for intervention.[39] An unusually direct appeal came from the editor of the *Observer*, David Astor. He implored the secretary of state for foreign affairs, R. A. Butler, to intervene in order to prevent the execution of the Rivonia defendants. The letter referred to Mandela as "one of the most impressive of all the African leaders." Astor noted that he had been told that the sentence could be one of life imprisonment, but that "this is only likely to happen as a result of political and diplomatic pressure—particularly from London and Washington."[40]

The Foreign Office replied patiently but without budging. The response written by Secretary Butler to David Astor noted that there had already been representations to the South African government in general terms. He added, "I do not think that it would be wise for us to make any further representation while the trial is still in progress. To do so would imply that Mr. Justice de Wet was to some extent the tool of the South African government and if we made representations now the South African government could only respond favourably by admitting in effect that they were able to influence the judge's decision." Butler was convinced that Pretoria would be sure to reject any entreaties on the part of the British government, and this would compromise later efforts that might be made if and when death sentences were handed down.[41]

The same conclusion was reached in Washington, where the State Department was hit by a similar barrage of correspondence from various sources seeking their intervention. In April 1964, as the trial was drawing to a close, McGeorge Bundy, special assistant to President Johnson, received a letter from the *Observer*'s David Astor identical to that sent to British Foreign Secretary Butler.[42]

But there were voices arguing for caution in all of the United States's dealing with South Africa. Many of these came from the Pentagon. In May, General Maxwell D. Taylor, chairman of the Joint Chiefs of Staff, sent a National Security Action Memorandum to the president reiterating the view that "the objectives of the U.S. toward South Africa should include its alignment with the Western Powers." "As long as Communist penetration and racial discord in Africa remain an active threat to Free World interests," wrote Taylor, "stability in South Africa is desirable and the United States should do everything that its political and moral position permits to contribute to this."[43] Taylor had been one of the first proponents of sending American ground troops into Vietnam.

Surviving documents demonstrate that the conflicting pressures from the left—including the dominant voices in the United Nations—and the concerns of military and economic interests caused Johnson to move cautiously. Johnson, who had taken office after the assassination of President Kennedy on November 22, 1963, was just finding his sea legs, especially on foreign policy issues. Judge Charles Fahy, a U.S. Court of Appeals judge, was sent to South Africa. Fahy attended some of the trial sessions and met with counsel for both sides and with Judge de Wet. His report back focused on the general political situation and the possibility that moderate forces within the National Party might succeed in moving the government away from the most severe racial policies. Otherwise, he wrote, South Africa was headed toward "a violent upset." Fahy hoped that his presence would, he wrote, "encourage the independent stand of the judiciary and will indicate a sympathetic U.S. interest, thus indirectly affecting the Rivonia Trial."[44] The same memorandum, written directly to Bundy, noted that the accused could receive death sentences, but that those sentences were "not likely." One reason was the absence of proof that the sabotage admitted by the defendants had resulted in injury. Moreover, he reported, the American embassy in Cape Town "thinks it unlikely that death sentences will be imposed and even more improbable that they would be carried out."[45]

Both the Americans and the British made one attempt at direct—albeit circumspect—intervention, with mixed results. Contact by both governments was initiated based upon a request from the widely respected and moderate Nigerian foreign minister Jaja Wachuku. Wachuku had asked both foreign offices to convey the message to the South African government that the execution of Mandela or others would greatly weaken the position of those such as the Nigerian government who were trying to counsel moderation. After consultation with each other, the American and British ambassadors communicated Wachuku's message to two prominent South African government officials.

In April 1964, American ambassador Joseph C. Satterthwaite met with the South African foreign secretary, G. P. Jooste. Jooste was the permanent head of the foreign office—as opposed to the foreign minister, then Hilgard Muller, who was a member of Parliament. Satterthwaite began by simply reading a statement from Wachuku setting forth his concerns that the execution of the Rivonia defendants—and especially Mandela—would present a problem for African moderates. Satterthwaithe added that many, both within the Johnson administration and outside, were concerned about the possibility of a death sentence.

Satterthwaite describes Jooste as taking several notes and appearing calm, then reacting in an agitated fashion, insisting that any comment on a trial in process was interference with South Africa's domestic affairs and judicial procedure. The American ambassador described Jooste's comments: "Why it was that South Africa was only country in world which is being subjected to such treatment? Observing that South African courts were known for their fairness and objectivity, he asked whether the United States government, which is [the] leader in fighting Communism, would stand for a minute for any interference by South African government in any trial of subversives going on in the United States." Jooste added that defendants in Rivonia Trial were being tried for crimes against the constitution and laws of South Africa. South Africa had not tried to interfere when Julius and Ethel Rosenberg had been sentenced and executed for espionage in 1953 in the United States by passing along pleas for clemency. Satterthwaite responded to this "outburst" by noting that he was simply making an observation, not a representation. Jooste then calmed down and recognized that the American had been "moderate in tone."[46]

British ambassador Hugh Stephenson met with Foreign Minister Muller with regard to the Wachuku request. It is probable this conversation formed the basis for the Foreign Office's statement to those seeking intervention in the Rivonia Trial that the British government had made its views known in "general terms." Muller's response to Stevenson was different, at least in tone, from the reception Satterthwaite got from Jooste. When Stephenson mentioned Wachuku's position to Muller, Muller responded that this was "very interesting." He remarked that Wachuku had made a very helpful speech in the General Assembly, pointing out that white people "were also Africans." Stephenson reported that his impression—though only an impression—was that death sentences would not be carried out.[47]

Stephenson's conclusion was that the British could not let it be known that it had made any sort of representation to the South African government on this subject or, he wrote, "we shall gravely prejudice chances of their commuting death sentences."[48] Satterthwaite was of the same opinion, telling the State Department that any further meddling by the United States while the trial was in process would "only be counter-productive and could indeed contribute to a state of mind on the part of the South African government which might lead it to reject appeals for clemency if death sentences should unfortunately be imposed."[49]

The Johnson administration took its ambassador's recommendations to heart. In March 1964, the president received a letter from the chairman of the United Nations Special Committee on Apartheid, asking him to exert all possible influence to induce the government of South Africa "to spare the lives of the persons threatened with the death penalty in South Africa."[50] Based on Satterthwaite's conversation with Jooste, the State Department recommended, and the president agreed, that there was to be no reply at all to the United Nations committee. A briefing memorandum for the president with regard to the committee's request had him indicating only that he had received the letter and that it would be "given serious consideration, because we are deeply concerned about problems arising from the South African policy of apartheid."[51]

There would be no further official American or British efforts to influence the judgment or conviction of the Rivonia defendants. Nonetheless, the South African government must have been aware that the execution of Mandela or any of the defendants would hinder the ability of the United States and the United Kingdom to shield South Africa from further international sanctions. Did this have an effect on Pretoria? There is no documentation to prove that it did. But the instinct for self-preservation may have led the government to realize that its goals might be achieved without death sentences.

To execute the defendants would certainly rid white South Africa of some troublesome antigovernment leaders forever. Yet the adverse international reaction would likely exceed by far anything that Pretoria had previously endured. It would trigger immediate and effective economic sanctions. On the other hand, life sentences would get these very troublesome men out of the way almost as effectively. And the Pretoria government could reasonably argue that the convictions had been obtained in accordance with the rule of law. The acquittal of one of the less important defendants—say, for example, Rusty Bernstein—would be further evidence of the fairness of the system.

As the trial approached its end, there were clear indications that Pretoria had backed off from the death penalty—if indeed it had ever really wanted it. Shortly before judgment was to be handed down, the British embassy reported that Major General Hendrick van den Bergh, the head of the South African Special Branch, did not expect death sentences.[52] Both the U.S and British governments took heart at statements made by Percy Yutar in conversations that "in his personal opinion the prosecution would not (repeat *not*) ask for death sentences."[53] The British embassy commented that Yutar was under the direction and control of the minister of justice.[54] If he was speaking the truth, the minister did not want death sentences to be passed. The judge could still sentence the defendants to death, but the absence of a specific request from the prosecution was a sign that there would be no executions.

Defense advocate George Bizos was much relieved by a late-evening (and possibly alcohol-induced, according to Bizos) comment made in passing by British consul general Leslie Minford. As Bizos was leaving a dinner party, Minford put his hand on Bizos's shoulder. "George, there won't be a death sentence."[55] British journalist Anthony Sampson has stated that Minford had "intelligence links."[56]

Minford's confidence doesn't seem to have been the product of any inside information; it was simply his own conclusion. He had merely kept close tabs on the trial, attending many of the sessions and of course meeting regularly with defense counsel, especially Vernon Berrange and Bizos.[57] He had also met with foreign observers, including the ICJ's John Arnold. In May 1964—shortly before judgment—Minford prepared a lengthy analysis of the trial's probable outcome, predicting that Bernstein was likely to be acquitted, and that acquittal was possible for Kathrada and Mhlaba. He was certain that Mandela, Sisulu, and Mbeki would be found guilty and that a death sentence was still possible for them.[58] Minford also passed to defense counsel research done by another lawyer on death sentences in South African sabotage cases, indicating that there had been no death sentences where the actions of the defendants were not shown to have resulted in a loss of life.[59] Again, however, neither Minford nor anyone else at the British embassy appeared to have inside information.

On June 2—less than two weeks before judgment and sentencing were to occur—Minford asked for permission from the government to inform the defense of the British "interest" in the case—apparently referring to the conversations that Ambassador Stephenson had had with Foreign Minister Muller.[60] There is no record of a response to that request, but Stephenson was authorized to speak informally to the South Africans in the event that the judge did hand out death sentences.[61] Minford may therefore have received some nod of approval to communicate with Bizos before sentencing, or, perhaps, his friendly dinner-party comment was his way of letting the defense counsel know that the British were on top of things and that the lives of the defendants were likely to be spared. Minford may have been making an educated guess to calm Bizos's fears and to plant the seed of the idea that intervention by the British had at least played a part in saving the defendants' lives. Surviving records are not definitive in the matter.

By May 1964, the American State Department was also reasonably confident there would be no death penalties. The British Foreign Office had been warned by a reporter for the *Observer* that African leaders were planning "concerted action and for simultaneous demonstrations through the Continent if Nelson Mandela was executed."[62] The reporter, Colin Legum, said that he thought it was quite possible that these demonstrations might take the form of attacks on British and U.S. embassies in African countries.

When warned by the British of this possibility, the American State Department responded that there was a "good chance that Mandela would not receive a death sentence." American officials wondered whether Legum might simply be trying to scare them into "taking the matter up with the South Africans."[63]

One can only speculate as to whether any pressure—either within South Africa or from abroad—had any effect on Judge Quartus de Wet. There was nothing that kept him from reading the South African newspapers, including their coverage of the attacks on his country in the foreign media and the United Nations. As a South African and an Afrikaner, he was much more likely to be influenced by that press than by the *New York Times* or the *Times* of London. Defense lawyers remain adamant in their belief that de Wet's eventual decision was not influenced by the South African executive branch. And, at least on the day of the sentencing, as we shall see, de Wet was willing to disclose to a defense lawyer his decision on punishment.

But for the defendants themselves, there was no assurance that they would not be both convicted and hanged. For his part, Mandela prepared notes on what he would say when the court sentenced him to hang.

12

Judgment and Sentencing

ON JUNE 11, 1964, exactly eleven months after the Rivonia raid, the court reconvened to pronounce its judgment. Two thousand black Africans crowded Church Square in front of the Palace of Justice, joined by a small but noisy group of whites, most wearing blazers identifying them as students at the Afrikaans-language University of Pretoria. The blacks carried signs and sang in support of their leaders. The students demonstrated in favor of a conviction and death. Very few of those demonstrating had right of entry to the courtroom; a series of checkpoints controlled access to the courtroom, limiting admission to those associated with the police.

The proceeding itself was astonishingly brief. The audience and counsel were seated. The accused were brought up from the cells below. Judge de Wet entered in his red robes and, in a quiet voice difficult to hear in most of the gallery, read a short statement announcing his ruling on the charges.

All defendants, other than Ahmed Kathrada and Lionel Bernstein, were convicted on all counts. Kathrada was convicted only on count 2, conspiracy to violate the Sabotage Act. Bernstein was found not guilty of all charges and ordered discharged. The judge gave no reasons for his rulings from the bench, but filed a seventy-two-page judgment explaining his decisions. Sentences were to be handed down the next day.[1]

After the judge left the bench, courtroom decorum gave way to confusion. The accused turned and waved to their families, shouting out the judgment for those who might not have heard the judge's pronouncement. An elated Hilda Bernstein rushed toward the dock to touch her husband. Rusty Bernstein pushed his way out of the dock, trying at least to reach counsel table. Prison officials restrained him, demanding that he return to the cells down below where "everything would be fixed up." Knowing he would be rearrested, Bernstein wanted that arrest to take place in open court, with the whole world watching. He got his way. The defendants' old nemesis, Captain Swanepoel, placed him under arrest under new—and as yet unspecified—charges and ushered him below with the other now-convicted defendants.[2] The Sabotage Act specifically negated the defense of double jeopardy.

The accused left the courthouse in the police convoy. As they left, Albertina Sisulu, Walter's wife, led the crowd in singing the African anthem *Nkosi Sikelel' iAfrica*. To the jeers of the University of Pretoria students, the supporters raised their fists in the illegal African National Congress salute and shouted *"Amandla."* The convicted returned their salute with their hands thrust through the bars of the van carrying them, responding *"Ngawethu."*[3]

The typewritten judgment contained few surprises.[4] The documentary evidence had been overwhelming. Most of the defendants had admitted the critical charges against them. Judge de Wet made short work of the cases against Mandela, Sisulu, and Mbeki. All had effectively admitted guilt of count 2 (conspiracy to violate the Sabotage Act), count 3 (violation of the Suppression of Communism Act), and count 4 (receiving money to commit the offenses set out in the other counts). Mandela had admitted to being one of the founders of MK. He also described his tour of Africa, during which he had undergone military training and made arrangements for MK recruits to receive military training. Sisulu and Mbeki testified to and conceded their involvement in planning sabotage and transporting of recruits for guerrilla training abroad. Mbeki's testimony had admitted enough for him to be found guilty on all four counts.

Neither Mandela through his statement nor Sisulu in his testimony admitted guilt on count 1 (acts committed in violation of the Sabotage Act). Indeed, Mandela had been in prison for much of period when the acts occurred. Sisulu testified that he was not a member of the MK High Command and therefore not directly involved in the perpetration of the acts. But Mandela's imprisonment and Sisulu's denial made no difference to the judge. It was enough for the court that Mandela was one of the MK leaders and had therefore set the machinery for sabotage in motion. Similarly, as a member of the ANC National Executive, Sisulu had been intimately involved in the militant organization's planning activities. Both were guilty of the charges in count 1 as if they had committed the acts themselves.

Judge de Wet took the added step—unnecessary for conviction—of tainting Mandela with the accusation that he had Communist sympathies. Bruno Mtolo testified that Mandela had told the Durban Regional Command that ANC and MK members who visited other African countries should be careful not to admit that they were Communists or that they sympathized with Communists. Based in large measure on Mtolo's testimony, the judge made clear that he believed both Umkhonto and Mandela to be under the sway of Communists.

In finding Sisulu guilty on count 1, de Wet took the opportunity briefly to review the Mtolo's testimony. Mtolo, or "Mr. X," told of his personal involvement in more than twenty acts of sabotage, as well as extensive activities in recruiting young men for guerrilla training abroad. He described in detail the hierarchy of the ANC, the Communist Party, and, most importantly, MK. Mtolo told of meetings with several of defendants, including Sisulu, Mbeki, and Kathrada, as part of his clandestine activities. Despite rigorous cross-examination by Vernon Berrange, the court found Mtolo to be "an honest and truthful witness." He struck the judge as "highly intelligent and to have a remarkable memory." In particular, he was impressed that Mtolo did not appear to minimize his own guilt in relation to the part he played in the illegal activities. De Wet found the discrepancies exposed in cross-examination to be immaterial. There was simply no need to mention the self-serving motivations for Mtolo's testimony and the lies he told to justify his turning against the accused. The bulk of his story was convincing to the court, and in the end that was all that mattered.

Denis Goldberg presented only slightly more of a challenge. He had admitted to his extensive involvement in procuring explosives and related material for use in sabotage and, potentially at least, guerrilla warfare. He had been involved in the purchase of the safe house at Travallyn and a van for the use of those hiding there. His own testimony was enough to justify conviction on at least the conspiracy and Suppression of Communism Act counts.

Goldberg had really contested only one aspect of his involvement in the conspiracy—that he had been involved in a camp at Mamre near Cape Town where young men were trained in guerrilla warfare and had given a map to the now-deceased saboteur Looksmart Ngudle. The court analyzed the evidence of Goldberg's involvement in the camp and his explanation that the camp had been designed for health and educational purposes rather than for paramilitary training. Two witnesses testified about the training received at the camp. As we've seen, Goldberg denied that any such activity took place, arguing that he would not have taken the risk of inviting young men he hardly knew to participate in this kind of activity. De Wet was persuaded to reject Goldberg's denials by comparing witnesses' testimony about the activities at the camp to documents found at Liliesleaf Farm dealing with the recruitment of persons for instruction and training. The activities described were those set out in the prospectus.

He did not believe that the similarity between methods indicated in the exhibit and the methods employed at Mamre were coincidental. The map Goldberg gave to Ngudle showed the location of a sabotage target, the Kenilworth power station near Cape Town. A police officer testified that he saw Goldberg give something to Ngudle. Ngudle was found with the map. The court found that convincing enough. As to count 4, receipt of money for illegal purposes, the court found it sufficient that Goldberg associated himself with MK and that "he must have known that money was collected and used for subversive purposes."

The court similarly had no trouble finding Raymond Mhlaba, Elias Motsoaledi, and Andrew Mlangeni guilty on all counts, though none of these men fully conceded their guilt. Mhlaba testified that he was on assignments from the ANC at the time of the events charged but refused to say what those assignments were. Of all the defendants, including both those who gave testimony and those who made statements from the dock, the court found only Mhlaba to be "untruthful and unreliable." His own testimony, coupled with testimony of others tying him to both sabotage and recruitment, doomed him to conviction. Joel Joffe had been concerned that he had been an ineffective witness.[5] He was right.

As we've seen, neither Motsoaledi nor Mlangeni had testified—both made statements from the dock. Neither fully conceded their guilt. But their own statements contained admission of involvement in the affairs of the ANC and that, plus the testimony of others, though effectively cross-examined, was enough to tie them to the overall plan of sabotage and recruitment of trainees.

The court had the most trouble convicting Ahmed Kathrada. Contrasting what the court found sufficient for his conviction with what it found insufficient in the case against Lionel Bernstein provides insight into Judge de Wet's thinking. The evidence against both Kathrada and Bernstein was extremely weak. Neither admitted to anything that might be construed as a concession under any of the counts of the indictment. They were involved with the other defendants, yes, but the extent of their involvement was unclear. Yet the court found enough evidence to convict Kathrada of conspiracy to violate the Sabotage Act (count 2), even as the same evidence had been found insufficient to justify the conviction of Lionel Bernstein on any count.

The difference was that the state's witnesses put Kathrada at Liliesleaf Farm for some time prior to his arrest. Bruno Mtolo saw him there, running off copies of a document on a duplicating machine. The document was a proclamation of Freedom Day. Among other things, it referred to Prime Minister Ben Bella of Algeria's calls for a "blood bank to aid our struggle." Kathrada and his counsel were concerned about that reference; based on the court's judgment, they were right to be concerned. The court also was influenced by Kathrada's admission that he had stayed at the safe house at Mountain View prior to his arrest and that he disguised himself as a Portuguese man. Although never admitting his involvement in sabotage or guerrilla training, Kathrada had conceded to extensive involvement in ANC and Communist Party matters, as well as to knowledge of the formation and purpose of Umkhonto. He may have expressed reservations about sabotage, but he did nothing to condemn it. He was also aware that guerrilla warfare had been discussed. He further admitted his knowledge that young people were being sent out of the country for training.

The court found significant the evidence that Kathrada had drafted a speech to the Indian people of South Africa calling for solidarity with the ANC. He refused to concede that this speech contained "vicious" accusations but agreed with Yutar that the language used was "somewhat immoderate." His testimony and those of state witnesses put him in the middle of discussions of ANC and other Liberation Movement activities. All of this was enough to find Kathrada guilty of conspiracy, although not of the other counts.

Lionel Bernstein was also very much part of the group meeting at Liliesleaf Farm. Like Kathrada, he was arrested in the July 11, 1963, raid on Liliesleaf Farm. He was a Communist and a longtime participant in the liberation struggle. He had certainly visited Liliesleaf on occasions other than the day of the raid, but on at least some of those occasions, he was there working as an architect focusing on the renovation of the farm. He also went to discuss political matters, including, for example, the border dispute between India and China. He was involved in preparing propaganda against the ninety-day-detention law.

Nonetheless the court also found that he had arrived at Liliesleaf only a few minutes before the raid. The defense cross-examination was successful in destroying Sergeant Dirker's testimony that Bernstein's car engine was cold immediately after the raid. Judge de Wet noted that even if he went to the farm to be consulted on Operation Mayibuye, there was no indication Bernstein would have approved of the plan or would have associated himself with the conspirators. Even if he had given the conspirators literature concerning the Soviet Union and China so that they could decide on their policy should they succeed in overthrowing the government, this did not make him "a co-conspirator in relation to the charges in the indictment."

As discussed in chapter 7, the court in its final judgment also set out its reasons for the acquittal of James Kantor. Other than his partnership with Harold Wolpe, a person clearly involved in the most dangerous of the plans, Kantor was not shown to have had any knowledge or involvement in the activities. But that the state had known from the beginning.

All of the black men on trial were convicted. Two of the three whites were acquitted.

The defense had one day to make final preparations for mitigation. But the certainty of a conviction for at least some of the defendants had already given the defense team an opportunity to plan ahead. By the time the judgment was given, some of the defendants' lawyers began to believe that their clients' lives would be spared. The judge had made a point of finding that they had not decided on guerrilla warfare. He recognized that they had at least planned their acts of sabotage so as to avoid risk of death or injury. Bram Fischer expressed a restrained optimism to Denis Goldberg during Walter Sisulu's cross-examination.[6] George Bizos had been heartened by Leslie Minford's dinner party comment.[7] There was to be one more positive sign, although it would not come until shortly before the mitigation argument itself. Speaking to the judge in chambers before his argument, Harold Hanson, who argued the defense plea in mitigation, asked Judge de Wet directly whether there would be a death sentence. De Wet replied: "No."[8]

But neither Bizos's encounter nor Hanson's last-minute conversation with the judge were known to the defendants. The possibility of hanging was very much on their minds. And it couldn't have been otherwise. In March, after all, three ANC operatives, including the very visible and well-regarded Vuyisile Mini, had been sentenced to death.[9] Their charges included complicity in the murder of a state witness, but the case had arisen out of sabotage activities similar to those of which the Rivonia accused had now been convicted. And in general sentences for antigovernment activities were escalating. Less than six months before, an eighteen-year-old had been jailed for ten years for attempting to leave the country illegally to be trained by the ANC as a mechanic.[10] Another had received twenty years for recruiting a man to leave the country for training. Several young men had been sentenced to ten years for attending a single meeting at which sabotage had been discussed.[11] The evidence showed that the convicted men had done or said nothing. If such punishments could be handed out for comparatively minor offenses, far worse could be in store for the defendants.

The possibility of death prompted the defendants to think about two things. First, would they appeal a death sentence? Second, what should they say either before or after they were sentenced? The answers to both questions came with little hesitation from Mandela, Sisulu, and Mbeki. None of the three would appeal, since it might be viewed as an act of weakness by others in the liberation struggle. Their goal was to inspire their followers and to show that no sacrifice was too great for their cause.

Were the defendants asked why a death sentence should not be pronounced, Mandela would reply on behalf of the group.[12] If the court thought that by sentencing him to death it would end the liberation movement, it was mistaken. He was prepared to die for his beliefs, and his death would be an inspiration to his people in the struggle. He had said in a document entered as an exhibit in the case, "There is no easy walk to freedom. We have to pass through the shadow of death again and again before we reach the mountain tops of our desires."[13] Mandela went so far as to sketch out his comments should de Wet sentence him to death. The note, which has survived the years, reads:

1. Statement from the dock.
2. I meant everything I said.
3. The blood of many patriots in this country has been shed for demanding treatment in conformity with civilized standards.
4. [The fourth paragraph is indecipherable even to Mandela himself. George Bizos reports that Professor Tim Couzens deciphered the fourth point as "The army is beginning to grow" and that Mandela agrees with the deciphering.][14]
5. If I must die, let me declare for all to know that I will meet my fate like a man.[15]

But Mandela, Sisulu, and Mbeki's decision did not extend to efforts that might be made to save the lives of the others. No decision was made whether or not to appeal the death sentence for any of the others. None of the others had the stature of leaders of the struggle; efforts to save their lives would have little influence on public feeling.

All of the defendants consented to counsel's arguing for mitigation of sentence. Bram Fischer declined to deliver the plea in mitigation.[16] He could not bear the stress of arguing against the ultimate punishment for those who were not only the leaders of the movement in which he fervently believed but also his comrades and friends. Instead, the chore was given to Harold Hanson, who had earlier appeared in the case on behalf of James Kantor.

A number of individuals had been approached as potential mitigation witnesses. A few agreed; many declined. It would take courage to speak for men who, in the eyes of much of the white population of the country, had planned and committed horrific acts.[17] Ultimately, the defense team decided to call only one witness, the author of the much praised 1948 novel *Cry, the Beloved Country*, Alan Paton.

In addition to his international literary acclaim, Paton was an outspoken opponent of apartheid. But even more importantly to the defense, he was also an opponent of violence and an ardent anti-Communist. Paton had condemned acts of sabotage and openly clashed with some of the defendants over the militancy of their policies. He served as leader of the Liberal Party, an opposition political party opposed to the government's racial policies but advocating a peaceful solution to South Africa's racial problems. He was also a devout Christian, a lay minister of the Anglican Church.

Despite his differences with the defendants over the means to end apartheid, Paton, when asked by Bram Fischer to testify in mitigation, asked only, "Are their lives in danger?" When told that they were, Paton responded without hesitation: "In that case, there is no question at all. I will give evidence if I am called."[18]

The day of sentencing, June 12, 1964, drew the same crowds in Church Square in front of the Palace of Justice, including several thousand blacks, a smaller but boisterous group of University of Pretoria students heckling the blacks, and police controlling every entrance and exit from the area. Defense counsel and the families of the now-convicted prisoners struggled to gain admittance to the courtroom. After Joel Joffe protested to a senior security officer, a handful of relatives and close friends of the accused were also admitted.[19]

The proceedings began when Advocate Hanson rose to address the court. His task was to argue for mitigation but in no way to apologize for what his clients had done. Hanson was told to emphasize the moral justifications they felt for their actions. Paton's testimony was to buttress that claim.[20]

In his examination-in-chief, Paton spoke of the aspirations of the African people to lead a decent life. Putting aside any differences he may have had with their methods, he spoke glowingly of the defendants. Mandela was the heir apparent of the Nobel Prize recipient Chief Luthuli, regarded as the elder statesman of black South Africa. He spoke of Sisulu and Mbeki as men well known for their courage, determination, and ability. "I have never had any doubt as to their sincerity, and to their very deep devotion to the cause of their people, and I also believe one other thing, their desire to see that this country became a country in which all people participate."

Asked why he had elected to give this testimony, Paton said at first, "Because I was asked to come." "But primarily I came here," he added, "because, having been asked, I felt it was my duty to come here, a duty which I am glad to perform. I also came here because I am a lover of my country, and it seemed to me, my lord, with respect, that the exercise of clemency in this case is a thing which is very important to our future."

Paton went on to set forth his opposition to violence. He did not believe that it could achieve the ends he and others sought for the country. But, echoing the words of the defendants, he added that he understood how the failure of peaceful methods pursued by the accused for many years made them feel that their only alternatives were resignation or resistance. He did not believe those were in fact the only choices, but he understood why some would believe that. In a theme later picked up by Hanson in his argument to the court, Paton added that the history of the Afrikaner people showed that they, too, had refused to accept the position of subservience when the time for action had come. This was a clear reference to the resistance of the Afrikaner people to Great Britain in the years that followed the Anglo-Boer War.

As Hanson ended his examination of Paton, Judge de Wet chimed in: "There are many, many examples, Mr. Paton, of people who have resisted and been convicted of high treason, and executed, when they have done what the accused in the present case have done." He mentioned the Gunpowder Plot in England in 1605 as an example. However legitimate their grievances, they were not entitled to break the law, and they should understand that "what happens to people like that, historically, is that they get convicted of high treason, and condemned to death."

Defense counsel's optimism suddenly faded. It was furthered dampened by Yutar's cross-examination and the judge's apparent reaction to it.

Before the sentencing hearing, Yutar had received a twenty-four-page security police dossier on Paton containing every public appearance that he made since 1953.[21] No association, no speech, and no trip abroad was left unreported. The result was chilling. Despite all indications to the contrary, the South African authorities had concluded that Paton was "a violent anti-Government politician with a pronounced anti-white bias. . . . He is a rabid liberalist and negrophilist." The word "negrophile" or its variations was seldom used, even in South Africa in the 1960s. Ironically, it does appear in *Cry, the Beloved Country*.[22]

A careful reading by a neutral observer of the dossier on Paton's activities would not support the report's conclusion that Paton was "violent." It would simply confirm the commonly held view that he was a devout Christian deeply concerned about racism and the country that he loved deeply and absolutely. But Percy Yutar was not a neutral observer. If Judge de Wet's comment to Harold Hanson was serious, the issue of life versus death had already been decided by the court. At this point, Yutar likely also knew that there would be no death penalty. His goal was to expose even nonviolent, Christian objectors to apartheid as enemies of the state and of the white people of South Africa. Nothing in Paton's record indicated Communist leanings. Indeed, everything pointed to his rejection of Communism as an unworkable totalitarian system. Yet it was to the government's advantage, and therefore to the benefit of Yutar's ambition, to portray Paton as at least a fellow traveler of figures such as Joe Slovo. And his brutal cross-examination was undertaken with that goal.

Yutar began the cross-examination with an explanation to the court of what he was about to do. Recognizing that it was unusual to cross-examine a witness appearing in mitigation, he explained that he did not as a rule do so. He did not do so to "aggravate the sentence" but instead, he said, to "unmask this gentleman, and make perfectly clear that his only reasons for going into the witness box, in my submission, is to make political propaganda from the witness box." Yutar was willing to concede openly that his cross-examination had nothing to do with the issue before the court and everything to do with public opinion.

Yutar first asked Paton whether he was a Communist or a "fellow traveler." Paton denied he was either. He did acknowledge that he shared with the Communists the goal of more equitable distribution of land and wealth and better economic opportunities for all people. But he added that he disapproved entirely of totalitarian methods. He was then asked whether he thought the ANC was dominated by Communists. He answered that it was not. Yutar asked him whether he associated with a lawyer, Roley Arenstein, a known Communist. Paton's dossier indicated that the two had met. Paton admitted that he knew Arenstein through Defence and Aid, an organization providing funds to those charged with antigovernment activities. Defence and Aid provided funds for the Rivonia Trial defense and would later be made illegal. But it was not an illegal organization at the time of the trial.

Yutar asked Paton about his views on the world boycott of South African trade. He admitted that he once advocated such a boycott but now saw enough change in South Africa to be more optimistic. He denied that he had campaigned against his country; rather, he had campaigned against the policies of his government. He had spoken against apartheid, yes, but that was not—yet—treason. Yutar sought to establish that Paton had been able to speak against the government policies with "perfect freedom." Paton resisted acknowledging this, pointing out the extreme difficulty imposed by the intimidation of the security police against people who sought to participate in such meetings.

The cross-examination was not without its effect, especially on Paton himself. He became angry and defensive. The judge took no steps to intervene in the attack. Later, Paton told a newspaper that no one had foreseen that Percy Yutar would impugn his integrity. "It is not my nature to be secretive; on the contrary I rather pride myself on the openness of my political life and actions." He described Yutar's questioning as "vitriolic," and looked to de Wet to intervene, which the judge did not. "I am inclined to think that he enjoyed it, and that he thought the 'unmasking' to be well merited."[23]

Mandela would, at least publicly, forgive Yutar for most of his conduct at the trial. He was simply doing his job. But no one would forgive Yutar for attacking this gentle, religious, and patriotic man, and for no purpose other than self-advancement.[24]

A newspaper reported that Judge de Wet had been smiling during Yutar's cross-examination of Paton. When Hanson rose to address Paton in argument, de Wet appeared not to be listening.[25] In his argument, Hanson picked up on themes articulated by Paton. He stressed the history of antigovernment activities in South Africa and the resistance of the Afrikaner people themselves against British imperialism. In their time, the Afrikaners had engaged in armed uprising, rebellion, and treason. Such acts were ultimately treated with leniency by the British-controlled government. Hanson concluded by noting that it was not the crime alone that left its imprint on the history of the country but the lenient sentence that the court imposed on those found guilty.[26]

Yutar rose and said he would not address the court on sentence but wanted to affirm publicly his faith in the fairness of the court. Yutar later claimed that his failure specifically to ask for death at this moment had saved the lives of the defendants. In any event, de Wet brushed aside Yutar's words and without hesitation nodded to the accused to rise. He began to speak in a voice too soft to be heard by any except the defendants and the lawyers.

I have heard a great deal during the course of this case about the grievances of the non-European population. The accused have told me, and their counsel have told me, that the accused, who are all leaders of the non-European population, have been motivated entirely by a desire to ameliorate these grievances. I am by no means convinced that the motives of the accused were as altruistic as they wished the Court to believe. People who organize a revolution usually plan to take over the Government, and personal ambition cannot be excluded as a motive.

The function of this Court, as is the function of a Court in any country, is to enforce law and order, and to enforce the laws of the State within which it functions.

The crime of which the accused have been convicted, that is the main crime, the crime of conspiracy, is in essence one of high treason. The State has decided not to charge the crime in this form. Bearing this in mind, and giving the matter very serious consideration, I have decided not to impose the extreme penalty, which in a case like this would usually be the proper penalty for the crime.

But consistent with my duty, that is the only leniency which I can show.

The sentence in the case of all the accused will be one of life imprisonment. In the case of the accused who have been convicted on more than one count, these counts will be taken together for the purpose of sentence.[27]

After this brief pronouncement, Yutar rose to say something, but before he could finish Judge de Wet left the courtroom.[28] The Rivonia Trial was over.

Those in the gallery had not heard the court's remarks. Andrew Mlangeni's wife, Juni, called out, "How long, how long?" Andrew replied: "Life."[29] Annie Goldberg, Denis' mother, asked, "Denis, what is it?" Goldberg replied, "Life, life. To live."[30]

Helen Joseph was a leading antiapartheid activist who had been a defendant in the Treason Trial and had been frequently subject to various forms of house arrest. In her autobiography, *Side by Side*, she describes listening for the results of the sentencing on her transistor radio. She had stayed home from work on that day because she could not bear to be sitting in her office awaiting word on whether it would be life or death. When she heard the words "life imprisonment," she could only whisper, "They live, They live!" But she added, "Then I thought of the agony and the wives and the irony of it all, that they would be so thankful for the life imprisonment of their husbands which would make a mockery of their marriages. Life imprisonment for the convicted men meant just that. There would be no remission. Life meant for the terms of their natural lives."[31]

Joel Joffe articulated the feelings of the defense lawyers after hearing the judge's pronouncement: "We looked at each other. There was nothing more to say. We had managed to save their lives, which I suppose is the most that we could have hoped to achieve. But there was nothing to cheer us in the fact that, though our friends were going to live, they would live out their lives in a South African jail."[32]

Nelson's wife, Winnie, announced the sentence to the crowd outside. Banners in support of the now-sentenced defendants were unfurled: "Our future is bright." "We stand by our leaders." The police seized the banners, tore them up, and threw them in the gutters. As the crowd cheered, someone threw water on them from the upper level of a building. There were photographers from South Africa and the international press recording the scene. One television cameraman, who was certainly from abroad—there was no South African television in 1964—exchanged blows with an unidentified white man. Another white man who tried to intervene in the fight was thrown into a police van. Winnie Mandela got into her car to leave. Before she got it in, Toni Bernstein, Rusty's daughter, put her arms around her and kissed her.[33]

After about an hour, the defendants left in a motorcade with the chanting of the black crowd and the jeering of the students following them. Counsel had been told that they would have an opportunity to see the defendants again, but they were instead whisked off to prison.[34] All of the defendants except Denis Goldberg were sent to Robben Island. Goldberg, the lone white man convicted, was sent to prison in Pretoria. They were not to meet with their lawyers again for several days, by which point they had decided not to appeal any of the conviction and sentences.

Less than two weeks later, the defense team issued a statement confirming that there would be no appeal. It explained that because of existing legislation, a successful appeal against the convictions would mean the immediate rearrest and recharging of the accused. No purpose would be served by appealing, the statement added, "because of the power vested in the Minister of Justice to detain for indefinite periods persons who have served their sentences."[35]

13

Reaction

MOST OF WHITE South Africa greeted the trial's outcome with approval and relief. A front-page story in the *Sunday Times*—carrying the headline "Rivonia: The Inside Story"—called the trial "a story of intrigue, treason, muddle, money fiddling, betrayal and brilliant detective work." The story was based on an interview with Major General van den Bergh, the head of the security police.[1] Even the antigovernment *Rand Daily Mail's* headlines were "8 Rivonia Men Guilty—Reds, A.N.C., Spear [Umkhonte we Sizwe] Were Linked—Judge";[2] "Most Sabotage Acts Proved";[3] "Judge Says It Was Treason."[4] A *Daily Mail* editorial called the entire business a "remarkable coup." A later edition of the liberal newspaper referred to the Liliesleaf Farm raid as involving "brilliant police detection and fantastic intrigue."[5] The coverage of the outcome of the trial in other South African papers, English and Afrikaans, was all in the same vein. The security police had saved the nation from a Communist takeover.

There was, however, little open regret that the defendants had not been sentenced to death. Life imprisonment, which everyone assumed meant for the full terms of their natural lives, would be sufficient to keep these men from starting a guerrilla war. And further, the trial—which had after all resulted in the acquittals of Lionel Bernstein and James Kantor—had demonstrated that South Africa's judicial system was a model for the world to respect and admire.

Much of the South African press's reaction was directed at how the trial and its outcome were being portrayed in the rest of the world. Reaction abroad remained fully supportive of the defendants and their cause, although there was some grudging praise for the independence of the South African judiciary. There was of course relief that no death sentences had been handed down, but demonstrations erupted protesting the defendants' life sentences.

The largest demonstrations were in London. Thabo Mbeki, son of defendant Govan Mbeki and himself a future president of South Africa, led a march from the University of Sussex in Brighton, where he was studying, to London to protest the verdicts. He had collected 664 signatures on a petition to protest the expected death penalty. The marchers, waylaid by thunderstorms, stopped at Gatwick Airport (to the irritation of many of the arriving and departing passengers).[6] The numbers of protesters eventually marching on the Houses of Parliament reached close to fifteen thousand. Thabo Mkeki told the press that he had expected the death sentence "as a gesture by the South African government against people seeking to interfere in their affairs."[7] The philosopher Bertrand Russell told the protesters in Trafalgar Square, "The lives of Nelson Mandela and his brave colleagues have been saved by worldwide outcry."[8]

As was expected, the strongest reaction came from black Africa, the Communist world, and left-leaning organizations. The Soviet Communist Party denounced the sentences—although it also took pains to add that the defendants were not members of the Party.[9] Twenty-one Norwegian youth organizations issued protests.[10] The Birmingham England Anti-Apartheid Committee described the sentences as "savage."[11] Emperor Haile Selassie of Ethiopia condemned the sentences as "inhuman and cruel."[12] Labor groups throughout the West bitterly denounced the outcome. The World Council of Peace awarded the Jolio Curie Peace Gold Medal to the Rivonia Nine "in recognition of their courageous efforts for peace, democracy and human equality in South Africa," and called on all peace workers "to take immediate action for the release of the heroic men of Rivonia."[13] Dr. Joost de Blank, former Anglican archbishop of Cape Town, presented a petition to the United Nations, prepared by the World Campaign for the Release of South African Political Prisoners and bearing more than ninety thousand signatures, calling for the release of all South African political prisoners.[14] On the day after the sentences, the South African ambassador to the United Kingdom, Dr. Carel de Wet—no known relation to Judge de Wet— cancelled a planned visit to Oxford University, where he had been scheduled to speak to the Conservative Association about South Africa's policies. About three hundred demonstrators had intended to present a petition to de Wet condemning the Rivonia sentences.[15]

Not all the protests came from the far left. Britain's conservative *Daily Telegraph* reported, "This is not the end, rather the beginning of debate on the larger moral issues," including whether in any nation "the patriotism of those repressed tends to appear in the eyes of the rulers as treason."[16] A writer in the companion newspaper, *The Sunday Telegraph*, commented that, while the Rivonia Trial, "which was conducted with scrupulous fairness," was ostensibly about deciding whether Mandela and the other defendants had planned revolution, the "real issue was outside the competence of any South African judge to decide": "It was whether a people deprived of any peaceful means of asserting their rights are justified in resorting to violence—a question that by its very nature transcends the jurisdiction of a national court of law."[17]

The *New York Times* editorialized that most of the world regarded the convicted men as "the George Washingtons and Benjamin Franklins of South Africa." The protests that erupted were "only incidentally directed at the sentences. Basically they reflect the outraged conscience of the world."[18]

Two days after the sentences, the conservative *Sunday Times* of London carried an analysis of the trial written by its foreign editor, Frank Giles, which began: "So Mandela will not hang. On humanitarian grounds alone we can be thankful for the sentences in the Pretoria trial. We can also note, for possible future reference, that the weight of world opinion may have some effect upon the course of events in South Africa." The column went on to note that while the author had no faith in the value of economic sanctions, the outcome of the trial increased the "moral obligation to keep up the pressure of world opinion" on the South African government.[19]

Attacks on the outcome in the United Nations were led by Russia, China, India, and the newly independent African states.[20] The *Los Angeles Times* reported that, while the sentence was deplored unanimously by the African members of the world body, there was quiet relief that no death penalties were imposed and "a reluctant and unspoken recognition that the United Nations is impotent to do anything more about the matter."[21] On June 9, before the judgment and sentencing, the African bloc had been successful in obtaining a Security Council resolution condemning the trial and calling for amnesty for the Rivonia Trial accused. Great Britain and the United States had abstained. As a measure of how successfully leniency had played in world opinion, after the trial the African bloc was less successful in obtaining a similar resolution condemning the judgment and sentences. The best that could be accomplished was the passage of a Norwegian-Bolivian proposal condemning apartheid generally, calling for liberation or clemency of persons imprisoned or restricted for having opposed that policy, and calling for the formation of an "expert committee" to study the feasibility of sanctions. The British had initially opposed even the formation of such a committee, but the American staff reported to the State Department that talks with the United Kingdom representatives had convinced them that such a committee was a useful "time-saving device."[22]

To no one's great surprise, the British government treaded carefully in its reaction to the Rivonia verdict. Despite the outrage felt throughout much of Britain, there were other voices either in support of the outcome or urging a hands-off approach. Shortly before judgment, several prominent British leaders, including Foreign Secretary Butler, received a detailed analysis of the testimony and documentary evidence at the trial from the South African ambassador.[23] Shortly after the trial, a group, described by the Foreign Office as "right-wing Conservatives," visited the office to argue that they were concerned about "unwarranted interference with South Africa's internal affairs." Britain "should concentrate on an attack on Chinese and Russian Communism and leave South Africa alone."[24]

After judgment but before sentencing, Ambassador Stephenson told the Foreign Office that, whatever they might think of South Africa's laws, "to the best of our knowledge it was scrupulously fair from a legal point of view." Some of the convictions were "almost unavoidable on the basis of documentary evidence produced during the trial and sweeping admissions made by the accused." He added that, for parliamentary purposes, he did not think it would be wise to question the verdicts.[25] After sentencing, Stephenson discussed the case with his American counterpart, Satterthwaite. Both expressed their profound relief that no death sentences had been passed. They agreed that it was essential that they should say nothing to suggest that pressure from either country had influenced the court's decision. Stephenson told his government that they were convinced that neither American nor British pressure had influenced the outcome, and that no government would have given "lesser sentences than these." "It is clear that in practice a Government cannot be expected to release these men unless and until they consider that they safely can afford to do this."[26]

The State Department told the British that they had no plans to try to secure a reduction in sentences. It believed that such action would be inappropriate in light of the statement issued by the defendants' lawyers that an appeal would be worthless because the defendants would simply be rearrested or detained without charge.[27]

Initially, Stephenson was of the same view.[28] However, in July 1964 the Foreign Office advised him to take the opportunity of his next normal interview with the South African minister of foreign affairs to express views in favor of the abatement of the sentences.[29] Shortly thereafter, the ambassador met with Foreign Minister Muller. He expressed his relief that there had been no death sentences but called Muller's attention to the widespread criticism concerning the length of the sentences. Indeed, he had been instructed to represent to the Foreign Minister the desirability of abating the sentences. Muller responded that the judge had been entitled to pass death sentences in the normal exercise of his duties and on his own judgment, but that he, too, "was glad that a death sentence had not been passed." He added that the government had been under great external pressure to control the outcome of the trial. However, there had in fact been no intervention whatever. He added that the feeling in the country was very high. The trial had shown that the government's views of the Communist involvement and the precautions that they had taken were fully justified. He went on to say that "the South African public would not take a decision to abate the sentences now, particularly since events since Rivonia had shown that other subversive elements were still at work." His reference was to a bombing that had taken place at the Johannesburg rail station shortly after the trial, hospitalizing twenty-three people and killing a seventy-seven-year-old grandmother. The bombing was not linked to any activity on the part of the Rivonia defendants. Muller conceded that there might be some reduction of sentences later, "when time proved that opposition to the Government was being conducted legally."[30]

Anything and everything positive said about the trial—especially comments about the South African judiciary—was seized on by the South African press. Of particular focus were statements in the British papers the *Guardian* and the *Daily Herald*, given that they were left-leaning. A front-page article in the *Star* carried the headline, "Rivonia Judge Praised in U.K. Press." The story reported that the *Guardian* and *Herald* had praised Justice de Wet, the *Guardian* noting, "He has shown before now that he is not Dr. Verwoerd's office boy."[31] The *Star* article failed to mention the *Guardian*'s editorial in the same edition in which it referred to the worldwide revulsion at South Africa's apartheid system and strongly criticized the British government for its feeble voice in opposition to it.[32] In a story on the United Nations debates on resolutions condemning the Rivonia outcome and on possible sanctions, the Johannesburg *Sunday Times* noted, with obvious glee, that the United States had obviously moved to the right under President Johnson in resisting the Afro-Asian bloc recommendations. The article attributed the change in American policy to a reduction of influence by Robert F. Kennedy, who stayed on as attorney general in the Johnson administration until September 1964 but was known to be in conflict with his brother's successor, as well as with Johnson's friendship with big business interests. It referred to the formation of the committee to study sanctions as a "face-saving" measure[33]—not an inaccurate comment, as the State Department's own correspondence reveals.[34] A story in the Johannesburg *Sunday Express* on June 21 declared that British reaction to the Rivonia Trial sentences had been "shrill, predictable and largely ineffective. South Africa's image, dark enough already here, has not been made worse." The analysis was based largely on Britain's weak response to Security Council resolutions dealing with sanctions.[35]

A columnist using the pen name "Dawie" in the Afrikaans-language *Die Burger* may have summarized the feelings of many white South Africans toward the international protests that were mounted against the sentences. "The climax was to come yesterday. The agitators will, of course, make the best of the life sentences, but they really wanted the death penalty for the most important black accused, Mandela and Sisulu." A death sentence would have allowed these agitators to "really open the tap of excitement and hate against the whites of South Africa."[36]

Apparently a major outlier from the world press opinion, praising Judge de Wet but condemning the South African government policies, was the archconservative and passionately anti-Communist *Chicago Tribune*. In August, 1964, the Johannesburg *Star* reported that a *Tribune* editorial commented on the Security Council resolution adopted shortly before the judgment, calling many members of the United Nations "busybodies and mischief-makers." The editorial was reported as noting that evidence at the trial seemed indisputable: the accused were taking part in a conspiracy plotted by the South African Communist Party with the full knowledge and support of Moscow. The *Star* report quoted the *Tribune* as saying, "The evidence would seem to indicate that the Communists are seeking to use South Africa's racial troubles as [a] means of creating even more turmoil and confusion and eventually capturing the Government. This puts the trials in an entirely different perspective."[37] No such editorial or article has been retained in the *Tribune* archives.

The South African government's public response to the international protests was predictably defensive and intractable. Prime Minister Hendrik Verwoerd declared that those found guilty were "Communist criminals in the same way as any Communist spy found in the United States and sentenced to death"[38]—again, an oblique reference to the Rosenbergs. In July, Verwoerd issued a statement that stressed that the government had no intention of submitting to outside pressure. Verwoerd added, "If the death sentence had been passed and upheld by the Appeal Court—had an appeal been lodged—the sentences would also have been carried out notwithstanding any pressure. . . . It must be emphasised again that sabotage in South Africa is Communist-inspired and enjoys the sympathy of world Communistic aspirations."[39] On the floor of Parliament, he said: "I want to state clearly and unequivocally that in this case we have not got to do with opposition against the South African Government policy or a championship of the freedom and rights of the people. We have to do with a Communist uprising."[40]

Even the leader of the opposition South African United Party, Sir de Villiers Graaf—who was no supporter of apartheid—commented favorably on the result. On the floor of Parliament, he called the verdicts "just" and "necessary." Graaf added that the "findings were arrived at by one of South Africa's great judges, a man who has proved himself not only a learned jurist but a wise man. In his judgment he pointed out that these men were guilty of treasonable activity. I want to say that if I have any regret, then my only regret is that they were not charged with high treason."[41]

Nonetheless, despite the rejection of the protests by the South African government and press, and despite the praise offered for the independence of country's judiciary, there were also some signs that the defendants' cause had not entirely been lost, even in white South Africa. Again, the press coverage reflects this. The subtle shift that Joel Joffe saw after the Mandela statement seemed in evidence at least in a few of the country's English-language newspapers. While the *Rand Daily Mail* had praised the judge in a front-page editorial the day after the trial ended, calling the sentences "wise and just," and arguing that the decision was law at its best— "justice tinged with mercy"—it added that "account had surely to be taken of the plea put forward that the accused believed there was no alternative to violence in the redress of grievances which they sought. This belief may or may not be well founded but no one who knows South Africa can fail to understand how some non-Whites could come to hold it." The editorial went on to comment that a death sentence would have had a disastrous effect abroad. The editorial argued that the "pervading lesson of Rivonia" was that violence should be rejected as a means of political change, and that the task of working out a just and viable relationship between white and black in South Africa remained more urgent that it was before. "If Rivonia has helped to make us more aware of this, then some good may yet come out of evil."[42]

The *Pretoria News* echoed this. It noted that the trial ended in manner befitting the high and unsullied reputation of the South African judiciary, but that there was a larger lesson to be drawn from Rivonia. "The trial has enforced the law, but has done nothing to solve the problems of our multi-racial society which gave rise to the acts of violence that have now been punished. Men and women of all races live together in this country and are here to stay. It is imperative that they should find a way of living together peacefully with justice and fair play for all."[43]

The South African government was sufficiently concerned with some of the reaction at home and much of the reaction abroad that, within a few months, it supported the publication of two books defending the trial and its outcome. One book, *Rivonia: Operation Mayibuye*, was written by H. H. W. de Villiers, a retired judge. The book traces the trial from the raid through the sentencing and the international reaction, including a chapter on the escape of Wolpe and Goldreich. The book's thesis was that if the Communists behind the actions of all of the defendants had not been thwarted by superb police work, they would have succeeded in turning South Africa into a Marxist state. The book also included a chapter seeking to outline the "tough problem" of dealing with race in South Africa and seeking to justify the government's racial policies. De Villiers noted the almost universal condemnation of the trial in the international press—all except for the *Chicago Tribune* editorial noted above, which had gotten the story right.[44] De Villiers took issue with Percy Yutar on only one point—in his view, the charge against all of the accused should have been high treason.[45]

The second book, *Rivonia Unmasked*, by Lauritz Strydom, included a foreword by Justice Minister B. J. Vorster and introductory remarks by Yutar. Vorster wrote that the message of the book was that "we can rejoice as a nation and give thanks to God that the attack on the Republic and its way of life did not succeed." Yutar wrote that he had never received instructions from the minister of justice or anyone else in government. He noted that he was "deeply shocked" by what he had read in the documents. He concluded his introduction by asserting, "The public of South Africa owes a great debt of gratitude to the South African police." Like de Villiers's book, *Rivonia Unmasked* takes the Rivonia incident from the raid through the trial, also emphasizing the damning documentary evidence as well as the testimony of "Mr. X," Bruno Mtolo, who testified to numerous acts of sabotage at the direction of the defendants. The chapter on Alan Paton's testimony describes it as revealing "extreme leftist" views.[46] The international protests against the Rivonia outcome were "a tidal wave of world hysteria."[47]

Both books end the same way—not with the outcome of the trial and the reaction to it in South Africa and abroad but with that bomb that was set off in the new Johannesburg train station while visitors were converging on the city for a rugby match between South Africa and France. The conclusion of both authors was that the threat to the lives of South Africans—exposed in the Rivonia Trial—was very real. In fact, the bomb was proved to be planted not by the ANC or the Communist Party but by a young white liberal named John Harris.[48] Nonetheless, Strydom commented, "We have now seen Communism in action." He ends with a quote from Dr. Verwoerd. "When therefore it is said in those circles that Mandela may yet, like Kenyatta, become the leader of the future, then I say, GOD FORBID!"[49]

The books, in short, were pure government propaganda. An embassy memorandum to the British Foreign Office, written by staff member named Snodgrass, was highly critical of the de Villiers book. Snodgrass pointed out its glaring omissions: the book mentions neither the dismissal of the first indictment nor anything about the defense case, including Mandela's statement. The de Villiers book's only mention of the defense case is a reference to Paton's testimony. Snodgrass's memorandum also notes that the book fails to mention the establishment by the defense that there was a policy to avoid loss of life. De Villiers had indulged in an "unconvincing tirade against Communism and all its works," and the result was "an insult to the intelligence of an objective reader."[50]

The South African government had won the battle of Rivonia in many respects. The most effective and prominent of the black leaders, Mandela and Sisulu, were now safely out of the way for the rest of their lives. And indeed there would be no serious threat of civil unrest until the Soweto Uprising of June 16, 1976, which was led by an entirely new generation of activists—approximately twenty thousand students took part, and their clash with security forces resulted in the deaths of 176. The activism that came to a head in the Soweto Uprising began a period of ever increasing domestic and international pressure that ultimately led to real change in the country. But that was all very much in the future. After the Rivonia Trial the government had won over white public opinion within South Africa and had driven black resistance deep underground. Most white South Africans were convinced that the police and the judicial system had saved them from a Communist-inspired revolution. While some seeds of concern had been planted—as illustrated by the *Rand Daily Mail* and *Pretoria News* editorials—among more moderate whites, the majority were unwavering in their support of the government.

To some extent, that victory extended overseas as well. The life sentences and acquittals of James Kantor and Lionel Bernstein had convinced some—and not just vehement anti-Communists—that South Africa's courts had operated fairly and independently. Still, most knowledgeable people abroad realized that no matter how independent the judiciary was, it was enforcing apartheid. And more importantly in the long run, the international publicity the Rivonia Trial had generated had created heroes, living heroes. Those convicted at Rivonia were not hanged and therefore did not become martyrs. Instead, they became the absent leaders of a fight that would pick up steam for the next twenty-five years. The British and the Americans could protect the South Africans from sanctions for only so long. Eventually, the pressure that began with Rivonia would create a crisis, and with it an opportunity.

14

Thinking about the Judgment and Sentence

THE GUILT OF most of the accused in the Rivonia Trial was never in doubt. They were unlikely to have been found innocent under the Sabotage Act, given its provisions for shifting the burden of proof to the defense. But the prosecution didn't really need the harsh provisions of that act. The defendants—with the exception of Lionel Bernstein, James Kantor, and perhaps Ahmed Kathrada—admitted, either in their statements to the court, as in Mandela's case, or by their testimony, that they committed acts prohibited under the statute for political purposes.

The case against Kathrada was weaker than the others convicted. Denis Goldberg believes to this day that it was no stronger than the case against Bernstein, who was acquitted. Goldberg also reports that Bernstein said after the judgment that it had been a miscarriage of justice for him to be acquitted and Kathrada convicted.[1] Kathrada was sentenced to a term of life imprisonment based upon his conviction of a single count: conspiracy to violate the Sabotage Act. Kathrada's testimony established his involvement in planning meetings at Liliesleaf Farm on a regular basis and his staying at the Mountain View safe house disguised as a Portuguese man. He admitted knowledge of the formation of Umkhonto we Sizwe. Bruno Mtolo had testified that Kathrada was present at the farm during Mtolo's visit there and that he was duplicating documents.

Bernstein was at the farm on the day of the raid, too, but there was no testimony of his being a regular part of the strategy sessions that occurred there. On the other hand, Kathrada had admitted writing a document referring to a "blood bank to aid our struggle." Bernstein had no such document attributed to him. Applying South African case law, the court found Kathrada guilty of conspiracy based upon his "knowing" of aid to the actions of the other defendants. He "knew in essence" what their work was and had aided them in that work. Under the South African law of conspiracy, as the court saw it—a law as vague in South Africa as in other countries, including the United States and United Kingdom—there was sufficient evidence of Kathrada's guilt by association to justify his conviction.

But a conviction of Bernstein or even Kantor could probably have been sustained under South African law as well. Not only was Bernstein at Liliesleaf on the day of the raid, he admitted to being there on other occasions, if only in his capacity as an architect. He also conceded his involvement with the other defendants in various political discussions, although not to being part of planning for sabotage or guerrilla warfare. It doesn't take much involvement with coconspirators to be found guilty of being part of their scheme. Bernstein was at the scene of the discussions of action against the government and associated with those who admitted planning sabotage.

The law of conspiracy is truly guilt by association, and there was enough association here to sustain a conviction. Rusty Bernstein's identification with the conspiracy under count 2 of the indictment was less than Kathrada's, but only by a small degree. No one would or should have been surprised had he been convicted of the same count that sent Ahmed Kathrada to prison for life.

Even James Kantor had been at risk of conviction under South African law as it existed at the time. The evidence, as we've seen, established the significant involvement of Kantor's brother-in-law and law partner, Harold Wolpe, in the setting up of the Liliesleaf Farm headquarters and of the antigovernment planning that took place there. There was no proof of any involvement by Kantor himself, or even of his knowledge of Wolpe's actions. But as discussed in chapter 7, the South African law of partnership—§ 381(7) of Act 56 of 1955, as paraphrased by Judge de Wet in his judgment, provides: "Where a partner has in carrying on the business of affairs of that partnership, or in furthering or in endeavouring to further its interest, committed an offence, any other partner is deemed to be guilty of that offence unless it is proved that he did not take part in the commission of the offence, and that he could not have prevented it."[2]

Kantor was dismissed at the close of the state's case. At that time, he had introduced no evidence that he did not take part in the commission of the offence or that he could not have prevented it. De Wet chose to find, consistent with South African precedent, that such proof could be found in the evidence of state witnesses. Yutar had conceded that Kantor had played no direct part in the conspiracy. There was no evidence that he had associated with the conspirators, and the court found that it was "highly improbable" that he had any knowledge of the purpose for which the property at Liliesleaf farm had been purchased.

In the most careful legal analysis of the evidence contained in his judgment, de Wet rejected the language from cases cited by the prosecution and instead relied on cases that absolved persons from responsibility for the acts of others in their businesses where they had no knowledge of their partners' illegal activities. Yet the very fact that the court felt it necessary to give a painstaking analysis of the applicable case authority indicates that others might have taken a different view of the law. It is difficult to quarrel with the court's legal reasoning, especially in light of the fact that Kantor was so clearly uninvolved in any antigovernment actions. He was an innocent man, certainly as a matter of raw justice. But if the judge had found Kantor guilty of conspiracy, rightly or wrongly, there would have been no certainty of a reversal on appeal by an appellate court predisposed to uphold the lower court's decision.

In the end, the trial probably turned out exactly the way the apartheid regime wanted. The acquittals of Kantor and Bernstein, as we've seen, gave some credibility to the trial as a fair and independent decision based purely on the facts. Despite Yutar's tireless attempts to prove the contrary, neither man was especially dangerous to the government. Kantor, who was deeply traumatized by his arrest, detention, and trial, was likely to leave the country forever, and in fact did so. Even assuming that new charges against Bernstein failed, he, too, was likely to escape to another country where his antiapartheid activities would have modest effect on the existing regime. He also fled the country within a few months of his acquittal. And, of course, both Kantor and Bernstein were white. The conviction of Denis Goldberg gave sufficient credit to the racial impartiality of South African justice.

Some in the South African leadership had undoubtedly hoped for a death sentence; it would have insured against their further resistance by these individuals. Indeed, at some point the death sentence was probably the prevailing goal of the administration in Pretoria. But the argument that hanging the defendants would only make them martyrs was a compelling one, and the wisdom of that argument cannot have been lost on Prime Minister Verwoerd and Justice Minister Vorster. Life sentences for the antiapartheid leadership would get them out of the way, likely forever, without their martyrdom.

Most important, the prosecution evidence at the Rivonia Trial— particularly the unrefuted documentary evidence—effectively made the government's case to its white population and to the world that South Africa was under serious threat from the Communists. The sentences the defendants received made little difference for propaganda purposes.

The key questions are the following: Was the fact that the trial turned out the way that the government likely wanted a coincidence, or did the Ministry of Justice help create that result by instructing Yutar to indict the defendants for sabotage rather than treason? Or, even more sinisterly, did Justice Minister John Vorster or someone reporting to him tell Justice de Wet to hand down life sentences rather than the death penalty and to acquit Kantor and Bernstein? There is no direct evidence the either Yutar or de Wet was controlled (leaving aside influenced) by the government or even that there was communication between them during the trial. There is no smoking gun.

Nonetheless Joel Joffe believes that Yutar took his orders directly from the Ministry of Justice. Indeed, there would have been nothing wrong with a prosecutor taking directions from those more senior to him in the bureaucratic hierarchy. But in writing a defense of his actions after Mandela had become president of the republic, Yutar denied that he had consulted anyone in the ministry with regard to the charges brought against the accused.[3] Most people connected to the trial find that hard to believe.

Justice de Wet was a different story. Any communication between the judge and someone connected with the Ministry of Justice about the case would have been improper. Some connected with the trial have concluded, and even assumed, that de Wet was told by the powers in Pretoria to reach the decision he reached. Nicholas Wolpe, son of Harold Wolpe and now director of the Liliesleaf Farm Museum, has reached that conclusion based upon conversations with his father and mother.[4] But the closest thing to even circumstantial evidence of de Wet's communication with anyone in the government was the conversation between British counsel general Leslie Minford and advocate George Bizos at that dinner party shortly before judgment. But the passing comment does not and cannot prove that de Wet was communicating with the government. Minford's memorandum to the British Foreign Office shortly before judgment indicates that he still believed that a death sentence was a possibility.

None of the defense lawyers alive today—Joel Joffe, Arthur Chaskalson, and George Bizos—believe that de Wet acted under orders from the government or even communicated with it. In his memoir, Joffe states: "I do not believe Mr. Justice de Wet took or would take instructions from anybody, nor do I account for his behavior by the popular idea that he was 'told.'"[5] He adds that de Wet was "an obstinate and self-willed man, who would not, I think, have taken kindly to either direct government or even indirect political intervention in his domain."[6] Bizos has said that de Wet was not a man who "would take an instruction."[7] Chaskalson expresses similar views.[8]

If one assumes that the judge was not instructed to reach the decision he made, the question of why he decided the case the way he did remains. From the time of their detention, the accused knew that death was a very real possibility under the Sabotage Act. Their lawyers, from the time of their initial conference with them, reminded them of the possibility of capital punishment. Counsel may have become more optimistic as the case went on, but the defendants feared the worst up until the judge's sentence was pronounced. As we have seen, Mandela went so far as to sketch out the remarks he would make when the death sentence was announced. George Bizos has commented that Justice de Wet was not a "hanging judge."[9] Both Arthur Chaskalson[10] and Joel Joffe[11] have the same belief, although none of the three fully attributes the final sentence to the judge's aversion to the death sentence.

More than thirty years after the trial, Percy Yutar—having just been entertained by Mandela at his presidential residence—sought to take credit for the leniency shown by the court. He based his argument on two decisions he made, carefully noting that the South African Ministry of Justice dictated neither decision. The first was the decision to indict the defendants for sabotage rather than treason.[12] Given the judge's specific reference in pronouncing sentence to the fact that the defendants had committed high treason but were not charged with it, there would seem to be some support for Yutar's claim that he had saved the defendants' lives by not charging them with treason. Yet sabotage carried the possibility of capital punishment just as treason did. Even Yutar conceded that his decision not to indict for treason was based on factors other than sparing the lives of the accused. He recalled that the 1956–61 Treason Trial, in which several of the accused had also been defendants, had "had an ignominious ending."[13]

Treason was a difficult crime to prove. As discussed earlier, there were important procedural distinctions between a Sabotage Act trial and one for treason. Under South African law, every overt act of treason had to be proved by two witnesses. There was no such onus under the Sabotage Act. Treason charges required a three-judge panel; a single judge could decide a Sabotage Act prosecution. Unlike treason, the prohibition against double jeopardy did not apply to Sabotage Act prosecutions. The burden of proof beyond a reasonable doubt was always on the prosecution in a treason case. Again, once an act prohibited by the Sabotage Act had been proven, the burden was on the defense to prove that the act had not been done for antigovernment purposes.

Yutar also pointed out in self-defense that he did not specifically ask for the death sentence in his closing argument to the court.[14] Both the British Foreign Office and the American State Department received with great relief the information that Yutar did not intend to ask for the maximum penalty. But it was not the practice in South Africa to recommend a specific punishment to the court.[15] And, given that practice, Yutar's closing came as close to asking for death as it could have without specifically asking for it. Remember that in his introduction to his closing remarks, Yutar referred to the defendants' actions as "classical case of high Treason," adding simply that "for reasons which I need not here detail, the state has preferred to charge the accused with sabotage." In the 1995 document explaining his actions and taking credit for the absence of a death sentence, Yutar states that he "very pointedly and significantly . . . did not add the usual statement 'which deserves the ultimate penalty.'"[16] The point was a subtle one that was lost at least on the defendants and their lawyers. Sabotage, of course, carried the same possible penalty. Had Yutar been trying to gain a conviction but not a death sentence, an argument equating the defendants' acts to high treason hardly seems the way to do it.

As we've seen, at the close of his argument, Yutar again referred to the case as one of "High Treason *par excellence*," adding, "Because of the people who have lost their lives and suffered injury as a result of the activities of the accused it is apparent that this case is now one of murder and attempted murder as well." Death sentences for murder were common in 1964, as Yutar well knew. The fact that there was no evidence that anyone had lost his or her life as a result of the defendants' actions seemed to escape the learned Dr. Yutar. But his willingness to equate the accused's actions with murder hardly seems like a veiled plea for clemency.

Mac Maharaj was another important antiapartheid leader who himself was jailed at Robben Island after what is known as the "Little Rivonia" trial, which took place in November 1964 and was largely a mopping up operation after the major players were jailed. Maharaj, now an ANC leader in the new South Africa, wrote an introduction to the 2007 reprinting of Joel Joffe's memoir on the Rivonia Trial.[17] In his introduction, Maharaj analyzes the trial and seeks to reach a conclusion as to why the defendants were not sentenced to death. He, like Joffe, points to the mistakes made by the prosecution in playing to the media rather than simply making its case. In Maharaj's words, "The prosecution botched its case."[18] Yutar tried to take on the accused on their own political turf and "was hopelessly outmaneuvered."[19] His analysis also points to the substantive pressure put on the South African government by the international community. Maharaj acknowledges Joffe's view that Justice de Wet would not countenance outside interference in his decision making. But, he adds, "that does not exclude the likelihood that he may have licked his finger and held it up to determine whether there was a breeze and its direction."[20] Joffe has a similar view. As he noted in connection with the judge's upholding of the second indictment, if Justice de Wet was independent of the government, Justice de Wet independently knew what the government wanted.[21]

And in addition to the international pressure likely to be considered by both the South African government and the court, Maharaj recognizes the "pressures that were mounted by the defense team and the accused themselves." He notes: "At the heart of 'the battle to prevent the death sentence' was the strategy of the accused, the dignity and forthright way in which they gave their evidence, withstood cross-examination and championed the cause of freedom and democracy from within the courtroom and the magnificent performance of the defence team led by Bram Fischer."[22]

Maharaj's explanation of the result is well supported by the record of the trial itself and a review of the South African and international context in which the trial took place. It is difficult to attribute the result of the case to anything other than a combination of factors, most of which Maharaj sets out in his introduction. But this important case deserves at least a more detailed dissection of the trial and the contemporary scene. Maharaj correctly identified most of the things that contributed to the judge's decision, but the degree of their significance to the ultimate outcome of the case is worth another look.

The prevalence of the death penalty in many U.S. states has spawned a group of dedicated lawyers who work exclusively on capital cases. Those specialists often conduct seminars for other lawyers who may be undertaking for the first time a case in which a death sentence has already been handed down and affirmed on appeal—the post-conviction process. In those seminars, a common theme is that it is up to the lawyers for the defendant to seek to "change the picture" of their client. The prosecution has usually been successful in portraying the client as a horrible person who has committed a brutal, senseless crime. The impression that the accounts of the

client's arrest, trial, and conviction have made on the general public un-
derstandably will affect any judge—no matter how open-minded—who
will hear post-conviction arguments. It is the difficult task of the lawyer to
"change that picture" and to create another one in which the client emerges
as an individual worthy of continuing existence. A case may turn not on
the character or circumstances of the convicted person but rather on a
point such as the ineffectiveness of his trial counsel. But the court's view
of the client is nevertheless an important aspect of the representation.

In this case, something happened in the course of the Rivonia Trial to
change the picture of the defendants in Judge de Wet's mind from both
his likely prejudices as a white Afrikaner and what he heard in the courtroom during the prosecution case. The state had painted the picture of the
accused as brutal revolutionaries bent on the destruction of all that de Wet
and most of the rest of white South Africa held near and dear. At some
point in the trial, that picture changed—at least enough for the judge to
see them as men whose lives were worth sparing. The answer may lie in
part, as Maharaj says, in the judge's sense of how the wind was blowing.
But it likely had more to do with what went on in the courtroom. The
credit for the transformation of the picture goes both to the defense
lawyers and to the defendants themselves.

Several key decisions were made by counsel, in consultation with their
clients, that turned the case around. First, for the most part there was no
attempt to counteract the state's evidence that was clearly true. The defense
challenged some peripherally significant aspects of the case, such as the
nature of Denis Goldberg's involvement in training camps. And the embellishments of many of the witnesses were undermined either by a successful attempt to show that the witness was lying or by calling to the
court's attention the fact that the police had coerced them with lengthy
and often brutal detentions. But such attacks served primarily to paint a
general picture of the world in which the accused had to function rather
than to show their innocence.

For the most part, the fundamental thrust of the case—that there
were at least some acts of sabotage that resulted from the defendants'
plans, that there was preliminary planning for guerilla warfare, and that
there was recruitment of young men who were sent abroad for training
in warfare—was conceded by the defense. By conceding the essence of the
charges, the defendants ensured their conviction. But by refusing to dodge
the charges, Mandela and his codefendants were able to establish their
primary purpose at the trial—to show that the apartheid government had

left them no choice. Their purpose was more to tell the world what was happening, but in doing so they also began the process of convincing the court that they were not the kind of people who should be hanged. Their candor surely played a role in de Wet's assessment of them.

Secondly, the defense hammered away at a few basic themes, none material to their guilt or innocence but undoubtedly important to the court in the sentencing phase. Most importantly, although the Operation Mayibuye document contained a frightening plan for a bloody guerilla war, the defense was able to convince the judge that the plan had never been adopted. They may have talked about its adoption, and some of the defendants may have been in favor of it, but it had never in fact been anything other than a suggestion for what may happen in the future if things did not get better. The judge was so convinced of the defense position on this issue that he interrupted the closing arguments of both Percy Yutar and Bram Fischer to acknowledge the point.

Likewise, counsel for the defense successfully convinced the judge that MK—and therefore the defendants—was not responsible for all of the acts of sabotage that had taken place. This fact was also acknowledged by the court during closing argument and lent support to another—perhaps even more important—point in the judge's failure to sentence the defendants to death. No act of sabotage actually attributed to them or their organizations had resulted in death or injury to any person. Even the star state witness, Bruno Mtolo, acknowledged that it was the MK policy to avoid injury to persons. Justice de Wet demonstrated that he was skeptical that the policy of no injury could always be successful, but the intent to avoid harm to people became clear to him.

In addition, although probably less important on the question of sentence and more important for the general picture of antiapartheid activism in general, the defense was able to separate MK from the African National Congress, and the ANC from the Communist Party. The separation of MK was important to future defendants who were shown to be members of the ANC but not participants in MK—although there would soon be legislation enacted to equate the two organizations. Separation from the Communist Party was important for the international perspective on the ANC. The government would still attempt to portray the entire plot as Communist-inspired, but any thoughtful analysis of the record demonstrated that the primary motivation of the ANC defendants was to overturn South African racial policies and to achieve equality for all people in the country. The Communist Party assisted their efforts, but the party did not dictate their actions, nor would it control the leadership once their goal had been achieved. Even with regard to the sentence, it would have been easier for the court to sentence hardened Communists to death than men whose primary motivation was to achieve a better life for people of their race.

Perhaps the most significant decision made by the defense—primarily by the defendants themselves—was for the accused to address the court either by way of a statement from the dock or by testimony. George Bizos, on point here as he was so often in the defense strategy sessions, had emphasized the value of the accused addressing the court in some way. Bizos says: "Above all I was aware that the judge had never had any meaningful contact with black people, particularly Africans, except at the level of master and servant. I believed that if our clients testified for days on end, he might still not be satisfied enough to let them go free, but the justice of their cause, their deeply felt sense of grievance, their intelligence and courage would become clear and could lead him to spare their lives."[23]

Although Yutar would make the point that Mandela's statement was not substantive evidence in the case, the judge heard every word of it, and de Wet, like everyone else who heard or would become familiar with the speech, could not have been unmoved by it. Even segments of white South Africa were impressed with his eloquence and the power of his expression of convictions. Mandela's statement made him into a man of substance— dangerous indeed to the power structure, but a human being.

Likewise, Walter Sisulu's testimony and especially his ability to engage the much better-educated Yutar in political debate and come out on top could not have escaped the court. The quality of the other defendants' testimony or statements—with the probable exception of Raymond Mhlaba— was similarly impressive, although no others fully matched the eloquence of the primary leaders, Mandela and Sisulu.

The positive effect of the defense decision to call most of the accused as witnesses was significantly enhanced by the conduct of the prosecution. George Bizos, alone among defense counsel, predicted that Yutar would argue politics with the defendants. His prediction was a characteristically prescient one, based not only on his knowledge of Yutar himself but on a correct perception that the prosecution was trying the case as much as a defense of apartheid and an attack on the antiapartheid movement as a criminal prosecution. The state's conviction of the accused was secure— not because the judge was in its pocket but because the evidence of guilt was overwhelming. Now, it must have seemed to Yutar, was the time to engage these intellectually inferior men in a political debate. He lost.

In his comments at sentencing Judge de Wet said that he did not fully buy the altruistic motives of the defendants, adding: "People who organize a revolution usually take over the government, and personal ambition can't be excluded as a motive." But simply because he believed that the defendants would someday become power hungry does not mean that he did not respect the integrity of their motivations at this time.

Those observing de Wet during Alan Paton's testimony, as we've seen, reported that he was either smiling in seeming approval of the attempted destruction of the noted author or ignoring the testimony entirely. His tolerance of Yutar's treatment of Paton may have been the result of a general dislike for the soft, liberal approach to South Africa's problems, or at least a resentment of this individual who had achieved international acclaim as an opponent of the existing South African order. And besides, if Leslie Minford and Harold Hanson were to be believed, Justice de Wet had already made up his mind to spare the defendants before the sentencing hearing even began. Ironically, Paton's testimony and Hanson's argument may have made them more at risk than they were before the hearing began.

Mac Maharaj comments that Yutar "botched the case" by failing to concentrate on the mountains of proof against the defendants and instead engaging them in political arguments. There is another way to look at the record. Yutar's sought-after conviction was secure. Both the prosecution's examinations-in-chief and its cross-examinations established sufficient evidence to convict and, indeed, to hang the defendants. Even more importantly, the state relied most heavily on the documentary evidence, which was clearly tied to the defendants and was sufficient to support the charges in the indictment. Yutar accurately pointed out in his 1995 statement that he asked each of the accused who testified whether any of the documentary exhibits produced at the trial were "false, fabricated or falsified." No defendant pointed to a single falsified document. Joel Joffe is critical, as a lawyer, of Yutar's closing argument, in which he read from four volumes summarizing the evidence, without analysis.[24] A sufficient response from Yutar would be that he didn't need to do anything else.

But in another sense, Yutar may have botched the case—assuming that he in fact wanted a harsher punishment. From the time of the argument on the first indictment, quashed by the court, it was apparent that the trial judge was unimpressed and even hostile to Yutar. As previously noted, the British barrister John Arnold told people at the British embassy that Yutar was, as he put it, a "nasty piece of work" whose method of prosecution would certainly be very counterproductive in a British court.[25] There were certainly times when the judge appeared clearly on the prosecution side, as when he took over a hostile line of questioning. But there was never an indication that he liked Yutar. His failure to refer to him as "Doctor Yutar" is an example. The British consul general, Leslie Minford, told the British Foreign Office of an incident when, because of a scathing cross-examination of Vernon Berrange, Yutar said that he would be forced to call other witnesses to establish evidence. Minford noted that "Mr. Justice de Wet is reported to have said with a smile that perhaps Mr. Yutar was not finding his task quite so easy after all."[26] Defense lawyers in criminal cases will not complain of the trial judge who treats them in a rough manner, so long as the judge treats the prosecution the same way. Such may have been the case at the Rivonia Trial.

Rivonia was a case in which the competency—indeed the brilliance—of defense counsel, coupled with the demonstrated quality of the defendants as human beings, saved those charged from the harshest penalty. This success, especially in light of the fact that the sole decision maker had absolutely no sympathy with the cause that motivated the defendants, was remarkable. Joel Joffe notes that after the sentences were handed down, all of the other lawyers shook Bram Fischer's hand. He says: "It had been his responsibility in the first place to save their lives, and it was his victory in the first place that they would live."[27] The comment is an accurate one. Bram Fischer was the person most responsible for saving the defendant's lives. But none of his efforts would be enough to save his own.

15

After Rivonia

ALL OF THE men convicted in the Rivonia Trial survived to be released by
the government, though they all served long and excruciatingly difficult
prison terms, ranging from Goldberg's twenty-two years to a total of twenty-
seven years for Mandela. For much of their time in prison, all of the convicted men, except Goldberg, were confined to the forbidding facility on
Robben Island; Goldberg was confined to a prison for whites in Pretoria. [1]

For those imprisoned on Robben Island, their incarceration eventually
presented opportunities to continue to participate in the struggle.[2] The
Rivonia defendants were at first isolated in single cells in a special unit.
Other inmates who were imprisoned for political crimes joined them
later. After 1965, the Rivonia defendants would come into contact only
with men convicted of political crimes. Murderers, rapists, thieves, and
the like were removed from the prison in 1965 after a brief experiment by
the authorities in granting such criminals special privileges to gain their
assistance in keeping the political convicts in line. The policy failed when
the authorities recognized that the political prisoners had begun to politi-
cize their criminal compatriots.

Unlike during their time in detention and solitary confinement after
their arrests, the prisoners could and did communicate with each other
during the long years of their imprisonment—although at times the
prison authorities attempted to make communication among the inmates
as difficult as possible. The persistence and ingenuity of the prisoners assured a continuing dialogue within the prison. The confinement with
like-minded inmates provided opportunities for intellectual and political
conversation, permitting the prisoners to lay the groundwork for success
after their release.

Many Robben Island prisoners took the opportunity to study and gain
university degrees through correspondence. Informal education, especially political education, took place on a regular and continuing basis,
with the older and better educated prisoners teaching and providing or

recommending reading materials. The extent to which prisoners were permitted to receive outside reading materials gradually increased from nothing at the beginning to a significant level near the end of their incarceration. Obtaining current newspapers or radio news was always challenging. These educational opportunities, combined with the dialogue among the imprisoned, turned Robben Island into a prestigious educational institution for influential black leaders in the postapartheid era.

Communicating with the outside world was more difficult for the prisoners. But every chance to do so was seized. Lawyers and the few others permitted visits received and passed on information—usually coded—to leaders of the struggle outside the country. Enough communication existed, particularly in the 1980s, for those convicted in the Rivonia Trial to have some input into the policies guiding the continuing struggle against the apartheid government. In 1982, after eighteen years on the island, all but Mbeki and Motsoaledi were transferred to the Pollsmoor Prison on the mainland, where life was marginally better.

This emphasis on the continuing political involvement of those convicted in the Rivonia Trial and other South African political prisoners is not meant to minimize their suffering. Although some of the brutality initially dished out on Robben Island subsided in later years, imprisonment on the island was particularly painful—even by South African prison standards. All were deprived of their freedom for almost all of the prime years of their lives. Their time in Robben Island was filled with backbreaking hard labor in the island quarry. All were denied contact and even written communication with their loved ones except in an extremely limited way.

Rather, this brief description of their continuing political involvement while in prison is intended only to present further evidence of the quality of the individuals imprisoned and their devotion to their cause. Their involvement in the struggle against the regime continued even during their prison years. The Rivonia defendants were more than simply symbols of resistance—they continued to be a part of it.

Most of the world knows the rest of the story for Accused No. 1 in the Rivonia Trial, Nelson Mandela. He was released from prison in 1990, after serving twenty-six more years on Robben Island and in other South African prison facilities. He went on to lead the negotiations that resulted in a new South African constitution and a truly democratic multiracial nation. In 1994, he became the first president of the new South Africa, serving as an effective leader who brought a degree of cohesiveness to the people of that nation beyond anyone's expectations.

All of the rest of those convicted at Rivonia went on to play important roles in the creation and beginning years of the new South Africa. Goldberg was the first to be released, in 1985. His release was predicated on him pledging not to be involved in armed conflict against the South African government and not to break the law. Goldberg went briefly to Israel, then to London, and then to Africa to meet with Oliver Tambo, the leader of the African National Congress in exile. During the years between his release and the end of apartheid, he traveled the world as an ANC spokesman, technically keeping his pledge to eschew armed struggle but supporting the cause nonetheless. He did not return to South Africa until 2002, after the death of his wife, Esme, who had wanted to remain in England. After his return, he worked for Ronnie Kasrils, who was named as an unindicted coconspirator in the Rivonia indictment and who became the minister of water affairs and forestry in the Mandela administration. Goldberg finally became the engineer he had always wanted to be. He is now retired and lives in the seaside village of Hout Bay south of Cape Town.[3]

The next to be released, in 1987, was Govan Mbeki. Mbeki was not transferred from Robben Island to Pollsmoor prison when the others had moved there in 1982.[4] There are mixed reports with regard to the relationship between Mbeki and Mandela, both on Robben Island and after their release. Mandela's biographer Martin Meredith reports on a rift between the two while in prison over the relationship between the ANC and the Communist Party. Mbeki insisted on stronger ties between the two than Mandela wanted. Meredith says that the feud was brought formally to end, but the "fault line remained."[5] Mark Gevisser, Govan's son Thabo's biographer, reports that Mandela and Mbeki "loathed each other." Gevisser also reports that "after his release, Mbeki had spread the word that Mandela had 'sold out' to his captors."[6] Although he discusses some disagreement over the beginning of negotiations with the government,[7] Mandela reports none of this animosity in his autobiography. Ahmed Kathrada denies that there was a strong break between Mandela and Mbeki on Robben Island.[8]

Upon his release, Mbeki resumed his role as a vocal critic of government policies, resulting in his confinement to his home city of Port Elizabeth for two years. After his restriction was removed, he continued his work with the ANC.[9] In the first postapartheid general election, Mbeki was elected to the Senate and became deputy president of that body. He died in 2001.[10] Despite any the differences between Mandela and Govan Mbeki, Govan's son Thabo was chosen by Mandela to succeed him as president of the Republic.

The remainder of the defendants, other than Mandela, were released in 1989. Of these men, Walter Sisulu, already seventy-seven years old, was the best known to both black South Africans and the outside world. Sisulu immediately renewed his activism. He became ANC deputy president in 1991, shortly after the party again became legal. He worked to quell the government-instigated black-on-black violence that threatened to tear South Africa apart in the years preceding the adoption of the new constitution. He retired from politics after the 1994 election and died in 2003.[11]

Ahmed Kathrada stayed politically active after his release. He was elected to Parliament in 1994 and served as a parliamentary counselor in the office of President Mandela. He is still active in South African political and cultural life.[12] Raymond Mhlaba became the premier of the Eastern Cape Province in 1994 and then served as high commissioner to Rwanda and Uganda until 2001. He died in 2005.[13] After their release from prison, both Andrew Mlangeni and Elias Motsoaledi were named to the ANC National Executive Committee. Mlangeni served as a member of Parliament from 1994 until 1999.[14] Motsoaledi died on the day that Nelson Mandela was inaugurated as president of South Africa, May 10, 1994.[15]

All of the defendants received numerous honors from the African National Congress and other organizations, in South Africa and beyond, for the contributions and sacrifices they had made to end apartheid and in the formation of a new, multiracial government for their country.

As noted previously, though he was acquitted, Rusty Bernstein was rearrested after the trial but, at the urging of Vernon Berrange, freed on bail. The new charges against him were not detailed but, if there had been a trial, certainly would have involved the Suppression of Communism Act. After being alerted that the police were about to sweep in on both him and his activist wife, Hilda, the couple escaped South Africa. They fled through Bechuanaland—now Botswana—eventually arriving in London, following a path not radically different than that of Harold Wolpe and Arthur Goldreich after their escape from the Marshall Square prison. The Bernsteins settled in England, where Rusty worked as an architect and Hilda as a writer and journalist. They—especially Hilda—continued their verbal activism on the part of the antiapartheid movement. Hilda broke from the Communist Party in 1968 after the Soviet invasion of Czechoslovakia. Rusty was much slower in following that path but eventually made the break from Moscow as well. Still citizens of South Africa, the Bernsteins returned in 1994 to participate in the election that made Mandela the nation's president. They returned to Britain after that trip. Rusty Bernstein died of a heart attack in 2002.[16]

In her moving memoir, *The World That Was Ours*, Hilda Bernstein describes a visit from Mandela after Rusty's death. Mandela, by then retired as president of South Africa, came to the Bernstein's semidetached house in Oxford together with his wife, Graça. He arrived with a contingent of armored cars and security men—causing a sensation in the quiet suburb. Hilda adds, "He stayed and talked about old times: he never forgot his old friends."[17] In 2003, Hilda and her youngest son and his family returned to South Africa to set up permanent residence. Hilda died in Cape Town in 2006.[18]

James Kantor also immigrated to England shortly after the dismissal of the charges against him. In England, he worked to get the British government to intervene with the South African government to spare the lives of his codefendants. He contacted the Bow Group, which had sought to urge the British Foreign Office to intervene on behalf of the accused, and asked Anthony Mitton of that group to arrange a meeting with the Foreign Office.[19] In May 1964—a few weeks before the judgment in the trial—Kantor contacted Phillip Mason, the director of the Institute of Race Relations, and told him that Mandela would be convicted and that Kantor thought he would be sentenced to death and not reprieved.[20] Although Kantor's requests and opinions were passed on to the diplomats, there was to be no meeting.[21]

For a long period, Kantor bore resentment against his sister, AnnMarie, and her husband, Harold Wolpe, whose escape had prompted the South African government to bring the charges against him. He later reconciled with his sister, but the two never fully discussed what had happened leading up to the Rivonia Trial. In England, Kantor gave up the thought of a law practice. After some period of difficulty, he became involved in some successful business schemes. His success enabled him to try to duplicate his Johannesburg lifestyle, with a comfortable house and a yacht. But his health never recovered from his experience in prison. He died of a massive heart attack in 1974 at the age of forty-seven.[22]

Kantor's fellow Rivonia defendants gratefully remembered his unwillingness to turn against them—even to save himself. Denis Goldberg has said in reference to Kantor, "It was quite phenomenal to have a person like this with us."[23] Mandela also remembers Kantor fondly in his memoir *Long Walk to Freedom*, recalling that, sitting in the dock, Kantor had passed him a note asking him to be the godfather of their expected child. Mandela replied: "I would be more than delighted, and the honour is mine, not the baby's. Now they dare not hang me."[24]

*　　*　　*

After his harrowing trek through Africa following his escape, Harold Wolpe settled in London. His wife, AnnMarie, who was permitted to leave the country despite her obvious involvement in her husband's escape, later joined him.[25] Wolpe continued his involvement in Communist Party and MK business. After a few years, he received a fellowship at the London School of Economics and became a lecturer in sociology. AnnMarie went back to school as well, and she and her husband both eventually wound up with teaching posts at Bradford University. AnnMarie became a world-renowned scholar in what was then the emerging field of feminist studies. She was a founding member of the *Feminist Review*. They both returned to South Africa after the changeover. Both taught at the University of the Western Cape, an institution whose origins under the apartheid regime were as a university for Coloured people. Harold died of a heart attack in 1996. AnnMarie still lives in Cape Town. Their son, Nicholas, is the founder and director of the museum at Liliesleaf Farm, which opened its doors to the public in 2008.[26]

Arthur Goldreich settled in Israel after his escape. Although South African–born and reared, he had fought in Israel's 1948 war of independence. In 1966, he became head of the Industrial and Environmental Design Department at Jerusalem's renowned Bezalel Academy. Goldreich did not give up his activism. He was a frequent critic of Israeli policies with regard to the Arab population of the occupied territories, comparing the treatment of the Arabs with the policies of apartheid South Africa. In a 2006 article in the British newspaper the *Guardian*, he called the Israeli policies "bantustanism," the term used in South Africa to separate blacks into separate "Bantustans," or homelands. He is quoted as referring to Israel's actions as "the brutality and inhumanity of what is imposed on the people of the occupied territories of Palestine."[27] Arthur Goldreich died in 2011 in Tel Aviv.[28]

Bob Hepple also settled in England after he avoided testifying against his compatriots by fleeing the country. Later, he would tell an interviewer at Cambridge University that he had never intended to testify for the state against men he "admired and respected."[29] For the most part, the other participants in the Rivonia Trial have forgiven him for agreeing to testify against the defendants. Not surprisingly, Mandela falls into that camp. He and Hepple met for the first time after the Rivonia Trial at a Buckingham Palace reception. As Hepple's wife was greeting the queen, Mandela recognized Hepple, said "Bob, is that you?" and gave him what Hepple describes as "one of his great bear hugs."[30] Joel Joffe has commented,

"I think it is very easy for [there to be] critical judgments of people who decide to give evidence against their colleagues and friends and certainly the accused felt very badly let down. But I have every sympathy, personally, with Bob and was sure that when he gave evidence, he would do his very best to avoid doing any harm whatsoever to the accused."[31] George Bizos too believes that Hepple would never have given testimony against the others. Denis Goldberg is not entirely forgiving, but adds that "over the years, I have come to understand." He notes that Hepple was under tremendous pressure, arising in part from the fact that his father had been a member of Parliament. Nevertheless, Goldberg remembers that he felt betrayed.[32]

In fact, Hepple's statement to the police—released as part of Percy Yutar's papers—shows that his testimony would have given very little to the prosecution's case other than the propaganda boost of having a white participant testifying as a state witness. Much of Hepple's contact was with Joe Slovo, who was out of the country by the time of the Rivonia arrests. Nothing in the remaining portions of statement revealed anything other than what the defendant's themselves admitted in their testimony. Ironically, Hepple's testimony would have had some detrimental effect on the state's case. He confirmed what the defendants themselves would say: Operation Mayibuye was not a topic of discussion on the day of the raid on Liliesleaf Farm. Instead, the men were about to begin a discussion of the legal aspects of the ninety-day-detention law.[33]

Hepple achieved enormous success in England as a legal academic specializing in labor law and related topics. He became a fellow of Clare College Cambridge in 1966, and eventually professor of law and master of Clare College. He returned to South Africa many times after 1994 to lecture on labor law. He has served as a visiting professor at the University of the Witwatersrand in Johannesburg and is an honorary professor at the University of Cape Town. He was knighted in 2004, and is now Professor Sir Bob Hepple.[34]

Justice Quartus de Wet did not participate in any postmortems of the trial. He gave no known interviews, nor did he contribute any writing to the two government-sponsored books written about it. He remained as judge president of the Transvaal province until his retirement. His only involvement with the Rivonia defendants or their counsel after the trial's end was to serve as judge at the disbarment proceedings brought against Bram Fischer. De Wet ruled against Fischer and ordered the distinguished and much-admired advocate disbarred.[35]

*   *   *

After the trial, Percy Yutar continued on the road to success as a prosecutor, eventually achieving his goal of becoming the first Jewish attorney general of South Africa. He first achieved that rank in 1968 in the heavily Afrikaner and extremely conservative Orange Free State.[36] In 1975, he was appointed attorney general for Transvaal, the heavily populated and developed province that included both the cities of Johannesburg and Pretoria.[37] He retired from his public position the next year.[38]

It was upon his retirement from being attorney general that he began to reap the animosity he had sown with his conduct as a prosecutor, especially in the Rivonia Trial. After leaving government, Yutar applied to join the Johannesburg bar. Sydney Kentridge, a close friend of the defense lawyers in the Rivonia Trial, led the resistance to the application. The opposition was based in part on the belief that his only reason in applying for membership to the bar was to make himself eligible to be a judge.[39] Yutar's application to the bar was ultimately accepted, but he did not become a judge.[40]

As the tide in South Africa turned against apartheid after Mandela's release in 1990, Yutar began to attempt to rehabilitate himself in the eyes of what would be the new South Africa. In the draft of a preface to a never-published memoir, he claimed that in 1983 he "spoke to no fewer than four Cabinet Ministers and urged them to take steps to have the accused released." As discussed in chapter 14, he also claimed in the same draft preface that his decisions to charge the defendants under the Sabotage Act and not with treason as well as his failure to ask specifically for the death sentence had saved the defendants' lives—points rejected by the accused's defense team.[41]

But by the time the draft preface was written, Yutar had already been hosted at lunch by then-president Nelson Mandela. The lunch took place in 1994 at the request of a film documentary crew. Mandela greeted him warmly and assured Yutar that he had played only a "minor role" in sending him to Robben Island and that he had only "done his duty."[42] Yutar, in turn, praised Mandela as "a saintly man."[43] Privately, Joel Joffe asked Mandela how he could treat Yutar so generously after his appalling conduct in the trial. Mandela responded that in reconciling the different races in South Africa, he could not "afford the luxury of revenge."[44]

Other Rivonia defendants were less forgiving of their former prosecutor. Walter Sisulu and Ahmed Kathrada declined invitations to the lunch. Sisulu commented: "Yutar wanted to show the Nat [National Party] government that he, as a Jew, was more vicious than anyone else."[45]

Even as he accepted Mandela's hospitality and called him saintly, Yutar still fervently maintained his belief in the guilt of all of the defendants. In his unpublished preface, he felt obliged, to be fair to his conscience and the interest of all South Africans, "to point out a real fear and concern that sorely troubled me at the time of the trial, namely that the African National Congress was, as proved at the trial, admittedly dominated by the South African Communist Party, a fact which had to be kept secret particularly from the outside world for fear of losing its support both financially and otherwise." He went on to catalogue documents introduced at the trial demonstrating Mandela's Communist involvement.[46]

Yutar was involved in another controversy when, in 1997, he sold for an undisclosed sum all of his papers concerning the Rivonia Trial to gold and diamond magnate Harry Oppenheimer for inclusion in the Brenthurst Library, which Oppenheimer built. The collection included the only complete transcript of the trial. Although there was an initial stipulation that the transcript not be available until after Mandela's death, it was made public shortly after its transfer to the Brenthurst. Yutar's sale of an important historic and public document to a private institution remains another black mark on his life. The collection has now been transferred to the South African National Archives.[47] Yutar died in 2002, aged ninety, with his great victory at Rivonia a permanent stain on his career.[48]

With the very notable exception of Bram Fischer, most of the lawyers for the defense went on to achieve success in law or—in the case of Joel Joffe—in life.

Vernon Berrange, to whom many of the important cross-examinations had been assigned, did not escape government harassment. He continued to practice as an advocate in Johannesburg for several more years, participating in several other important cases involving antiapartheid activists. But he was subsequently banned—his movements and associations severely restricted by government decree.[49] He moved to neighboring Swaziland and died in 1983.[50]

Harold Hanson, who argued the defense case on sentencing, continued his advocacy both in commercial and human rights matters. Bram Fischer retained him as his lawyer when disbarment proceedings were brought against him.[51] Hanson died in 1973.[52]

After the Rivonia Trial, Arthur Chaskalson continued his active representation of oppressed people. He helped establish the Legal Resources Centre, a nonprofit legal organization that continues to fight for human rights throughout South Africa. Chaskalson served as director of the center for fifteen years, from 1978 until 1993. When the new government took over in 1994, Chaskalson served as the first president of the newly establish Constitutional Court. In 2001, he became chief justice of South Africa.[53] He retired in 2005 but continues to be active in human rights work, working with the International Commission of Jurists,[54] which was bluntly criticized by the South African government for alleged attempts to interfere with the justice system in South Africa during the Rivonia Trial. Chaskalson lives in Johannesburg.

George Bizos continued his brilliant career as a civil rights lawyer after Rivonia and is still active today. He was involved in most of the important civil rights cases prior to the end of apartheid, after which he was a leader of a team working with the Truth and Reconciliation Commission, which investigated apartheid-era crimes with the power to grant amnesty. On behalf of many of the families of victims of apartheid-era oppression, Bizos's team opposed applications for amnesty filed by persons who had committed violence against opponents of the old regime. As the leader of the team representing the South African government in the first case before the Constitutional Court, he argued, successfully, that the death penalty was unconstitutional under the newly adopted constitution. He now serves as senior counsel at the Legal Resources Centre's Constitutional Litigation Unit. Most observers of the legal scene in South Africa recognize Bizos as the most important civil rights lawyer active today.[55]

Bob Hepple was not the only person connected to the trial to receive honors from the British crown. Joel Joffe, whose emigration to Australia was postponed by his involvement in the Rivonia trial, remained in South Africa for a short time. He stayed long enough to serve as the attorney in the Little Rivonia Trial later in 1964, at which several of the remaining ANC leaders were tried and convicted. In 1965, he and his family again attempted to emigrate to Australia. Their furniture was sent there and they left the country on an exit permit. However, before they left the country, Joffe's South African passport was withdrawn, making him ineligible to go to Australia.[56] They eventually were able to settle in the United Kingdom, where Joffe fully left the practice of law. The United Kingdom government initially denied Joffe entry. However, Jimmy Kantor, already in the country, persuaded member of Parliament Dick Taverne, QC, to intervene with the immigration authority, and entry was granted.[57] Joffe and some other South African émigrés went into the financial services industry together. They achieved great success in their venture. Joffe's financial success enabled him to retire in 1991 to devote his time fully to charitable causes. He served as chair of the important British charity Oxfam from 1995 to 2001. He was named a commander of the British Empire (CBE) in 1999 and was made a life peer in 2003. He is now the Baron Joffe of Liddington, serving as a cross-bench member of the House of Lords.[58] Joffe is best known in the House of Lords as a strong advocate of physician-assisted suicide.[59]

Although the road was often difficult and painful, there were relatively happy endings for most of the Rivonia defendants and their lawyers. But there was no happiness in the future for Bram Fischer, the leader of the defense at the Rivonia Trial.[60] Fischer faced a personal tragedy within hours of the trial's end. The day after the trial, Fischer and his wife and closest confidant, Molly, were traveling with a young family friend, Liz Lewin, from Johannesburg to Cape Town for some rest. While driving, Fischer swerved to avoid a cow in the road. The car tumbled down a riverbank and perched precariously at the edge. Fischer and Lewin crawled out through a window and then attempted to pull Molly through the window. Before they could free her, the car pitched forward into thirty feet of water. Molly drowned, despite repeated efforts by Bram to save her.

Fischer was devastated by his loss—so much so that he could barely talk about it. The day after her funeral, he and Joel Joffe visited the Robben Island prisoners to talk about a possible appeal. Walter Sisulu asked about Molly and Fischer could only reply, "Molly is all right." The men were later told of her death by a prison guard.

Fischer's tragedy was then compounded by threats to his own freedom. Within weeks, he was detained under the ninety-day law. He was released after three days but was soon arrested again—this time under the Suppression of Communism Act. In an illustration of the incredible paradox that was Bram Fischer, he was granted bail to enable him to go to London to argue a complex patent-rights case for an American company in front of the Privy Council—the highest court of the British Commonwealth. His many friends in exile in London attempted to convince him not to return to South Africa. But he returned not only as a matter of personal honor but to continue his work to reconstruct resistance to the government. Back home, Fischer faced trial on the Suppression of Communism Act charges. His defense team included both Vernon Berrange and Harold Hanson. The state had succeeded in getting a Communist Party colleague and friend of Fischer's, Piet Beyleveld, to testify against Fischer and the other defendants. With the verdict of guilt inevitable, this time Fischer decided to jump bail in order to continue to work underground for the cause to which he had devoted the last years of his life.

He remained at large for 290 days. His attempts at organizing a network of activists were unsuccessful—the government had effectively disrupted the resistance. Many of his most active associates had already left the country. During his time as a fugitive, the Johannesburg Bar Council brought a disbarment proceeding against him—based in large part on his jumping bail. The application was heard and granted by Justice Quartus de Wet on November 2, 1965. Fischer was rearrested and again brought to trial on charges of involvement in plans to overthrow the government. He was defended by George Bizos. Like Nelson Mandela, Fischer addressed the court from the dock on his reasons for seeking to overthrow the apartheid state. Unlike Mandela, he spoke as an ethnic Afrikaner. He stated his fears for the Afrikaner people and of the deep hatred engendered against them among all "non-whites." He wanted at least one Afrikaner to protest actively. He added: "If one day it may help to establish a bridge across which white leaders and the real leaders of the non-whites can meet to settle destinies of all of us by negotiation and not by force of arms, I shall be able to bear with fortitude any sentence which this court may impose upon me."[61]

On May 9, 1966, Fischer, aged fifty-eight, was sentenced to life imprisonment, almost exactly twenty-eight years before Nelson Mandela, who was to lead negotiations very much like those for which Fischer prayed, was inaugurated as president of South Africa. Fischer spent the rest of his life in a South African prison. Suffering from terminal cancer, he was released a few months before his death so that he could spend his last days with his family. His brother's house was designated a South African prison for the purpose of housing Bram Fischer. Fischer—the person most responsible for saving the lives of the Rivonia defendants—was the only one connected with the trial to die in prison.

Nelson Mandela notes: "In many ways, Bram Fischer, the grandson of the prime minister of the Orange River Colony, made the greatest sacrifice of all. No matter what I suffered in my pursuit of freedom, I always took strength from the fact that I was fighting with and for my own people. Bram was a free man who fought against his own people to ensure the freedom of others."[62]

The South African government could rightly proclaim that the Rivonia Trial was a significant success for the regime. The heart of the leadership of the African National Congress, the Communist Party, and their joint enterprise, MK, was in prison—presumably for life. The Rivonia arrests, trial, and sentences, coupled with continued aggressive action by the police and draconian laws, broke the back of antigovernment resistance for a generation. Some important, but second-line, leaders were imprisoned in the Little Rivonia Trial later in 1964.[63] Much of the rest of the leadership fled the country to avoid prosecution or detention under the ninety-day— soon to be 180-day—detention law. Resistance would flounder for more than a decade until the emergence of new and youthful leaders in the mid-1970s, most notably Steve Biko and the Black Consciousness Movement, and various young activists after the 1976 Soweto Uprising.

Shortly after the trial, British ambassador Hugh Stephenson wrote a confidential report on the Rivonia Trial for the Foreign Office. He noted that most of the white South African public, anxious for its own safety, was relieved that the Security Services had protected it from dangerous saboteurs. He noted that the government welcomed this reaction and apparently accepted such an analysis as the whole truth. Stephenson wrote: "By attributing all of their security troubles to the machinations of international Communism, they are able to deny, with apparent conviction, that their own policies bear any responsibility."[64] He observed the existence of a "large and vocal body" of opposition opinion but concluded that even the older politically conscious Africans prefer to accept the spiritual wounds of apartheid rather than risk losing everything through revolutionary action.[65] "I have little doubt that Government claims to have broken underground African opposition are at present justified." But Stephenson added that new, more militant leaders were likely to emerge, and concluded:

> Unless the Government shows an awareness of which it has hitherto given no practical sign, that something more radical than the conversion of reserves into "Bantustans" [black homelands] is needed to satisfy African demands, nothing can prevent Government action and African counteraction from taking a progressively more violent form on both sides. It is too early to say when further subversive action will occur, or what form it will take; but that it will come, I have no doubt.[66]

Stephenson's description of the impact of Rivonia on the revolutionary movement and most of white South Africa was indeed accurate. His prediction of further violence was also on target, although the future—in large measure because of the survival of the Rivonia defendants—turned out less bleak than he forecast.

Furthermore, although the Rivonia Trial at least temporarily gave the South African government some breathing room from militant opposition, its international propaganda efforts surrounding the trial were far less successful. The trial was good publicity only to the extent that much of the Western media gave a grudging nod of respect for the independence of the South African judiciary. But most of the world sympathized with the defendants' motives and the oppression that spurred them to commit sabotage and plan for guerrilla warfare. Justice de Wet may have gotten kudos from the world press, but the ruling powers in Pretoria continued to be castigated at every opportunity.

The failure of the trial to generate support abroad for the South African government removed an incentive for similar trials in the future. There would be very few public trials as long as the Nationalists continued to rule the country. The Little Rivonia Trial and the Delmas Treason trial of the late 1980s[67] were the only notable exceptions. Enemies of the regime were dealt with by long detentions without trial and—as in the case of Steve Biko—by murder.[68]

The publicity generated in the world press by Rivonia actually had another effect—one very different from what the regime expected. Instead of generating strong support for the government as a bulwark against dastardly Communist plots, the already strong opposition to apartheid in the African, Asian, and Communist blocs picked up support in the West. The points made by the defendants in their testimony and especially Nelson Mandela's statement from the dock were widely reported in the Western media. The United States and the United Kingdom were not ready immediately to approve meaningful sanctions against South Africa, but pressure on both governments was building. Rivonia had fully exposed apartheid for the evil it was. Opponents of the South African regime were to refer to that exposure over and over again in various international forums—most importantly the United Nations General Assembly. Perhaps the same pressure would have built had there been no trial or no statements from the leaders of the antiapartheid movement at that trial. But the articulation of the plight of black people in South Africa at the Rivonia Trial accelerated the process.

Would the forces abroad fighting apartheid have achieved an even greater propaganda victory if the defendants had been sentenced to death and ultimately hung? As we've seen, the columnist Dawie suggested in the Afrikaans-language newspaper *Die Burger* that the "agitators" had "really wanted the death penalty for the most important Black accused."[69] There is no doubt that the deaths of Mandela and the others would have been a rallying point for both antigovernment forces within South Africa and world the antiapartheid movement. A death sentence might even have given rise to armed conflict of at least some kind within the country.

But ultimately the life sentences gave an enormous boost to those seeking change in South Africa—a boost unlikely to have occurred if the leaders had been killed. Any armed insurrection would almost certainly have failed in 1964 and in the years that followed. No person active in the antiapartheid movement believes that the opposition was then ready for a shooting war with the modern, entrenched South African military. Operation Mayibuye, even if it had been approved, was at most the pipe dream of a few militant leaders. The operation depended both on the ability of MK to land thousands of guerrilla fighters on South African shores and, ultimately, the intervention of other countries on their side.

Looking back in history, neither seems likely. The deaths of Mandela and the others would certainly have been met with mass demonstrations in South Africa and around the world. But for those demonstrations to lead to the overthrow of the government—with or without a bloody guerrilla war—would be much more difficult. The leaders would have been remembered as martyrs, but such memories are difficult to sustain as impetus for action over the long run. Rather, the continued life of Nelson Mandela and his compatriots gave the antiapartheid forces everywhere a rallying point, a hope for the future that would sustain the opposition for more than twenty-five years.

Most important, the Rivonia defendants—and most particularly Nelson Mandela—were alive to lead the negotiations for a new South Africa and to lead the nation after the changeover. With all due respect to the other Rivonia defendants, Nelson Mandela's continued life and leadership was most responsible not only for the end of apartheid but for the peaceful way in which it ended. Perhaps another leader of Mandela's caliber would have emerged, but such leaders are few.

The scourge of Communism was a major prosecution theme in the trial. Indeed, government analyses of the case—including Percy Yutar's own writings—make defense against Communist takeover the principal purpose of the trial. Neither the Rivonia Trial nor anything else in South Africa contributed to the downfall of the Soviet Union. But the fall of the Soviet Union contributed significantly to the end of apartheid in South

Africa. By 1990, it was no longer important to the United States and the United Kingdom that there be a bulwark against Communist aggression in Southern Africa. F. W. De Klerk, then the president of South Africa, could read that handwriting. Support for his government from the Western powers would diminish or disappear. His only course was some sort of peace with the antiapartheid forces on the best terms he could get. Mandela was in prison but alive and still very much the face of the antiapartheid movement. Furthermore, with the threat of Communism gone, his taint of association with the Communists was not nearly as significant as it had been. Mandela became the ideal negotiating partner for De Klerk.

But Nelson Mandela was far more than the most opportune person to represent the oppressed black people of South Africa. He proved to be a leader of extraordinary ability and foresight. It is difficult to imagine that there would have been anyone else with his combination of diplomacy, strength of conviction and interpersonal skills. He dealt effectively with the fears of his fellow ANC members that he was selling out to the whites. Doing so was no easy task—many of his earliest meetings took place while he was still in prison and unable to communicate fully with other ANC leaders. He took into negotiation a clear and unwavering bottom line: any new political picture in South Africa would require one person, one vote, not some proportional representation scheme that would leave the whites still effectively in power. But he was able to compromise on matters that were less important to black South Africa but enormously important to his white counterparts, including maintaining the existing civil service and judiciary. Only a person of Mandela's diplomatic and interpersonal gifts could have carried off such give and take. He was not alone in the negotiations by any means, but he was critical to them.[70]

Skill in negotiating a peaceful end to apartheid was not the only contribution that this extraordinary man made to the country that had treated him so harshly. As president of the Republic, he healed the wide racial divisions to an extent that few had thought possible. He worked not only to assure that the black people of the nation would achieve their political rights, but also—as much as was possible given the history of the country—to convince the white population that they could maintain much of the way of life to which they had become accustomed. He saw South Africa as a "rainbow nation" and strove to make that image a reality. He set the tone in his inaugural address, telling the nation: "We enter into a covenant that we shall build a society in which all South Africans, both black and white, will be able to walk tall, without any fear in their hearts, assured of their inalienable right to human dignity—a rainbow nation at peace with itself and the world."[71] His goal has not yet been achieved, but most agree that South Africa today has better race relations than most thought possible before the apartheid regime ended.

It is difficult to imagine a scenario for South Africa had Mandela not been alive to shepherd the negotiations and lead the country in the first years of true democracy. Bloody warfare was always a possibility; indeed, full-scale warfare was almost a reality in the early 1990s. Mandela's ability to calm the black population reeling from government involvement in clashes between the Inkatha Freedom Party and the ANC was crucial in stemming the violence. Many credit Mandela for keeping the country from racial warfare in the wake of the April 1993 assassination of the charismatic black Communist Party general secretary Chris Hani—shortly after stalled negotiations for a new constitution had restarted. Hani was killed by a white man, a Polish immigrant. A white neighbor of Hani's had identified the killer's car. As the threat of violence rose, Mandela spoke on television, appealing to blacks and whites to close ranks. "A white man, full of prejudice and hate, came to our country and committed a deed so foul that our whole nation now teeters on the brink of disaster. But a white woman, of Afrikaner origin, risked her life so that we may know, and bring to justice, the assassin." The populace calmed and the negotiations were accelerated rather than aborted.[72]

In the absence of a Mandela—even an imprisoned Mandela—it was far more likely that somewhere down the line, a leadership would have emerged that would have pushed for a guerrilla war. Who would win such a war is less significant than the certainty that it would have been bloody. Moreover, prior to the fall of the Soviet Union, support from the Communist bloc for such a war was not out of the question. A confrontation between East and West on the South African veld was not inconceivable. No one knows how things would have worked out, and any scenario is uselessly speculative. But one can say with assurance that it is unlikely that anything in South African and world history would have come out better without Nelson Mandela.

Mandela's importance on the world scene transcends what he was able to accomplish in his own country. He is the embodiment of courage and persistence in the face of adversity. Twenty years later, on February 7, 2010, the *New York Times* printed the reactions of seven other people who, like Mandela, had served long prison terms at the hands of repressive regimes around the world.[73] Nelson Mandela, his imprisonment, survival, and release, greatly bolstered all of them in their struggles for freedom in their own countries. Nguyen Dan Que, a doctor in Vietnam imprisoned three times, told the *Times*, "Mr. Mandela's struggle was to me—as it is to activists through the world—a shining, vivid example of the courage it takes to fight for liberty." The story of Nelson Mandela, the international symbol of the fight against governmental repression, will boost the spirits of those fighting for freedom for centuries to come.

But the legacy of Rivonia lies not simply in the saving of a leader who would bring a peaceful conclusion to a potentially violent situation. In addition, the trial demonstrated some good and some very bad features of South African law in the early 1960s—features that were taken into account in the promulgation of South Africa's new constitution in the mid-1990s. The good feature was the country's history of an independent judiciary. Justice de Wet, for all of his faults and racial bigotry, acted independently, and that independent action may have saved the lives of the Rivonia defendants. The new constitution carefully maintains that independence with a judicial selection process that, while far from perfect, is as good as any in the world. An independent Judicial Service Commission, composed of judges, lawyers, and laypersons, is primarily responsible for the selection of judges. The process, at least in theory, is as far removed from politics and favoritism as in any democracy.

What was wrong in Rivonia was that the laws on which the prosecution was based—principally the Sabotage and Suppression of Communism Acts—deprived individuals of basic human rights. Compounding the horror was the ninety-day-detention law that made a mockery of the rule of law both before Rivonia and for many years thereafter. Furthermore, the laws that led to the defendants' antigovernment activities—all of the complex body of law that created and maintained apartheid—violated most of the world's values. A primary function of the new South African constitution is to prevent the adoption of laws that would violate human rights—both in the field of criminal law and in racial justice. For the first time in its history, South Africa has a Constitutional Court with the power to declare an act of Parliament contrary to the constitution and therefore void. The laws that defendants were charged with violating and the laws that they were protesting could not have survived under South Africa's new constitution and the scrutiny of its new Constitutional Court.[74]

The Rivonia Trial and its aftermath—the eventual release of the defendants to take up leadership roles in the nation—also set the scene for another important aspect of South Africa's postapartheid era. Instead of prosecutions of those involved in apartheid era crimes—including actors on both sides—a Truth and Reconciliation Commission was formed. The purpose of the commission was to expose what had happened during that time, most particularly the violence and oppression of government-sponsored activities. Rather than severe punishment, there was disclosure and often amnesty. For the most part, people involved in the evils of those days were permitted to go on with their lives. Many were unhappy with the clemency, but most in South Africa had had their fill of recriminations and punishments such as those dished out at the Rivonia Trial.[75]

Finally, what, if anything, does the Rivonia Trial's outcome mean for the debate on the wisdom of capital punishment? Execution is final and irrevocable. The convicted person is still dead—even if the nation or the world changes its mind with regard to his or her guilt or villainy. There is no doubt that Mandela and most of his codefendants were guilty of crimes against the state—crimes that would have been punishable in any democracy, let alone in the oppressive South African regime. But had Mandela and his codefendants been hanged, no change in the political scene could have brought them back to help guide the nation in its transition to democracy. South Africa's Constitutional Court, in its very first case, *State v. Makwanyane*,[76] unanimously held that the constitution prohibited capital punishment. The government of Nelson Mandela supported the appeal of the condemned defendants for the abolition of the death penalty. Two of the Rivonia defense lawyers were very much involved in the court's decision. George Bizos argued the government's case;[77] Arthur Chaskalson, the court's president, wrote the leading opinion on behalf of the court. Chaskalson noted in his opinion: "The rights of life and dignity are the most important of all human rights."[78] Those rights were the basic ones for which the Rivonia defendants were fighting and for which they were willing to give their lives if necessary. If the government had killed these men, it would have struck a blow against life and dignity from which South Africa, and the world, might not have recovered.

Acknowledgments

I OWE SPECIAL thanks to four of the participants in the Rivonia trial for their time and encouragement. Denis Goldberg submitted to two lengthy interviews and entertained me at his Houk Bay, South Africa, home. George Bizos and Arthur Chaskalson graciously gave me time to talk about the case and their roles in it. I am especially grateful to Joel Joffe for long conversations, for his helpful reading of a draft of the manuscript, and for his useful comments. I also thank Joel and his wife, Vanetta, for their hospitality at Liddington Manor.

My research into documents, contemporary newspaper reports, and photographs was greatly facilitated by librarians and others at the University of the Witwatersrand (especially Michele Pickover) in Johannesburg, the Brenthurst Library (especially Diana Madden) in Johannesburg, the National Archives of South Africa in Pretoria and Cape Town, the British National Archives in London, and the Lyndon Baines Johnson Library in Austin, Texas. I also want to give special thanks to the people at the Liliesleaf Farm Museum in Rivonia—particularly Nicholas Wolpe and Adrienne van den Heever—for their help in finding documents, for loaning me copies of transcripts of interviews with participants, and for providing photographs used in this book. Nick Sexton, Donna Nixon, and Jim Sherwood of the University of North Carolina Law Library provided valuable research assistance.

Conversations with others who have written about some of the same events, including Stephen Clingman and Mark Gevisser, were extremely useful. The superb historian William Leuchtenburg gave me encouragement and advice throughout the project.

My warm thanks go to Faith and Thom Mandiwana for hosting me on several occasions while I was conducting research for the book. Their hospitality, nourishment, and transportation were greatly appreciated. Their continuing friendship is priceless.

Although not directly involved in the research for this book, many people have been responsible for my many visits to South Africa and for my love for that country and its people. I owe much gratitude to everyone associated with the Black Lawyers Association of South Africa—with special thanks to the late Godfrey Pitje, Mojanku Gumbi, Justice Moloto, Dikgang Moseneke, Sibusiso Gamedi, and so many others. I also acknowledge the companionship of the many American lawyers who have given selfishly of their time to teach trial advocacy in South Africa, especially Jim Ferguson, Geraldine Sumter, and Rudy Pierce.

I imposed on the time of several people who provided valuable feedback on early versions of this book as well as encouragement: Gene Nichol, Rosemary Waldorf, and Tom Wolf. Mike Tigar can be credited and blamed for encouraging this project in the first place and for his helpful reading and comments on drafts. My 2010–11 research assistant, the ever-helpful Meghan Jones, did important editing work on the later drafts of the book. Earlier research assistants Christina Simpson, Kimberly Velez, and Joanna Holguin, also provided valuable assistance. I am also indebted to Alida Nortier, at the time a law student at Stellenbosch University, for finding and translating articles from the Afrikaans language newspaper *Die Burger*.

Many thanks to my agent, Valerie Borchardt, for her work, and for her encouragement of this project. My editor, Tim Bent, did an outstanding job. Any legalese that remains in the book is my fault, not his.

I am always grateful to the University of North Carolina School of Law and all the people associated with it for their support in all my endeavors. Special thanks go to Dean Jack Boger for his encouragement of this project.

And finally, and most important, I thank members of my family for their help and support. My son Jonathan, who continues to work to keep North Carolinians from the death penalty, is an inspiration to me. My son Dan, who also inspires me by his work to ease the pain of poverty in this country, provided a helpful reading of an early draft. But most especially, I thank my wife, Margie, for her critical readings of many drafts of the book, for her constant encouragement and good humor, and for her companionship both on trips abroad and at home.

Notes

INTRODUCTION

1. There was an earlier and shorter Anglo-Boer War fought in 1880–81 over the British annexation of the Boer's Transvaal Republic, led by Paul Kruger, into the larger British colony. The Boers inflicted reverses on the British army causing Britain to reverse the annexation and to grant a degree of independence to the Transvaal. See Pakenham, *The Boer War*, 11.
2. Sparks, *The Mind of South Africa*, 128, citing A. C. Martin, *The Concentration Camps* 1900–1902 (Cape Town: Timmins, 1957), 31.
3. The population estimates are from the South African Bureau of Statistics, reprinted in Austin, *Britain and South Africa*, 3.

CHAPTER 1

1. In addition to the record of the Rivonia Trial, the background material on the purchase and use of the Liliesleaf Farm property comes from a number of sources including Hilda Bernstein, *The World That Was Ours*; Rusty Bernstein, *Memory Against Forgetting*; Clingman, *Bram Fischer*; Frankel, *Rivonia's Children*; Joffe, *The State vs. Nelson Mandela*; Kathrada, *Memoirs*; Mandela, *Long Walk to Freedom*; Meredith, *Fischer's Choice*; Meredith, *Nelson Mandela: A Biography*; Sampson, *Mandela*; Wolpe, *The Long Way Home*. Frankel's book *Rivonia's Children* was especially useful in providing information with regard to Liliesleaf Farm, as well as the events immediately preceding and during the raid; *Rivonia's Children* both collects material from other sources and provides original material based on interviews.
2. Frankel, *Rivonia's Children*, 85.
3. Strydom, *Rivonia Unmasked*, 21.
4. Mandela, *Long Walk to Freedom*, 243.

5. This name is a reference to the Scarlet Pimpernel, a fictional character—an elusive hero using many disguises—that was widely popular during the first half of the twentieth century. His first appearance was in the play and novel by Baroness Emmuska Orczy, *The Scarlet Pimpernel*, first published in 1905. The work was set during the Reign of Terror following the start of the French Revolution.

6. De Villiers, *Rivonia: Operation Mayibuye*, 6.

7. Ibid.

8. Frankel, *Rivonia's Children*, 24.

9. Bizos, *Odyssey to Freedom*, 212.

10. Meredith, *Fischer's Choice*, 64.

11. Letter from Ambassador Sir Hugh Stephenson to Sir Geoffrey Harrison at Foreign Office, December 30, 1963, reporting on visit of John Arnold, QC and Tom Kellock, UK National Archives, FO371/177122, JSA 1641/1.

12. Frankel, *Rivonia's Children*, 28.

13. Ibid., 27–28.

14. The accounts of the raid on Liliesleaf Farm and the events immediately leading up to it from the police perspective are taken from the two books written on the Rivonia Trial by persons sympathetic to the prosecution. De Villiers, *Rivonia: Operation Mayibuye*, 1–3; Strydom, *Rivonia Unmasked*, 14–25. Some of the background information was also included in the testimony of various police officers at the Rivonia Trial.

15. The accounts of the raid from the perspective of those arrested are taken from a number of sources, including those set out in note 1. The details of the documents found in the raid come from a review of the documents themselves in the Rivonia Trial record.

16. Author's interview with Denis Goldberg, October 7, 2008.

17. Frankel, *Rivonia's Children*, 32.

18. Strydom, *Rivonia Unmasked*, 30.

19. Frankel, *Rivonia's Children*, 34.

20. Kathrada, *Memoirs*, 142.

21. Ibid., 7–10.

22. Ibid., 24.

23. Hilda Bernstein, 120, 133.

24. Ibid., 140.

25. Author's interview with Denis Goldberg, October 2008.

26. Hilda Bernstein, *The World That Was Ours*, 155–57.

27. Frankel, *Rivonia's Children*, 124.

28. The account of the Wolpe and Goldreich escape is taken from several sources, including those set out in note 1, with particular reliance on Wolpe, *The Long Way Home*, 122–84.

29. Frankel, *Rivonia's Children*, 129.

30. Letter from Lord Dunrossil (John William Morrison), official observer at the Rivonia Trial, September 27, 1963, UK National Archives, FO 371/167541: JSA 1641/28.

31. Interview with Nicholas Wolpe, October 5, 2009.

32. "Vorster: They Were Two of Our Biggest Fishes," *Star* (Johannesburg), August 28, 1963.

CHAPTER 2

1. Joffe, *The State vs. Nelson Mandela*, 10.

2. Ibid., 11.

3. Ibid., 12.

4. Rusty Bernstein, *Memory Against Forgetting*, 285.

5. The account of the recruitment of Joel Joffe as the attorney and the selection of Bram Fischer, George Bizos, and Arthur Chaskalson is taken from Joffe's memoir, *The State vs. Nelson Mandela*, 10–12. Others remember the formation of the defense team differently. George Bizos writes in *Odyssey to Freedom* that Hilda Bernstein and others first contacted Bram Fischer, who called Joffe and Bizos to a meeting in Arthur Chaskalson's office (205). Stephen Clingman writes in *Bram Fischer* that Fischer and Chaskalson had already decided to enter the case by the time Hilda Bernstein approached Joffe. Clingman states that Hilda Bernstein was asked to approach Joffe, who in turn "chose" Fischer as lead counsel (302).

6. Meredith, *Fischer's Choice*, 36.

7. Bizos, *Odyssey to Freedom*, 243.

8. Hilda Bernstein, *The World That Was Ours*, 183.

9. Meredith, *Fischer's Choice*, 35.

10. Mandela, *Long Walk to Freedom*, 340.

11. Meredith, *Fischer's Choice*, 35.

12. Joffe, *The State vs. Nelson Mandela*, 17.

13. Ibid.

14. Bizos, *Odyssey to Freedom*, 205.

15. Joffe, *The State vs. Nelson Mandela*, 67.

16. Bizos, *Odyssey to Freedom*, 212.

17. No such statement appears in the records of the UN debates, although the entire South African justice system was condemned by many of the African speakers. See chapter 11.

18. Collins, *Faith Under Fire*, 226.

19. "The Yutar Legend," *Sunday Chronicle* (Johannesburg), August 29, 1965.

20. De Villiers, *Rivonia: Operation Mayibuye*, biographical appendix.

21. *Sunday Chronicle* (Johannesburg), August 29, 1965.

22. De Villiers, *Rivonia: Operation Mayibuye*, biographical appendix.

23. Frankel, *Rivonia's Children*, 184.

24. Rebecca Weiner, "The Virtual Jewish History Tour: South Africa," *Jewish Virtual Library*, http://www.jewishvirtuallibrary.org/jsource/vjw/South_Africa.html. The Jewish population of South Africa is now closer to 75,000.

25. *New York Times*, obituary, July 21, 2002.

26. Memorandum by Minford, May 12, 1964, UK National Archives, FO 371/177122, JSA 1641/35, 3.

27. Sampson, *Mandela*, 81.

28. Kathrada, *Memoirs*, 140.

29. Memorandum by Minford, 3.

30. O'Malley, *Shades of Difference*, 138.

31. The stories come from interviews by the author with George Bizos, February 9, 2007, and Arthur Chaskalson, February 16, 2007.

CHAPTER 3

1. Joffe, *The State vs. Nelson Mandela*, 12–13.

2. "Rivonia Documents May Lead to Arrest," *Rand Daily Mail*, July 16, 1963.

3. "More Arrests Expected after House Raid on Rand," *Die Burger*, July 16, 1963.

4. "Vorster on 'Wealth' of Clues Found in Rivonia Raid Justifies 90-Day Law," *Star* (Johannesburg), July 16, 1963.

5. "11 Accused in South Africa of Planning Revolt," *New York Times*, October 10, 1963.

6. UK National Archives, FO 371/177122, JSA 1641.

7. Statement by United States Ambassador Adlai Stevenson to the United Nations Security Council, August 2, 1963, available online, www.anc.org.za/show.php?id=4993.

8. United Nations Security Council debate, 1054th meeting, August 6, 1963.

9. Quoted in Gonze, Houser, and Sturges, *South African Crisis and United States Policy*, 13.

10. United Nations Security Council Resolution 134, April 1, 1960, available online, http://daccess-dds-ny.un.org/doc/RESOLUTION/GEN/NR0/157/23/IMG/NR015723.pdf?OpenElement.

11. United Nations Security Council Resolution 181, August 7, 1963, available online, http://daccess-dds-ny.un.org/doc/RESOLUTION/GEN/NR0/200/54/IMG/NR020054.pdf?OpenElement.

12. Circular Telegram from the Department of State to Certain Diplomatic Posts, Diplomatic Posts, July 19, 1963, *Foreign Relations of the United States*, 1961–63, vol. 21, *Africa*, doc. 317.

13. See, e.g., Memorandum from the Joint Chiefs of Staff to Secretary of Defense McNamara, April 13, 1964, *Foreign Relations of the United States* 1964–68, vol. 24, *Africa*, doc. 583.

14. Ibid.

15. United Nations General Assembly, 18th session, 1238th plenary meeting, October 11, 1963, remarks of Mr. Thomas on behalf of the United Kingdom, no. 93.

16. *New York Times*, October 13, 1963.

17. Ibid.

18. Bizos, *Odyssey to Freedom*, 211–12.

19. Austin, *Britain and South Africa*, 37–38.

20. Ibid. 42.

21. Hyam and Henshaw, *The Lion and the Springbok*, 276.

22. See ibid., chap. 12.

23. Ibid., 318. Controversy over sports competition between Great Britain and apartheid South Africa reached a boiling point in 1969 and 1970 with the tour of Britain by the South African rugby Springboks and the cancellation of the South African cricket team's tour of England. ibid., 325–27.

24. Ibid., chap. 13.

25. Ibid., 269–70 See also Arianna Lissoni, "The Anti-Apartheid Movement, Britain and South Africa: Anti-Apartheid Protest vs. Real Politik" (PhD diss., University of London, 2000).

26. Hyam and Henshaw, *The Lion and the Springbok*, chap. 13.

27. Sampson, *Mandela*, 171.

28. Austin, *Britain and South Africa*, 127.

29. Gonze, Houser, and Sturges, *South African Crisis and United States Policy*, 47.

30. *FRUS* 1964–68, vol. 24, doc. 583.

31. See, e.g., Hilgard Muller, "The Official Case for Apartheid," *New York Times*, June 7, 1964.

32. UK National Archives, FO 371/167541, JSA 1641/34.

33. Letter from Lord Dunrossil to Foreign Office, October 19, 1963, UK National Archives, FO 371/167541, JSA 1641/28.

34. Ibid.

CHAPTER 4

1. Joffe, *The State vs. Nelson Mandela*, 14.

2. The Sabotage Act, Act 37 of 1963.

3. Joffe, *The State vs. Nelson Mandela*, 16.

4. Ibid.

5. Author's interview with Joel Joffe, February 4, 2007.

6. Joffe, *The State vs. Nelson Mandela*, 14–15.

7. Ibid.

8. Author's interview with Denis Goldberg, October 7, 2008.

9. Joffe, *The State vs. Nelson Mandela*, 21.

10. Frankel, *Rivonia's Children*, 56.

11. The account of the lawyers' meeting with Attorney General Rein is taken from Joffe, *The State vs. Nelson Mandela*, 22–23; and Bizos, *Odyssey to Freedom*, 205–6; as well as the author's interviews with both lawyers.

12. The account of the lawyers' first meeting with their clients is taken from Joffe, 23–32; Bizos, *Odyssey to Freedom*, 206–7; Kathrada, *Memoirs*, 166–67; Mandela, *Long Walk to Freedom*, 305–6; Meredith, *Fischer's Choice*, 82–83; and author's interviews with Joel Joffe, George Bizos, Arthur Chaskalson, and Denis Goldberg.

13. Joffe, *The State vs. Nelson Mandela*, 30.

14. Bizos, *Odyssey to Freedom*, 206.

15. Kathrada, *Memoirs*, 166.

16. Mandela, *Long Walk to Freedom*, 306.

17. Ibid.

18. Author's interview with George Bizos, February 9, 2007.

19. Joffe, *The State vs. Nelson Mandela*, 30.

20. Ibid. 30–31.

21. The account of the visit to Women's Prison is from Joffe, *The State vs. Nelson Mandela*, 31–32; Bizos, *Odyssey to Freedom*, 207; and Meredith, *Fischer's Choice*, 83.

CHAPTER 5

1. Frankel, *Rivonia's Children*, 183.

2. Meredith, *Fischer's Choice*, 83.

3. Mandela, *Long Walk to Freedom*, 307.

4. Bizos, *Odyssey to Freedom*, 209.

5. Hilda Bernstein, *The World That Was Ours*, 188–89.

6. Joffe, *The State vs. Nelson Mandela*, 35.

7. Ibid.

8. Ibid., 37.

CHAPTER 6

1. The first indictment is available online as part of the Rivonia Trial Collection, Library of the University of the Witwatersrand, www.historicalpapers.wits.ac.za/?inventory/U/Collections&;c=AD1844/I/8062, Aa3.

2. The account of preparations to attack the first indictment and the request for particulars is from Joffe, *The State vs. Nelson Mandela*, 41–44; Bizos, *Odyssey to Freedom*, 211–15; Meredith, *Fischer Choice*, 85; Clingman, *Bram Fischer*, 307; and author's interviews with Joel Joffe, George Bizos, and Arthur Chaskalson.

3. Joffe, *The State vs. Nelson Mandela*, 46.

4. Ibid., 43.

5. Clingman, *Bram Fischer*, 306.

6. Joffe, *The State vs. Nelson Mandela*, 59. Accounts of this incident also appear in other sources including Clingman, *Bram Fischer*, 306–7; Mandela, *Long Walk to Freedom*, 313; Meredith, *Nelson Mandela*, 257; and Frankel, *Rivonia's Children*, 198–99. The accounts vary slightly, although the essence of the story is the same.

7. The account of this hearing is taken from several sources, primarily Joffe, *The State vs. Nelson Mandela*, 44–57; and Bizos, *Odyssey to Freedom*, 215–18. See also Clingman, *Bram Fischer*, 308–9; Frankel, *Rivonia's Children*, 200–203. Some, but not all of the arguments of counsel and the remarks of the judge are contained in the record of the hearing, Rivonia Trial Collection, A1.6.

8. Joffe, *The State vs. Nelson Mandela*, 45.

9. Meredith, *Fischer's Choice*, 85–86.

10. Joffe, *The State vs. Nelson Mandela*, 46.

11. Ibid., 47.

12. Ibid., 47–48.

13. Ibid., 48; Bizos, *Odyssey to Freedom*, 216.

14. Rivonia Trial Collection, A1.6, 90.

15. Joffe, *The State vs. Nelson Mandela*, 48, 216–17.

16. Rivonia Trial Collection, 91.

17. Ibid., 92.

18. Ibid., 93.

19. Joffe, *The State vs. Nelson Mandela*, 51.

20. Rivonia Trial Collection, A1.6, 95–96.

21. Ibid., 121.

22. Rivonia Trial Collection, A1.68, 3.

23. Joffe, *The State vs. Nelson Mandela*, 53.

24. Ibid., 54–57.

25. Ibid., 61.

26. Rivonia Trial Collection, A2.1.

27. Joffe, *The State vs. Nelson Mandela*, 63.

28. Ibid., 65.

29. Ibid., 66.

30. Author's interview with Joel Joffe, August 11, 2010.

31. Joffe, *The State vs. Nelson Mandela*, 64–65.

32. Bizos, *Odyssey to Freedom*, 220.

33. Meredith, *Bram Fischer*, 89.

34. Joffe, *The State vs. Nelson Mandela*, 68.

35. Author's interview with Denis Goldberg, October 7, 2008.

36. See, for example, Press Conference Statements by John Arnold, Q.C., December 16, 1963, UK National Archives, FO 371/167541, JSA 1641/64, 3; and Memorandum from Consul-General Leslie Minford, UK National Archives, FO 371/177122, May 12, 1964, JSA 1641/35, 8.

CHAPTER 7

1. Joffe, *The State vs. Nelson Mandela*, 71–72; Bizos, *Odyssey to Freedom*, 221.
2. Joffe, *The State vs. Nelson Mandela*, 72–73; Bizos, *Odyssey to Freedom*, 221–22; Meredith, *Fischer's Choice*, 92.
3. Joffe is of the same opinion: *The State vs. Nelson Mandela*, 73.
4. Percy Yutar's opening address can be found in the Rivonia Trial Collection, Library of the University of the Witwatersrand, www.historicalpapers.wits.ac.za/?inventory/U/Collections&;c=AD1844/I/8062, A4.
5. Author's interview with Joel Joffe, August 11, 2010.
6. Bizos, *Odyssey to Freedom*, 228.
7. Clingman, *Bram Fischer*, 313.
8. Joffe, *The State vs. Nelson Mandela*, 77–78.
9. The documents introduced at the trial are available in the Record of the Rivonia Trial, *Criminal Court Case No. 253/1963 called The State versus N Mandela and Others, heard in the Supreme Court of South Africa (Transvaal Provincial Division)*, South African National Archives. The records were formerly housed at the Brenthurst Library in Johannesburg and reviewed by the author at that location.
10. See, for example, Federal Rules of Evidence, Rule 901, available at www.utd.uscourts.gov/forms/evid2009.pdf.
11. For example, see Florence Ntonmela statements from witnesses, reading of exhibits, Rivonia Trial Collection, A8.2.
12. State's Concluding Address, A Factual Analysis of the Documentary Exhibits Handed In, And of the Oral Testimony Given, By the State Witnesses, Rivonia Trial Collection, A30a1.
13. Rivonia Trial Collection, Aa5 (Exhibit R71).
14. Record of the Rivonia Trial, South African National Archives, R46.
15. Judgment, Rivonia Trial Collection, Library of the University of Witwatersrand, http://web.wits.ac.za/Library/HistoricalPapers.htm, A32.3, 25.
16. Record of the Rivonia Trial, South African National Archives, R54.
17. Ibid., R16, R17.
18. Ibid., R18–R19, R24.
19. Ibid., R25.
20. Record of the Rivonia Trial, South African National Archives, Exhibit WW.
21. Second Indictment: Indictment, Rivonia Trial Collection, A2.1. See also Annexure A to the Second Indictment (labeled on website as "Second Indictment: Annexure B: Particulars of commission of acts"), Rivonia Trial Collection, A2.2.
22. Judgment, Rivonia Trial Collection, A32.3, 31–32.
23. Clingman, *Bram Fischer*, 304.
24. Evidence: J. Mashipane, Rivonia Trial Collection, A11.1, 6–8.
25. Ibid., 35.
26. Joffe, *The State vs. Nelson Mandela*, 78.

27. Evidence by Harry Mbambani et al., Rivonia Trial Collection, A7.2; Evidence by Suliman Essop et al., A7.1, D21–D25.

28. Part II: The persons who were parties to the conspiracy and the implementation thereof, Rivonia Trial Collection, A30a2, 179–80.

29. Joffe, *The State vs. Nelson Mandela*, 135.

30. Ibid., 135–37.

31. Ibid., 136–37.

32. Ibid., 86.

33. The surviving transcript does not reflect Yutar's request to call Mhtembu "Mr. Y." Justice de Wet refers to him by that designation in the judgment. Judgment, Rivonia Trial Collection, A32.3, 51.

34. Evidence by Harry Mbambani et al., Record of State witness, Bruno Mtolo, Rivonia Trial Collection, A7.2, E24.

35. Bruno Mtolo's testimony can be found in the Rivonia Trial Collection, A15 and A16.

36. Author's interview with Joel Joffe, August 11, 2010.

37. Evidence: J Du Preez, Rivonia Trial Collection, A13.5, 22–23.

38. Ibid., 36–38.

39. Ibid., 13–14.

40. Evidence: DJ Card, Rivonia Trial Collection, Library of the University of Witwatersrand, http://web.wits.ac.za/Library/HistoricalPapers.htm. A12.3.

41. Ibid., 19.

42. Ibid., 20.

43. For example, Ibid., 13.

44. Joffe, *The State vs. Nelson Mandela*, 140–42.

45. Ibid., 140.

46. Ibid., 142.

47. Ibid., 139.

48. Ibid., *The State vs. Nelson Mandela*, 139–42; Bizos, *Odyssey to Freedom*, 241–42.

49. Joffe, *The State vs. Nelson Mandela*, 213–15.

50. Goldberg Testimony, Record of the Rivonia Trial, South African National Archives.

51. The account of Davids' testimony is from Joffe, *The State vs. Nelson Mandela*, 111–20.

52. Goldberg Testimony, Record of the Rivonia Trial, South African National Archives.

53. Judgment, Rivonia Trial Collection, A32.3, 43.

54. Ibid., 44. See further discussion in chapter 10.

55. Author's interview with Denis Goldberg, October 7, 2008.

56. See Rivonia Trial Collection, A17.1–A17.11.

57. IE Makda testimony can be found in the Rivonia Trial Collection, A17.1, 18–19.

58. Joffe, *The State vs. Nelson Mandela*, 144.

59. Judgment, Rivonia Trial Collection, A32.3, 12. See further discussion in chapter 14.
60. Ibid., 12.
61. Ibid., 11–13.

CHAPTER 8

1. Joffe, *The State vs. Nelson Mandela*, 148.
2. Clingman, *Bram Fischer*, 314.
3. Mandela, *Long Walk to Freedom*, 268–90.
4. The Defense Opening Address and Nelson Mandela's Statement can be found in the Rivonia Trial Collection, Library of the University of the Witwatersrand, www.historicalpapers.wits.ac.za/?inventory/U/Collections&;c=AD1844/I/8062, A19.
5. Joffe, *The State vs. Nelson Mandela*, 157.
6. Sources vary as to the length of the speech. Joffe remembers it as five hours long (*The State vs. Nelson Mandela*, 160), as does Kathrada (*Memoirs*, 177). Mandela remembers it as lasting "over" four hours (*Long Walk to Freedom*, 322). His biographers (Meredith, *Nelson Mandela*, 268; Sampson, *Mandela*, 192) put the time as four hours.
7. Bizos, *Odyssey to Freedom*, 243; Sampson, *Mandela*, 191.
8. Author's interview with Denis Goldberg, October 8, 2009.
9. Joffe, *The State vs. Nelson Mandela*, 160; Meredith, *Nelson Mandela*, 268.

CHAPTER 9

1. "11 Accused in South Africa of Planning Revolt," *New York Times*, October 10, 1963.
2. Walter Sisulu's Evidence, Rivonia Trial Collection, Library of the University of the Witwatersrand, www.historicalpapers.wits.ac.za/?inventory/U/Collections&;c=AD1844/I/8062, A20.
3. Bizos, *Odyssey to Freedom*, 249.
4. Ibid.
5. Joffe, *The State vs. Nelson Mandela*, 186–87, See also Ahmed Kathrada's Evidence on resuming (copy), A24.2, 131–34.
6. Joffe, *The State vs. Nelson Mandela*, 180.
7. Clingman, *Bram Fischer*, 317.
8. Bizos, *Odyssey to Freedom*, 254.
9. Joffe, *The State vs. Nelson Mandela*, 180.
10. Second Indictment: Indictment, Rivonia Trial Collection, Library of the University of Witwatersrand, http://web.wits.ac.za/Library/HistoricalPapers.htm, 1.
11. Joffe, *The State vs. Nelson Mandela*, 181.

12. Ibid., 218–19.
13. Ahmed Kathrada's testimony can be found in the Rivonia Trial Collection, A24.1, 24.2.
14. Esop Amod Suliman's evidence, Rivonia Trial Collection, A6.4, C3–C4.
15. Joffe, *The State vs. Nelson Mandela*, 190.
16. Raymond Mhlaba's testimony can be found in the Rivonia Trial Collection, A25.1.
17. Joffe, *The State vs. Nelson Mandela*, 194–95.
18. Lionel Bernstein's testimony can be found in the Rivonia Trial Collection, A26.1, 26.2.
19. Govan Mbeki's testimony can be found in Rivonia Trial Collection, A28.1.
20. Joffe, *The State vs. Nelson Mandela*, 30–31; author's interview with Denis Goldberg, October 7, 2008.
21. Joffe, *The State vs. Nelson Mandela*, 221.
22. Ibid., 219.
23. Ibid., 220.
24. Goldberg Testimony, Record of the Rivonia Trial, *Criminal Court Case No. 253/1963 called The State versus N Mandela and Others, heard in the Supreme Court of South Africa (Transvaal Provincial Division)*, South African National Archives, 50.
25. Joffe, *The State vs. Nelson Mandela*, 220.
26. Ibid., 222–24.

CHAPTER 10

1. Joffe, *The State vs. Nelson Mandela*, 229–30. The bound volumes of Percy Yutar's closing appear in Record of the Rivonia Trial, *Criminal Court Case No. 253/1963 called The State versus N Mandela and Others, heard in the Supreme Court of South Africa (Transvaal Provincial Division)*, the records of the South African National Archives, and the Rivonia Trial Collection, Library of the University of the Witwatersrand, www.historicalpapers.wits.ac.za/?inventory/U/Collections&;c=AD1844/I/8062, A30a1, and A30a2. However, the oral presentations by Yutar and defense counsel are not recorded in those places. The references in this chapter are taken from Joffe, *The State vs. Nelson Mandela*, and Bizos, *Odyssey to Freedom*.
2. Joffe, *The State vs. Nelson Mandela*, 230.
3. Ibid.; Bizos, *Odyssey to Freedom*, 269.
4. Joffe, 236; Bizos, *Odyssey to Freedom*, 269.
5. Joffe, *The State vs. Nelson Mandela*, 231–32.
6. Joffe, *The State vs. Nelson Mandela*, 234–36; Bizos, *Odyssey to Freedom*, 270–71.
7. Joffe, *The State vs. Nelson Mandela*, 236; Bizos, *Odyssey to Freedom*, 270–71.
8. *Star* (Johannesburg), May 25, 1964.

9. *Pretoria News*, May 25, 1964.

10. Joffe, *The State vs. Nelson Mandela*, 232–33.

11. Joffe, *The State vs. Nelson Mandela*, 237; Bizos, *Odyssey to Freedom*, 271–72.

12. Joffe, *The State vs. Nelson Mandela*, 239; Bizos, *Odyssey to Freedom*, 272–73.

13. Bizos, *Odyssey to Freedom*, 273.

14. Joffe, *The State vs. Nelson Mandela*, 240; Bizos, *Odyssey to Freedom*, 273.

15. Joffe, *The State vs. Nelson Mandela*, 240.

16. Ibid., 241.

17. Ibid.

18. Ibid., 242.

19. Ibid., 242–43; Bizos, *Odyssey to Freedom*, 273.

CHAPTER 11

1. *Star* (Johannesburg), December 1963.

2. *Rand Daily Mail*, December 4, 1963.

3. *Rand Daily Mail*, December 12, 1963.

4. Ibid.

5. *Rand Daily Mail*, May 26, 1964.

6. *Die Burger*, May 21, 1964.

7. Joffe, *The State vs. Nelson Mandela*, 65.

8. "Hepple Flees S.A. After Threats," *Rand Daily Mail*, November 27, 1963.

9. "Police Pledges Not Kept," *Star* (Johannesburg), November 29, 1963; "Why I Fled—Hepple," *Rand Daily Mail*, November 29, 1963.

10. Bizos, *Odyssey to Freedom*, 246.

11. Author's interview with Joel Joffe, February 4, 2007.

12. *New York Times*, October 30, 1963.

13. *Guardian*, October 10, 1963.

14. Anthony Sampson, "South Africa—The Time Bomb Ticks," *New York Times Magazine*, April 12, 1964.

15. Remarks of Diallo Telli, of Guinea, 1238th Plenary Meeting, United Nations General Assembly, Eighteenth Session, October 11, 1963, 24.

16. Remarks of Quaison Sackey, of Ghana, 1238th Plenary Meeting, United Nations General Assembly, Eighteenth Session, October 11, 1963, 86.

17. Remarks of Jaja Wachuku, of Nigeria, 1238th Plenary Meeting, United Nations General Assembly, Eighteenth Session, October 11, 1963, 118.

18. Statement of Oliver Tambo at the Meeting of the Special Political Committee of the United Nations General Assembly, New York, October 8, 1963, www.anc.org.za/show.php?id=419.

19. Statement of Oliver Tambo at the Meeting of the Special Political Committee of the United Nations General Assembly, New York, October 29, 1963. www.anc.org.za/show.php?id=4202.

20. United Nations Security Council Resolution 182, December 4, 1963.

21. "Council Takes Up Apartheid Issue," *New York Times*, June 8, 1964.

22. United Nations Security Council, Resolution 190, June 9, 1964.

23. Bulletin of the International Commission of Jurists, December 1963.

24. Ibid.

25. *Sunday Times* (Johannesburg), October 20, 1963.

26. Memorandum from Leslie Minford, Consul General, to Lord Dunrossil, December 13, 1963, UK National Archives, FO 371/167541, 1641/62.

27. December 16, 1963, UK National Archives, FO 371/167541, 1641/64.

28. Ibid.

29. UK National Archives, FO 371/177122, JSA 1641/1.

30. Joffe, *The State vs. Nelson Mandela*, 127–30.

31. "Mandela named as president of London University Council," *Rand Daily Mail*, April 25, 1964. Sampson, *Mandela*, 193; Joffe, *The State vs. Nelson Mandela*, 228.

32. "Judge De Wet Threatened with Death before Rivonia Case," *Die Burger*, November 1, 1963.

33. Yutar Papers, Brenthurst Library, Documents 385/30/15 and 17. These documents are now located at the South African National Archives.

34. "Court Told of Plot to Bomb Home of Yutar," *Rand Daily Mail*, July 7, 1964.

35. Report of Leslie Minford, October 18, 1963, UK National Archives, FO 371/167541/ JSA 1641/34; Letter from Ambassador Hugh Stephenson, December 30, 1963, UK National Archives, FO 371/177122, JSA 1641/1.

36. UK National Archives, FO 371/177035.

37. Ibid., April 18, 1964, JSA 1001/23.

38. Ibid., April 24, 1964, JSA 1001/24.

39. Ibid., May 19, 1964, JSA 1002/28.

40. Ibid., FO 371/177036, JSA 1002/25.

41. Ibid.

42. Lyndon Baines Johnson Library, National Security File: Country File, Africa, Box 76.

43. Memorandum for Maxwell D. Taylor, Chairman of Joint Chiefs of Staff, to Secretary of Defense Robert McNamara, May 22, 1964, *Foreign Relations of the United States 1964–68*, vol. 24, *Africa*, doc. 589, http://history.state.gov/historical documents/frus1964-68v24/d589.

44. Memorandum for McGeorge Bundy, May 20, 1964, Lyndon Baines Johnson Library, National Security File: Country File, Union of Africa, Box 78.

45. Ibid.

46. Telegram From the Embassy in South Africa to the Department of State, April 22, 1964, *FRUS 1964–68*, vol. 24, doc. 585, http://history.state.gov/historical documents/frus1964-68v24/d585.

47. Memorandum from Ambassador Hugh Stephenson to Foreign Office, April 17, 1964, UK National Archives, FO 371/177122, JSA 1641/13.

48. Memorandum from Ambassador Stephenson to Foreign Office, April 22, 1964, UK National Archives, FO 371/177122, JSA 1641/21.

49. Telegram From the Embassy in South Africa to the Department of State, April 22, 1964, *FRUS 1964–68*, vol. 24, doc. 585, http://history.state.gov/historical documents/frus1964-68v24/d585.

50. Letter from Chairman of United Nations Special Committee on Apartheid, Diallo Tolli of Guinea, March 23, 1964, Lyndon Baines Johnson Library, National Security File: Country File, Union of Africa, Box 76.

51. Memorandum and briefing paper for McGeorge Bundy from Benjamin H. Read, April 16, 1964, Lyndon Baines Johnson Library, National Security File: Country File, Union of Africa, Box 76.

52. Telegram from embassy to Foreign Office, May 20, 1964, UK National Archives, Catalogue FO 371/177122, JSA 1641/40.

53. Telegram from embassy to Foreign Office, May 21, 1964, UK National Archives, Catalogue FO 371/177122, JSA 1641/34A.

54. Telegram from embassy to Foreign Office, May 20, 1964, UK National Archives, Catalogue FO 371/177122, JSA 1641/40.

55. Bizos, *Odyssey to Freedom*, 274.

56. Sampson, *Mandela*, 193.

57. Numerous telegrams and memoranda from Minford concerning the trial appear in the Foreign Office Records, UK National Archives, FO 371/167541, 177122, 177123, 177124, 177035, 177036.

58. Memorandum from Minford to Foreign Office, May 12, 1964, UK National Archives, FO 371/177122, JSA 1641/35.

59. Memorandum from J. M. O. Snodgrass to Ambassador Stephenson, May 12, 1964, UK National Archives, FO 1117/3.

60. Memorandum from Embassy to Minford, June 2, 1964, UK National Archives, FO 177123, JSA 1641/45.

61. Telegram from Ambassador Stephenson to Foreign Office, June 4, 1964, UK National Archives, FO 177123, JSA 1641/43.

62. Foreign Office Memorandum, May 8, 1964, UK National Archives, FO 371/177122 JSA 1641/26.

63. Memorandum from British Embassy in Washington to Foreign Office, May 12, 1964, UK National Archives, FO 371/177122 JSA 1641/31.

CHAPTER 12

1. The judge's oral statement of judgment is from Joffe, *The State vs. Nelson Mandela*, 244.

2. Joffe, *The State vs. Nelson Mandela*, 244–45.

3. Ibid., 245.

4. The full judgment can be found in the Rivonia Trial Collection, Library of the University of the Witwatersrand, www.historicalpapers.wits.ac.za/?inventory/U/Collections&;c=AD1844/I/8062, A32.3.

5. Joffe, *The State vs. Nelson Mandela*, 194.

6. Clingman, *Bram Fischer*, 319.

7. Bizos, *Odyssey to Freedom*, 274.

8. Clingman, *Bram Fischer*, 320.

9. "South Africa Hangs 3 Accused to Sabotage," *New York Times*, November 2, 1963. Author's communication with Arthur Chaskalson, June 20, 2007; author's interview with Joel Joffe, August 11, 2010.

10. One of the people convicted at that same trial and also sentenced to ten years in prison was Jacob Zuma, then age twenty-one, who would become president of South Africa in 2009. Author's interview with Joel Joffe, August 11, 2010.

11. Joffe, *The State vs. Nelson Mandela*, 246.

12. Ibid.

13. Ibid.

14. Bizos, *Odyssey to Freedom*, 278.

15. Rivonia Trial Collection, A2519.9. The note is also reprinted in several places including Bizos, *Odyssey to Freedom*, 278; Sampson, *Mandela*, 195.

16. Bizos, *Odyssey to Freedom*, 276.

17. Joffe, *The State vs. Nelson Mandela*, 247.

18. Meredith, *Fischer's Choice*, 102; Bizos, *Odyssey to Freedom*, 274.

19. Joffe, *The State vs. Nelson Mandela*, 248.

20. The testimony of Alan Paton can be found in the Rivonia Trial Collection, A32.5, 2.

21. Record of the Rivonia Trial, *Criminal Court Case No. 253/1963 called The State versus N Mandela and Others, heard in the Supreme Court of South Africa (Transvaal Provincial Division)*, South African National Archives, 385/30/2/1.

22. Paton, *Cry, the Beloved Country*, 151.

23. Bizos, *Odyssey to Freedom*, 283.

24. Author's interview with Joel Joffe, August 11, 2010.

25. Joffe, *The State vs. Nelson Mandela*, 253.

26. Rivonia Trial Collection, A32.2.

27. Judge De Wet's remarks in passing sentence, Rivonia Trial Collection, A 36.2.

28. Joffe, *The State vs. Nelson Mandela*, 254.

29. Ibid.

30. Frankel, *Rivonia's Children*, 268.

31. Joseph, *Side by Side*, 157.

32. Joffe, *The State vs. Nelson Mandela*, 254.

33. Frankel, *Rivonia's Children*, 268; Joffe, *The State vs. Nelson Mandela*, 255–56; Hilda Bernstein, *The World That Was Ours*, 282–83.

34. Joffe, *The State vs. Nelson Mandela*, 257.

35. Letter from ANC with statement concerning appeal against sentence, Rivonia Trial Collection, Bc8.

CHAPTER 13

1. *Sunday Times* (Johannesburg), June 14, 1964.
2. *Rand Daily Mail*, June 12, 1964.
3. Ibid.
4. *Rand Daily Mail*, June 13, 1964.
5. "Tip-off led to Raid on Rivonia," *Rand Daily Mail*, June 19, 1964, in the archives of the Liliesleaf Museum and Library, Rivonia; hereafter "Liliesleaf."
6. "Marchers Turned Out of Airport," *Sunday Times* (London), June 14, 1964.
7. "Demonstrations in Britain over Pretoria Sentences," *Times* (London), June 13, 1964.
8. Gevisser, *A Legacy of Liberation*, 93.
9. "Rivonia: The Inside Story," *Sunday Times* (Johannesburg), June 14, 1964.
10. Ibid.
11. "Demonstrations in Britain over Pretoria Sentences," *Times* (London), June 13, 1964.
12. *Rand Daily Mail*, June 15, 1964.
13. "Demonstrations in Britain over Pretoria Sentences," *Times* (London), June 13, 1964.
14. Ibid.
15. "S. African Ambassador Cancels Oxford Visit," *Guardian* (UK), June 13, 1964.
16. Bizos, *Odyssey to Freedom*, 283.
17. Quoted in *Rand Daily Mail*, June 15, 1964.
18. Editorial, *New York Times*, June 14, 1964. See also Bizos, *Odyssey to Freedom*, 283.
19. "Mandela Has Left a Spark to Ignite," *Sunday Times*, June 14, 1964.
20. "Rivonia: World Reacts," *Rand Daily Mail*, June 13, 1964 (Liliesleaf).
21. "Sentence Deplored by African Members of the United Nations and in Security Council," *Los Angeles Times*, June 13, 1964.
22. Memorandum from Assistant Secretary to State for International Affairs (Cleveland) to Secretary of State Rusk, June 18, 1964, *Foreign Relations of the United States 1964—68*, vol. 24, *Africa*, doc. 592, http://history.state.gov/historical documents/frus1964-68v24/d592.
23. June 10, 1964, UK National Archives, FO 371/177123, JSA 1641/54.
24. Foreign Office memorandum, UK National Archives, FO 371/177124 1642/77.
25. Telegram from Ambassador Stephenson to Foreign Office, June 12, 1964, UK National Archives, FO 371/177123, JSA 1641/53.
26. Telegram from Ambassador Stephenson to Foreign Office, June 12, 1964, UK National Archives, FO 371/177123, 1641/51.
27. Telegram from British Embassy in Washington to Foreign Office, June 27, 1964, UK National Archives, FO 371/177124, FSA 1641/74.
28. Telegram from Ambassador Stephenson to Foreign Office, June 27, 1964, UK National Archives, FO 371/177124, FSA 1641/75.

29. Telegram from Ambassador Stephenson to Foreign Office (referring to earlier Foreign Office communication), June 27, 1964, UK National Archives, FO 371/177124, JSA 1641/75A.
30. Telegram from Ambassador Stephenson to Foreign Office, July 23, 1964, UK National Archives, FO 371/177124, JSA 1641/59.
31. "Rivonia Judge Praised in U.K. Press," *Star* (Johannesburg), June 13, 1964 (Liliesleaf).
32. Editorial, *Guardian*, June 16, 1964.
33. "Rivonia: LBJ Backed S.A.," *Sunday Times* (Johannesburg), June 28, 1964 (Liliesleaf).
34. Memorandum from Assistant Secretary to State for International Affairs (Cleveland) to Secretary of State Rusk, *FRUS* 1964–68vol. 24, doc. 592, http://history.state.gov/historicaldocuments/frus1964-68v24/d592.
35. "Rivonia Reaction in U.K. 'Ineffective,'" *Sunday Express* (Johannesburg), June 21, 1964 (Liliesleaf).
36. Quoted in "They Banked on Death," *Pretoria News*, June 13, 1964; "'Ignore the Excitement,'" *Sunday Times* (Johannesburg), June 14, 1964 (Liliesleaf).
37. "Chicago Paper Sees Red Plot in S.A.," *Star* (Johannesburg), August 6, 1964.
38. "Verwoerd Raps Critics of Rivonia," *Star* (Johannesburg), June 16, 1964 (Liliesleaf).
39. "Rivonia: State Is Firm," *Rand Daily Mail*, July 29, 1964.
40. Telegram from Ambassador Stephenson to Foreign Office, June 17, 1964, UK National Archives, FO 371/177124, JSA 1641/64.
41. Strydom, *Rivonia Unmasked*, 162.
42. Editorial, *Rand Daily Mail*, June 13, 1964.
43. "Rivonia—And After," *Pretoria News*, editorial, June 13, 1964.
44. DeVilliers, *Rivonia: Operation Mayibuye*, 59–60.
45. Ibid., 29.
46. Strydom, *Rivonia Unmasked*, 142.
47. Ibid., 161.
48. Hilda Bernstein, *The World That Was Ours*, 304; Meredith, *Nelson Mandela*, 277.
49. Strydom, *Rivonia Unmasked*, 166.
50. Memorandum from J. M. O. Snodgrass to Foreign Office, September 29, 1964, UK National Archives, FO 371/177124, JSA 1641/90.

CHAPTER 14

1. Author's interview with Denis Goldberg, October 7, 2008.
2. Judgment, Rivonia Trial Collection, Library of the University of Witwatersrand, www.historicalpapers.wits.ac.za/?inventory/U/Collections&;c=AD1844/I862, A 32.32, 12.
3. Preface to Yutar's unpublished book "The Rivonia Trial: The Facts," from the library of the Liliesleaf Farm Museum, Rivonia.

4. Author's interview with Nicholas Wolpe, October 5, 2009.

5. Joffe, *The State vs. Nelson Mandela*, 66.

6. Ibid.

7. George Bizos interview at Liliesleaf Farm Museum, 2003.

8. Author's interview with Arthur Chaskalson, February 16, 2007.

9. Author's interview with George Bizos, October 9, 2007.

10. Author's interview with Arthur Chaskalson, February 16, 2007.

11. Author's interview with Joel Joffe, February 4, 2007.

12. Preface to Yutar, "The Rivonia Trial: The Facts."

13. Ibid.

14. Ibid.

15. Author's interview with Arthur Chaskalson, February 16, 2007.

16. Preface to Yutar, "The Rivonia Trial: The Facts."

17. Joffe, *The State vs. Nelson Mandela*, xii.

18. Ibid., xiv.

19. Ibid.

20. Ibid., 18.

21. Author's interview with Joel Joffe, August 11, 2010. See also chapter 6.

22. Author's interview with Joel Joffe, August 11, 2010.

23. Bizos, *Odyssey to Freedom*, 245.

24. Joffe, *The State vs. Nelson Mandela*, 229–30.

25. Report of Ambassador Stephenson to Foreign Office, December 30, 1963, UK National Archives, FO 371/177122, JSA 1641/1.

26. Memorandum from Leslie Minford to British Embassy, April 1964, UK National Archives, FO 371/177122, JSA 1641/7.

27. Joffe, *The State vs. Nelson Mandela*, 254.

CHAPTER 15

1. Author's interview with Denis Goldberg, October 7, 2008.

2. Accounts of prison life for those convicted at the Rivonia Trial come from various sources including O'Malley, *Shades of Difference*, 147–84; Mandela, *Long Walk to Freedom*, 334–444; Meredith, *Nelson Mandela*, 281–321; Kathrada, *Memoirs*, 195–273; Sampson, *Mandela*.

3. Author's interview with Denis Goldberg, October 7, 2008.

4. Meredith, *Nelson Mandela*, 344.

5. Ibid., 294–95.

6. Gevisser, *A Legacy of Liberation*, 213.

7. Mandela, *Long Walk to Freedom*, 466.

8. Kathrada, *Memoirs*, 291.

9. www.anc.org.za/showpeople.php?p=50

10. Obituary for Govan Mbeki, *New York Times*, August 31, 2001.

11. http://africanhistory.about.com/library/biographies/blbio-WalterSisulu.htm. See also "Walter Sisulu, Mandela Mentor and Comrade Dies at 90," *New York Times,* May 6, 2003.

12. Kathrada, *Memoirs.*

13. "Raymond Mhlaba, 85, Veteran of the African National Congress," *New York Times,* March 13, 2005.

14. Who's Who Southern Africa, "Andrew (Tloks) Mlangeni," www.whoswhosa. co.za/user/2114.

15. www.indepedent.co.uk/news/people/obituary-elias-motsoaledi-1438986.html.

16. Information with regard to the Bernsteins' life after the trial comes from Hilda Bernstein, *The World That Was Ours,* and Rusty Bernstein, *Memory Against Forgetting.*

17. Hilda Bernstein, *The World That Was Ours,* 387.

18. Obituary for Hilda Bernstein, *Guardian,* September 18, 2006.

19. Memorandum in Foreign Office files, April 21, 1964, UK National Archives, FO 371/177035, JSA 1001/24.

20. Memorandum in Foreign Office files, May 29, 1964, UK National Archives, FO 371/177123, JSA 1641/41.

21. Memorandum in Foreign Office files, April 21, 1964, UK National Archives, FO 371/177035, JSA 1001/24.

22. Frankel, *Rivonia's Children,* 332.

23. Goldberg interview at Liliesleaf Farm, 2003.

24. Mandela, *Long Walk to Freedom,* 313–14.

25. The accounts of the Wolpes' lives in England are from Frankel, *Rivonia's Children,* 332–34, and Wolpe, *The Long Way Home.*

26. Author's interview with Nicholas Wolpe, October 5, 2009.

27. "Worlds Apart," *Guardian,* February 6, 2006.

28. "Arthur Goldreich, a Leader of the Armed Fight to End Apartheid, Dies at 82," *New York Times,* May 27, 2011.

29. Lesley Dingle and Daniel Bates, "Professor Sir Bob Hepple," University of Cambridge, Squire Law Library, www.squire.law.cam.ac.uk/eminent_scholars/professor_sir_bob_hepple.php

30. Ibid.

31. Joffe interview at Liliesleaf farm, 2003.

32. Author's interview with Denis Goldberg, October 7, 2008.

33. Reviewed at Brenthurst Library, MS 385/271 (vol. 24). Statement now located at the South African National Archives.

34. Dingle and Bates, "Professor Sir Bob Hepple."

35. Clingman, *Bram Fischer,* 389–90.

36. "Yutar Appointed Attorney-General of the Orange Freestate," *Cape Argus* (Cape Town), June 8, 1968 (Liliesleaf).

37. "Yutar Appointed Attorney-General for the Transvaal," *The Friend* (South Africa), November 14, 1974 (Liliesleaf).

38. Obituary for Percy Yutar, New *York Times*, July 22, 2002.

39. "Bar would oppose Yutar as judge," *Star* (Johannesburg), February 27, 1978.

40. Author's interview with George Bizos, February 9, 2007.

41. Preface to Yutar's unpublished book "The Rivonia Trial: The Facts," from the library of the Liliesleaf Farm Museum, Rivonia.

42. Obituary for Percy Yutar, *Scotsman* (UK), July 29, 2002.

43. Preface to Yutar, "The Rivonia Trial: The Facts."

44. Edelgard Nkobi, epilogue to Joffe, *The State vs. Nelson Mandela*, 271.

45. Obituary for Percy Yutar, *Scotsman* (UK), July 29, 2002.

46. Preface to Yutar's unpublished book, "The Rivonia Trial: The Facts."

47. "Apartheid's History in Shreds," *Mail & Guardian* (South Africa), October 23, 1998.

48. Obituary for Percy Yutar, *Scotsman* (UK), July 29, 2002.

49. Paul Erasmus, Report to South African Truth and Reconciliation Commission, Incident 19, www.justice.gov.za/trc/decisions/2001/ac21230.htm.

50. Kathrada, *Memoirs*, 314.

51. Meredith, *Fischer's Choice*, 124–25.

52. Obituary for Harold Hanson, *Rand Daily Mail*, February 19, 1973.

53. www.sahistory.org.za/pages/people/bios/chaskalson-a.htm

54. Author's interview with Arthur Chaskalson, February 16, 2007.

55. Information with regard to George Bizos's career is from his autobiography, *Odyssey to Freedom*, from author's interview with Bizos, February 9, 2007, and from various conversations with lawyers currently in active practice in South Africa.

56. "Lawyer Joffe in No-Passport Fix," *Sunday Times* (Johannesburg), March 7, 1965.

57. Author's interview with Joel Joffe, August 11, 2010.

58. In his maiden speech in the House of Lords, Joffe thanked Dick Taverne, now Baron Taverne, for his intervention in his gaining entry into the country. Author's interview with Joel Joffe, August 11, 2010.

59. Information with regard to Joffe's career comes from various sources including author's interviews, February 4, 2007, and August 11, 2010. See also "A Matter of Life and Death," *Guardian* (UK), October 24, 2004.

60. Information with regard to Bram Fischer's life after the Rivonia Trial and his death comes from Clingman, *Bram Fischer*, and Meredith, *Fischer's Choice*.

61. Meredith, *Fischer's Choice*, 143–44.

62. Mandela, *Long Walk to Freedom*, 411.

63. See the account of that trial in O'Malley, *Shades of Difference*, 137–46.

64. Memorandum to Foreign Office from Ambassador Stephenson, September 8, 1964, UK National Archives, FO 371/177124, JSA 1641/78.

65. Ibid.

66. Ibid.

67. See the account of the Delmas trial in Bizos, *Odyssey to Freedom*, 442–69.

68. See Sparks, *The Mind of South Africa*, 221–22.
69. Quoted in "They Banked on Death," *Pretoria News*, June 13, 1964; "'Ignore the Excitement,'" *Sunday Times* (Johannesburg), June 14, 1964 (Liliesleaf).
70. For a full account of the negotiations leading to the end of the apartheid regime, see Sparks, *Tomorrow Is Another Country*.
71. Ibid., 229.
72. Ibid., 189.
73. "Nelson Mandela's Captive Audience," *New York Times*, February 7, 2010.
74. For the provisions of the new South African constitution see the South African government website: www.info.gov.za/documents/constitution/index.htm. See also Bizos, *Odyssey to Freedom*, 541–56.
75. For a complete description of the Truth and Reconciliation Commission, see the Commission website: www.justice.gov.za/trc/.
76. *State v. Makwanyane*, www.saflii.org/za/cases/ZACC/1995/3.html.
77. Bizos, *Odyssey to Freedom*, 522–23.
78. Opinion of Chaskalson, Judge President, Conclusion, *State v. Makwanyane*.

Selected Bibliography

PRIMARY SOURCES

Most of the details of the trial contained in this book come from the memoirs of participants. My primary source was Joel Joffe, *The State v. Nelson Mandela*, a complete and brilliantly written account written by the attorney who put together the trial team and who participated in the trial from the beginning. Joffe's book was originally published under the title *The Rivonia Story* (Cape Town: Mayibuye Books, 1995). Another important source was the autobiography of one of the young advocates for the defense, George Bizos. His book *Odyssey to Freedom* provided further details both on the trial itself and on the strategy of defense counsel.

I also have also incorporated information contained in the memoirs of three of the defendants. The most important was Nelson Mandela, *Long Walk to Freedom*, whose recollections of the trial were important both because it was his own trial and because of his legal training. Two other defendants, Ahmed Kathrada and Lionel Bernstein, wrote helpful autobiographies describing the trial: Ahmed Kathrada, *Memoirs*, and Lionel Bernstein, *Memory Against Forgetting*.

Also of great value were the extremely well-written and revealing memoirs of the wives of two of the persons originally charged, Hilda Bernstein, Lionel Bernstein's wife, and AnnMarie Wolpe, Harold Wolpe's wife: Hilda Bernstein, *The World That Was Ours*; AnnMarie Wolpe, *The Long Way Home*. Scenes and dialogue from these memoirs also appears in Glenn Frankel, *Rivonia's Children*. Frankel's excellent book also provided other details, especially with regard to chapter 1 of this book, "Arrests and Escapes."

I have also relied heavily on important biographies of two of the principal people involved in the trial, Nelson Mandela and Bram Fischer. Mary Benson, *Nelson Mandela: The Man and the Movement* (New York: Penguin, 1994); Martin Meredith, *Nelson*

Mandela: A Biography; Anthony Sampson, *Mandela*; Stephen Clingman, *Bram Fischer*; Martin Meredith, *Fischer's Choice: A Life of Bram Fischer*.

Books containing especially valuable information on South African history before and after the Rivonia Trial are William Beinart, *Twentieth-Century South Africa* (Oxford: Oxford University Press, 1994); Mark Gevisser, *A Legacy of Liberation*; Allister Sparks, *The Mind of South Africa*; Sparks, *Tomorrow Is Another Country*.

I also made use of two books sympathetic to the government: H. H. W. de Villiers, *Rivonia: Operation Mayibuye*, and Lauritz Stydom, *Rivonia Unmasked*. I also reviewed the personal papers of the prosecutor, Percy Yutar, when they were housed in the Brenthurst Library in Johannesburg. The papers have now been moved to the South African National Archives in Pretoria.

As well I made extensive use of the records of the British Foreign Office housed at the UK National Archives in London and of the U.S. Department of State and Office of the President housed at the Lyndon Baines Johnson Library in Austin, Texas, and online at http://history.state.gov/ and in *Foreign Relations of the United States* 1964–68, vol. 24, *Africa*.

The book also contains references to contemporary South African and international newspapers and magazines reporting on the trial and on the relationship of South Africa with the rest of the world. Many of the newspaper articles cited are contained in the archives of the Liliesleaf Museum and Library in Rivonia. I have indicated in the notes those articles that I found at that location by the designation "Liliesleaf."

I conducted interviews with several of the participants, including Denis Goldberg, Joel Joffe, Arthur Chaskalson, and George Bizos. Their insights have added significantly to the information already contained in their books.

Most of the quotations from the trial are taken from available transcript, most of which is now available through the web site of the University of the Witwatersrand, www.historicalpapers.wits.ac.za/?inventory/U/Collections&;c=AD1844/I/8062. Some portions of the transcript are no longer preserved. In such instances, I have used the recollections contained in Joffe, *The State vs. Nelson Mandela*, and Bizos, *Odyssey to Freedom*.

In my analysis of the trial and its aftermath, I have relied heavily on my own experience as a trial lawyer and as a teacher of Evidence and Trial Advocacy for almost fifty years. I also have also drawn on my twenty-five years of teaching trial advocacy in programs sponsored by the Black Lawyers Association of South Africa and my observation of trials in South Africa during that time.

SOURCES

Austin, Dennis. *Britain and South Africa*. London: Oxford University Press, 1966.
Barber, James. *The Uneasy Relationship: Britain and South Africa*. London: Heinemann for the Royal Institute of international Affairs, 1983.

Barros, Romeo Julius. *African States and the United Nations versus Apartheid: The Efforts of the African States to Affect South Africa's Apartheid Policy through the United Nations.* New York: Carlton, 1967.

Bernstein, Hilda. *The World That Was Ours.* London: Persephone; first published by Heinemann, 1967.

Bernstein, Rusty. *Memory Against Forgetting: Memoirs from a Life in South African Politics.* London: Viking, 1999.

Bizos, George. *Odyssey to Freedom: A Memoir by the World-Renowned Human Rights Advocate, Friend and Lawyer to Nelson Mandela.* Houghton, South Africa: Random House, 2007.

Clingman, Stephen. *Bram Fischer: Afrikaner Revolutionary.* Amherst: University of Massachusetts Press, 1998.

Collins, L. John. *Faith Under Fire.* London: Frewin, 1966.

De Villiers, H. H. W. *Rivonia: Operation Mayibuye; A Review of the Rivonia Trial.* Johannesburg: Afrikaanse Pers-Boekhandel, 1964.

Dudziak, Mary L. *Cold War Civil Rights: Race and the Image of American Democracy.* Princeton, NJ: Princeton University Press, 2000.

Frankel, Glenn. *Rivonia's Children: Three Families and the Cost of Conscience in White South Africa.* New York: Farrar, Straus & Giroux, 1999.

Gevisser, Mark. *A Legacy of Liberation: Thabo Mbeki and the Future of the South African Dream.* New York: Palgrave Macmillan, 2009.

Gonze, Collin, George M. Houser, and Perry M. Sturges. *South African Crisis and United States Policy.* New York: American Committee on Africa, 1962.

Goldberg, Denis. *The Mission: A Life for Freedom in South Africa.* Johannesburg: STE, 2010.

Hance, William A., ed. *Southern Africa and the United States.* New York: Columbia University Press, 1968.

Hyam, Ronald, and Peter Henshaw. *The Lion and the Springbok: Britain and South Africa since the Boer War.* Cambridge: Cambridge University Press, 2003.

Joffe, Joel. *The State vs. Nelson Mandela: The Trial That Changed South Africa.* Oxford: OneWorld, 2007.

Joseph, Helen. *Side by Side: The Autobiography of Helen Joseph.* London: Zed, 1986.

Kathrada, A. M. *Memoirs.* Cape Town: Zebra, 2004.

Mandela, Nelson. *Conversations with Myself.* New York: Farrar, Straus & Giroux, 2010.

Mandela, Nelson. *Long Walk to Freedom: The Autobiography of Nelson Mandela.* Boston: Little, Brown, 1994.

Meredith, Martin. *Fischer's Choice: A Life of Bram Fischer.* Johannesburg: Ball, 2002.

Meredith, Martin, *Nelson Mandela: A Biography.* London: Hamilton, 1997.

O'Malley, Padraig. *Shades of Difference: Mac Maharaj and the Struggle for South Africa.* New York: Viking, 2007.

Pakenham, Thomas. *The Boer War.* New York: Random House, 1994.

Paton, Alan. *Cry, the Beloved Country: A Story of Comfort in Desolation.* London: Cape, 1948.

Pomeroy, William J. *Apartheid Axis: The United States and South Africa*. New York: International Publishers, 1971.

Sampson, Anthony. *Mandela: The Authorized Biography*. New York: Knopf, 1999.

Shain, Milton. *The Roots of Antisemitism in South Africa*. Johannesburg: Witwatersrand University Press, 1994.

Smith, David James. *Young Mandela*. London: Weidenfeld & Nicolson, 2010.

South Africa Foundation. *South Africa and United States Policy*. Johannesburg: South Africa Foundation, 1966.

Sparks, Allister. *The Mind of South Africa*. London: Mandarin, 1990.

Sparks, Allister. *Tomorrow Is Another Country: The Inside Story of South Africa's Road to Change*. New York: Hill & Wang, 1995.

Strydom, Lauritz. *Rivonia Unmasked!* Johannesburg: Voortrekkerpers, 1965.

Williams, Oliver F. *The Apartheid Crisis: How We Can Do Justice in a Land of Violence*. San Francisco: Harper & Row, 1986.

Wolpe, AnnMarie. *The Long Way Home*. London: Virago, 1994.

Index